YVON DELBOS
AT THE QUAI D'ORSAY

Photograph courtesy of Agence France-Presse

YVON DELBOS
AT THE QUAI D'ORSAY,

French Foreign Policy
during the Popular Front
1936-1938

John E. Dreifort

THE UNIVERSITY PRESS OF KANSAS
Lawrence/Manhattan/Wichita

© Copyright 1973 by the University Press of Kansas
Standard Book Number 7006-0094-9
Library of Congress Catalog Card Number 72-85252
Printed in the United States of America

Designed by Fritz Reiber

FOR
Carol

Preface

For nearly two years, from June, 1936, to March, 1938, a confusing series of crises occurred that threatened to demolish the peace of Europe. The Popular Front government in France—an alliance of Socialists, Radical Socialists, and Communists headed by Léon Blum —faced with domestic social upheaval and the need to give priority to a French version of the American New Deal, found itself confronted with the disintegration of the French power position in international affairs. The effects of the Rhineland crisis, the Abyssinian War, the Spanish Civil War, and the Austrian Anschluss raised problems that frequently forced domestic issues into the background. Indeed, it has been said with considerable justification that "the Popular Front experiment neither failed nor was it overthrown. It was smothered by the looming clouds of international crisis."[1]

Nevertheless, when compared with the multitudinous works on the other great powers, historians of the interwar period have tended to ignore the history of French foreign policy during the 1930s. There are essentially two reasons for the dearth of studies on the subject. In the first place, it has been widely assumed that for much of the decade, particularly after 1936, French policy generally followed in the wake of Britain's leadership. Second, the chaotic state of French documentary source materials after the war has hitherto presented a serious handicap to those who may have wished to probe into the matter. With the publication of several volumes of the *Documents diplomatiques français, 1932–1939* and the availability of unpublished British Foreign Office and Cabinet papers, however, it has now become possible to reexamine the first assumption. Herein lies the primary objective of this volume. There is a need to trace and examine the development of French foreign policy prior to Munich and to assess its relationship to the general flow of European developments during the period. For as Pierre Cot put it, it is "impossible to isolate the foreign policy of France from that of the other European powers."[2]

This study focuses upon Yvon Delbos, the French Foreign Minister, and the role he played in the formulation and implementation of French foreign policy during the period under consideration. With the exception of the venerable Aristide Briand, Delbos held the portfolio of Foreign Minister for a longer continuous period than any other individual during the interwar years. He held the post through three ministries—from June 4, 1936, until March 10, 1938—a span of over twenty-one months. Although it is frequently difficult to trace roles, determine causes, and allocate responsibilities, it is clear that many of the strengths, weaknesses, and contradictions in French foreign policy during that period are a reflection of Delbos' supervision. That French foreign policy had its strong points is unquestionable. Unfortunately, however, these strengths tended to be overshadowed by the regrettable weaknesses that early became evident. On the other hand, although there was a good deal of hesitation, fumbling, and groping, French influence in international affairs cannot be rejected out of hand as being completely impotent. There is increasing evidence that France frequently took actions, exerted pressures, and displayed a certain statesmanship which had a substantial influence upon European diplomacy of the period.

Rather than a strictly chronological narrative, a topical approach is utilized to elucidate and evaluate Delbos' role. Thus, one is better able to isolate, focus upon, and reinterpret foreign policy decisions in the areas of most direct concern to Delbos and other French decision makers. The questions receiving most attention are policy towards the Spanish Civil War, particularly focusing upon the decision to pursue nonintervention and the events that led to the

Nyon Conference of September, 1937, and relations with Great Britain, the Soviet Union, Italy, Germany, and the small states of Eastern Europe. Although the French position in the Far East and relations with the United States were of concern to French policy makers, these matters were secondary in importance to the primary consideration of French security in Europe and are therefore treated in a cursory manner, solely to round out the picture.

While this work does not pretend to be a political biography, it does attempt to fill, in a small way, the lacuna that exists in studies of key persons of the critical interwar years. Inasmuch as reactions to problems reflect the background and attitude of an individual, some attempt is made to treat with this personal element by first examining Delbos as a man.

This book originated from a discussion with Samuel M. Osgood, Professor of French History at Kent State University. I am deeply thankful for his example of scholarship which interested me in French History. Without his invaluable criticism and unfailing concern this study could never have been successfully completed. His linguistic knowledge and mastery are responsible for whatever smoothness exists in the translation of the French sources utilized. I am greatly indebted to William R. Rock, who instilled in me a fascination for the history of international relations. Many of my opinions and judgments are a reflection of those that I have acquired, often unconsciously to be sure, from classes and discussions with Professor Rock. The study has greatly benefited from the useful criticism of Kenneth Calkins, who so willingly gave of his time to read through the entire manuscript. A word of thanks must also be extended to my colleagues at Wichita State University, especially to George W. Collins and James C. Duram, for their most helpful suggestions concerning sections of the manuscript. For his words of encouragement and advice through the years, I am particularly grateful to Stuart R. Givens. I wish also to thank Mrs. Bobbie Givens for her proficient work in typing the manuscript.

Professors Pierre Renouvin, René Rémond, and Georges Dupeux willingly contributed their thoughts and suggestions, which helped to improve this study. Special gratitude must be expressed to the following who were so generous with their recollections and assistance in interviews with this writer: MM. Robert Blum, Paul Bastid, Georges Bonnet, Robert Clergerie, Charles Corbin, Pierre Cot, André François-Poncet, Henri Laugier, René Massigli, Daniel Mayer, and Jules Moch. I also thank those members of the Association Les Amis d'Yvon Delbos who permitted me to quote from their unpublished written *souvenirs* of Delbos. To Henri Bonnet, former Ambassador and lifetime friend of Delbos, who ferreted out those essays and whose information and assistance was so graciously given, I am eternally grateful. I also wish to thank him for obtaining the photograph of Yvon Delbos that the Agence France-Presse has permitted me to use as the frontispiece.

I owe much to the many librarians and archivists who skillfully sought out the materials essential to this study. Of particular assistance were the staffs at the Bibliothèque de Documentation Internationale Contemporaine in Paris, the Public Records Office in London, and the Library at Kent State University. The French newspaper holdings at the Kent State University Library and its efficient interlibrary loan service were of inestimable assistance.

Much of the research and collection of research materials, which was conducted in France and Britain, was made possible through a Supplementary Graduate Award from Kent State University that was designed to cover my travel expenses. The grant of a University Fellowship for the academic year 1969–1970 helped to provide the financial wherewithal and time needed to complete the main body of this study. The Faculty Research Committee at Wichita State University generously furnished the financial support necessary for polishing the final version of the manuscript.

Above all, it is with deep-felt appreciation that I acknowledge that I could hardly have finished this work without the help of my wife, Carol. Although too frequently taken for granted, her tireless encouragement and patience and her invaluable assistance in typing have been far beyond the call of duty. To her I owe a special debt.

As is usually the case in such instances, however, I alone am responsible for any errors of fact and judgment that may exist.

J. E. D.

Contents

1

The Man from Périgord

The problems of France in the interwar years, especially that period leading to the debacle of 1940, have been the subject of considerable study. Whether dealing with the profound cynicism and ferment in domestic politics or with the indecision and insecurity in international affairs, the focus of attention has thus far been upon the very most central figures. Yet France was not run by a closed coherent elite. It is therefore desirable to study some of the lesser, though still influential, leaders of the period. Some of that, too, has been done; but one who has as yet escaped investigation is Yvon Delbos, a major journalist, deputy, and minister during the interwar years of the French Third Republic. This is surprising—both in light of his important role as a leading politician and his conduct as Foreign Minister of one of Europe's major powers at a most critical time. Furthermore, throughout the kaleidoscopic fortunes of the Third Republic he was one of the few French politicians whose reputation managed to survive untarnished. Before endeavoring to analyze and judge his contribution to the diplomacy during the Popular Front era from 1936 to 1938, we should examine various facets of Delbos' career and character in order to perhaps discover some clues as to what manner of man he was and how his unique personality emerged from a background that was in many ways so similar to that of other politicians of his generation.[1]

Born on May 7, 1885, at Thonac in the rich Dordogne Valley in the Périgord region of southwest France, Delbos was a product of his times, upbringing, and environment. Like his grandfather, his parents were both *instituteurs,* or school teachers of the lower middle

1

class. In a local two-room schoolhouse Monsieur Delbos taught the older students and Madame Delbos the young ones.[2] Although Yvon held his father in great respect, it was his mother who influenced him most through her gentleness, teaching, advice, and example. One observer recounted later, "His politics . . . [reflected] the images on which his childhood nourished in the home."[3]

He began his secondary studies at the Lycée de Périgueux in 1897, where he was at the head of his class in history, philosophy, and languages, especially Latin. In 1904 he moved on to the Lycée Henri IV in Paris, which had an excellent reputation for training the best young French minds. Delbos apparently took the change of atmosphere in stride, although retaining a nostalgia for the life in the provinces, gathering on Sundays with his fellow *Méridionaux* (southerners) to partake of the good Périgord wine that they somehow secured. Those were impulsive, carefree days—especially during the first year—for Delbos as he built a reputation for himself through his prowess as captain of the school's rugby team, to which he also devoted his Sundays, until forced to the sidelines with a broken clavicle sustained in one of the life-or-death struggles at the Park-des-Princes. What was left of his weekends was frequently passed on the mezzanine of the Café Soufflet at such noble pursuits as the French game of *manille*. One of his comrades from those days, Emile Bouvier, later reminisced, "We were coarse, virile, and pure. We did not demand great things in life: we lived from day to day, joyously."[4] Perhaps the climax of this *joie de vivre* was the uproarious celebration at the end of the first year at the lycée which culminated with Delbos and his comrades depositing one of their fellow underclassmen dead drunk on the doorstep of his concierge.

There was, of course, time enough to devote to serious study. Beginning with his second year, Delbos attacked his studies with renewed vigor, even while leading the rugby team to the national championships. He again distinguished himself for his ability in Latin, his excellent translations frequently serving as models for his classmates. At the same time he was given a firm preparation in history, philosophy, and literature.

The main goal pursued during his two years at the lycée had been to prepare for the entrance examinations for the famous Ecole Normale Supérieure. Indeed, admittance proved difficult; but Delbos, after failing in his first two attempts, won a scholarship and entered with the *promotion* of 1907. Ostensibly charged with providing three or four years of training for posts in higher education, the Ecole Normale most frequently had its graduates siphoned off by the government, thus helping to explain the first-rate French civil service. Others used the prestige of the school as part of a springboard for vaulting into positions of political prominence. In any case, few *normaliens* ever completely free themselves from the influence of the institution on the Rue d'Ulm. This was undoubtedly true of Delbos. Indeed, he formed many intimate and enduring friendships, including those with Henri Bonnet, André François-Poncet, and René Massigli, all of whom would ultimately achieve high rank within the Foreign Office apparatus. In fact, the last two were established at various levels there when Delbos assumed his post as Foreign Minister in 1936.

Once in his new environs, he applied himself with his usual vigor. He again distinguished himself in the classics and literature, and he became a disciple of Gustave Lanson—one of the prominent scholars, literary historians, and critics of French literature and a future director of the Ecole Normale—who noted Delbos' "well composed and well thought out" research papers. By this time Delbos' appetite was being increasingly whetted for writing about topics involving journalism and politics. This inclination was facilitated by other influences surrounding the university at this time. The influence of the nearby Ecole des Hautes Etudes Sociales, where Delbos presented several lectures treating with journalism, and frequent meetings of literary groups which included his friend and future collaborator Roger Dévigne, increasingly exposed him to large doses of political liberalism. For the first time stirrings of political awareness and ambition began to arouse Delbos. Moreover, the Ecole Normale was the home of Lucien Herr, resident Socialist and director of the library; and the institution, largely through Herr's efforts, had achieved something of a reputation as a preparatory school for leftist politicians. Indeed, such familiar figures as Jean Jaurès, the great pre–World War I Socialist leader, and Léon Blum, Delbos' future friend and colleague and Jaurès' successor at the helm of the Socialist party after the war, were numbered among Herr's converts.[5]

In addition, these were the tumultuous post-Dreyfus years when the Latin Quarter pulsated with excitement. The courtyard of the Sorbonne frequently served as a battleground between the anti-Semitic royalist Action Française and the liberal defenders of the Republic with whom Delbos and many of his comrades sided, and Delbos' rugby training probably served him in good stead. How deeply those experiences affected him is not known and can only be a matter for speculation; but it probably seemed to his young and impressionable mind, as it did to a great many others, that the institutions of the Republic, and indeed the Republic itself, were in danger of being destroyed. It seems clear, therefore, that his interest in journalism and his leftist political orientation were immeasurably furthered during his years at the Ecole Normale.[6]

His desire for social progress initially led him to join a collectivist student group rallying to the Socialist banner. Ultimately, however, he found that the excessive dogmatism of the movement did not suit his nature, and he moved toward radicalism, although retaining a persistent sympathy and warm affection for the Socialists.[7] As Jules Romains, the eminent French novelist and Delbos' classmate at the Ecole Normale, observed, Delbos during this period showed an "attachment for a party and, better yet, the desire to act and to fight politically, to measure himself against the adversary in the arena which comprises the journals of opinion, the committees, the parliament, and the rest."[8]

Despite the spirited politics and the exacting academic discipline, there was time enough to discover the delights of the Paris theater, to frequent the Left Bank cafés, and to enjoy female companionship. Delbos' athletic stature, combined with a certain *gentillesse,* made him popular with the young ladies. There were Sunday excursions into the Chevreuse Valley, and rugby continued to lure him onto the practice field. Combining an obvious Périgord talent in epicurean matters with a symbolic revolt against the rigid, austere atmosphere of the Ecole Normale, which was dominated by the Parisian elite, he presided over the *Commission du Pot,* which was elected by the students and charged with formulating the daily menus. He later retained amused memories of his first electoral campaign on behalf of the more plebian tastes of his southern comrades, heartily conducted under the banner of "soup and cheese at all meals," which won a sweeping victory over the snobbish proponents of "hors d'oeuvre and side dishes"! Although he was defeated the following year, after standing on his principle, and was forever after repulsed by Livarot and Munster cheeses, he had nevertheless gained considerable prestige among his fellow students for his principled leadership![9] One of his comrades recalled, "He brought among us his smooth humor, a solid optimism, allied with a large spirit of tolerance, which made for all an excellent comrade and which did not prevent him from devoting his entire being to causes which appeared to him deserving of being defended."[10]

As he progressed in his preparation for the *agrégation de lettres*, those formative years were filled with doubts, anxieties, and questions concerning his future as he was tugged first one way then the next. In 1910 he failed in the stiff competition for the *agrégation*, not an unusual fate for a candidate's first attempt, but he recovered brilliantly and was successful the following year. The question of a career then arose. Due to his family example and by virtue of his academic success, one would have thought that he would have sought a university position in his beloved southwest; and, indeed, at one time he probably had considered a teaching career. By this time, however, he was no longer interested in pursuing such a course. Furthermore, difficulties of a financial nature, which had plagued him during his years in Paris, created a barrier to a research career, for which he was well prepared. Yet a man with his training was in considerable demand by special interest groups and enterprises.

In reality, Delbos had already chosen his path, perhaps quite subconsciously. His noticeable interest in journalism and what Massigli has described as "a passion that he nourished for politics" while at the Ecole Normale dictated the direction that he would pursue.[11] In fact, during 1911, even before passing the *agrégation*, through Raoul Anglès, a fellow *normalien*, Delbos came in contact with Justin Perchot, a Senator and the proprietor of *Le Radical*, a political daily newspaper of small circulation whose offices on the Rue Montmartre were located in the same building as those of the Socialist organ *L'Humanité*. Signed on as an editor, writing political reports and commentaries as well as literary and theatrical pieces, Delbos swiftly made a name for himself, advancing rapidly to become Editor in Chief despite his youth.[12] One contemporary observer, André Wormser, remarked that his journalism displayed the qualities of "zest but without wickedness; courage but without bravado; sincerity. What he wrote, he thought and he felt. . . . In no circumstances did he say what he did not believe."[13]

More importantly, his name and signature soon came to be widely recognized in political circles. His relationship with the directors and his position on *Le Radical* soon caused him, evidently with little soliciting on his part, to be considered one of the bright "hopes" of the Radical Socialist party. His contacts with leading Radicals, such as President Emile Loubet, Joseph Caillaux, Edouard Herriot, and Paul Painlevé among others, and with the neighboring Socialists, such as Jaurès and Blum, as they conversed on the stairs at the Rue Montmartre, were numerous and important for the future. As Bouvier has noted, "From there to foreseeing a parliamentary career there was only one step." Thus, like so many others, Delbos followed the logical and well-worn path which "led him from the university, to journalism, and from journalism to political action."[14]

Those were enjoyable years when he lived a simple life on the Rue Hautefeuille, unaffected by his rapidly rising star. He retained a refreshing modesty and "discrete patience" which contrasted delightfully with the arrogance and vanity of the other young *arrivistes* with whom he competed. He never neglected his professional tasks and obligations, doing all of his own writing and replying by hand to all of the solicitations that he received. Moreover, he was always accessible and willing to listen to his subordinates and even his rivals. Most often his nonprofessional activities were restricted to intimate gatherings of friends at his two-room apartment or over dinner.[15] He never forgot his friends, and while he was Editor in Chief at *Le Radical* its columns were richly enhanced by a wide variety of literary contributions that they were encouraged to submit.[16]

Unfortunately, like many others of his generation, Delbos did not have long to pursue his promising journalistic and political interests or to enjoy *la belle époque* in which he lived. On August 2, 1914, the day before the German declaration of war on France, Delbos was mobilized and left for the front as a sergeant in the infantry. His war record was outstanding. He was wounded in 1914 and forced to the sidelines, but returned and qualified as a pilot in the air force. Seriously wounded again in 1917 and cited twice, he was demobilized only after the armistice.[17] He had survived; and although he had escaped the horrors of the trenches, the war could not fail to leave its mark physically and mentally. Delbos belonged to that generation of Frenchmen who had seen so many comrades fall in action at their side. The war left scars on French spirits and souls as no other event has. It revealed men to each other—their strengths and frailties, their conceptions of right and wrong, their virtues and vices, and their willingness or reluctance to contribute to the common struggle for existence were not easily disguised. Few men have ever come to know each other so intimately as did the men of the Great War. It can be safely said that the men of the interwar Third Republic would often disagree violently, but seldom did they misjudge one another. To be sure, the psychological impact upon Delbos must have been great; and although it is one of the unmeasurable considerations, one must wonder how much his outlook and decisions at a much later time can be explained in the light of the experience he shared with his fellow Frenchmen in the traumatic years of World War I.

The war-exhausted nation attempted to restore "normalcy" and to build a new international order. But peace found many Frenchmen of Delbos' generation unemployed and filled with doubts and uncertainty. To them the victory seemed hollow indeed. Unlike many of his compatriots, however, Delbos found the war only a momentary interruption to his professional pursuits. In 1919, with some friends including Henri Bonnet, Delbos founded *L'Ere nouvelle,* which they soon abandoned for financial reasons. It was then that he went to work for *La Dépêche de Toulouse,* one of the most powerful and influential of the provincial French newspapers.[18] Under the control of the Sarraut family, with whom Delbos had become acquainted, it had become one of the pillars of the Radical Socialist party. The political power of *La Dépêche* derived from its predominant position in the press of southern France. Radical politicians had to maintain good relations with the director of the paper, Maurice Sarraut, in order to get a favorable press. This helps to account for the clique of Radical politicians who gathered around the Sarraut brothers. It served to give that clique an identification different from those groups that gathered around Edouard Daladier, Camille Chautemps, and Edouard Herriot in the Radical party.[19] The experience Delbos gained in the editorial rooms of *La Dépêche,* ultimately becoming head of its Paris services, was another stage in his education. A conscientious and tireless journalist writing editorials and commentaries on domestic politics, he was able to organize and further develop his own political thoughts.[20]

As previously noted, it was but a short step for Delbos to join the Radical party and enter the French political scene. It has been said that "although every Radical politician did not come to the party as a professional journalist, it was the exception who did not become one."[21] A moderate man with inclinations toward a "liberal democratic" position,[22] and an active journalist for one of the leading Radical newspapers in France, Delbos fit rather well into the mainstream of the Radical Socialist party, although he must have despaired at the mercurial fluctuations of a party which often reversed itself during the interwar period as it straddled the line dividing Right from Left.

As early as the first postwar elections of 1919, Delbos had stood for elections to the Chamber of Deputies on the Radical list. Still relatively a political unknown in his native Périgord, he managed to place only fourth among six candidates. Undaunted, he ran again in the next elections five years later and was swept in as a Deputy for the Dordogne by the Left landslide of 1924. For over thirty years, until 1955, with one interruption caused by World War II, he continued to be reelected by imposing majorities and served as a Radical Socialist Deputy from Sarlat.[23]

Delbos made a smooth transition to political life. Upon entering the Chamber of Deputies, he soon became identified with the moderate Left among the Radical deputies. The men like Herriot, Daladier, and Chautemps who most frequently held posts through the endless shuffling of cabinets during the interwar period came from this and the moderate sections of the party. Peter Larmour has unfairly categorized Delbos with such men as Chautemps, Paul Bastid, and Hippolyte Ducos as "les radicaux de gestion." They were considered to be "conservative but not intransigent, tempered always by political expediency. . . . A description of one of them in action at a meeting of his local General Council runs: 'he passes through the room . . . smiling, witty, telling one of his inimitable anecdotes, shaking hands, shaking hands, shaking hands.' "[24] Indeed, although Delbos' connections within the Radical party were not solely dictated by ideology, they were influenced even less by political opportunism.

Larmour has identified four major cliques in the party, gathering around Herriot, Daladier, Chautemps, and the Sarraut brothers. The groups, however, could never really be clearly defined, and the influence of one of those great leaders of the party frequently carried over into another's following.[25] Delbos had a foot in at least two of the camps. Since Delbos was a Deputy from the Dordogne and journalist for *La Dépêche*, the influence of the Sarrauts hung heavy over him. On the other hand, many considered him to be Herriot's protégé and heir.[26]

The central institution of parliamentary radicalism was the so-called Group. Although it frequently tried to enforce effective discipline in the Chamber, any success was temporary at best. It did, however, have considerable importance in the allotment of committee seats, supporting party representatives during debates, nominating candidates for important offices of the Chamber, and frequently petitioning ministers with considerable success. Therefore, the presidency of the Group was a prize and the object of considerable competition among leaders of the party. The president spoke for the party in major debates. Delbos' election to the post over Daladier in 1934 is a good measure of his influence within the party. Other presidents during the period were such imposing figures as Herriot, Chautemps, and Daladier.[27]

In April, 1925, only a few months after his election to the Chamber, Delbos entered the second Paul Painlevé government as Undersecretary of State in charge of technical education and the Beaux-Arts. In October of the same year he received his first ministerial post with the portfolio of Minister of Public Instruction in the third Painlevé government. The fact that he became "ministrable" so quickly "in an age when there was no lack of capable statesmen, . . . was no mean achievement,"[28] and was a good indication of his political maturity and the esteem in which he was held by his colleagues. This cabinet experience was brief, however, as the government fell in November. For reasons that are difficult to ascertain, during the next ten years he refused several cabinet posts as government after government shuffled in and out of office. Delbos busily engaged in a wide variety of Chamber committee assignments, however; and as has already been indicated, he remained active in the Radical party during these years and continued to write political editorials for *La*

Dépêche. In addition, he served as Vice-President of the Chamber of Deputies from 1932 until 1936 and proved to be a courteous Speaker of the Chamber.[29]

During those years Delbos developed an extensive interest in international affairs. In 1927 he represented France at the Pan-European Congress. A zealous defender of the League of Nations, he became convinced, especially after Hitler's rise to power, that the defeat of the League and of collective security would lead to disaster.[30] He worked long and hard, writing and speaking on behalf of the League and proposing what he believed were necessary reforms in its structure. In the course of the late summer of 1932, he traveled through Soviet Russia, observing conditions, methods, and leaders. Upon his return, he presented his views about Russian social and economic conditions, and gave some insight into the workings of the Soviet system in his book *L'Expérience rouge.* He concluded, "For my part, it is a regime that, of course, I do not wish for France nor for any other foreign country. I consider, however, that it is necessary not to let [Russia] go running off in a sense of indignation, nor in a sense of panic." He felt that in the face of the increasing fascist threat, Russia was looking for a rapprochement with France. France had to reciprocate due to the deterioration of its own international position.[31] This showed a considerable amount of insight into the realities of the European situation at a time when most French, as well as other European, statesmen had little idea where events were to lead them. Delbos was already convinced of the need for a Franco-Soviet connection three years before the pact between the two powers came into being. It is clear that, even in this earlier period, Delbos did not allow ideological considerations to blind him to the needs of French security. In the course of his activities and frequent travels abroad on behalf of international peace, he became personally familiar with leading European officials and cognizant of prevailing public opinion concerning international problems of the day. Those experiences would serve him in good stead during his tenure as Foreign Minister and, indeed, must have been of importance in his selection for the post.

Ultimately, Delbos was persuaded to accept a cabinet position in January, 1936, in the interim government formed by his old friend Albert Sarraut. Given the portfolio of Minister of Justice, he was also Vice-President of the Council. The major crisis confronted by the

Sarraut government was the German occupation of the Rhineland. The weak interim coalition government procrastinated, waiting for a reaction from the British. But there was never any real question of retaliatory action once the Commander in Chief, General Gamelin, exposed the lack of any French military plan for a limited operation. Presented with the alternative of either full-scale war against the Germans or no action at all, only a handful of ministers favored active opposition to Hitler. [32] There is little agreement about the positions taken by various cabinet members at the important meetings of March 8 and 9, 1936. It has been suggested that Delbos actively favored retaliation, along with Sarraut, Henri Guernut, Georges Mandel, Joseph Paul-Boncour, and a few others.[33] One can only speculate that he recognized the significance of Hitler's unilateral violation of the Rhineland clauses of the Treaty of Versailles, especially in view of the mounting evidence concerning the aggressiveness of the Nazi regime. But in view of Delbos' later high regard for British support, it is highly unlikely that he would have pushed too strenuously, even at that point, for an action that Britain was disinclined to support. He needed only to recall the Ruhr episode of 1923 to understand the possibly painful consequences of a unilateral French action upon Franco-British relations. When the Locarno powers met in London, a half-hearted French suggestion of sanctions was quickly brushed aside. British influence was decisive when Neville Chamberlain told the French Foreign Minister, Pierre-Etienne Flandin, that "public opinion here would not support us in sanctions of any kind."[34] The failure of sanctions against Italy probably made any further use of them a dubious enterprise in any case. Larmour has suggested that "there was, in short, no pressure from the Radicals for doing anything, and a good deal of support for doing nothing."[35] One can go further, however, and argue that this was indeed typical of the mainstream of the French and British response.

After serving as Foreign Minister during the Popular Front, the main consideration of this study, Delbos continued to play an active role on the French political scene. Writing frequent editorials in *La Dépêche*, he voiced his opinion on a wide range of domestic and foreign issues, including Munich and the subsequent rape of Czechoslovakia. With the outbreak of the war and the ensuing French rout, Delbos became one of the most ardent of those opposing any armistice and accommodation with the Germans. After he joined the Paul Reynaud cabinet on June 5, 1940, he voted against any such surrender.[36] In fact, he was one of those ministers who, in the confused last days of the Republic at Bordeaux, sailed off on the *Massilia*, bound for Casablanca on June 20. The motivation for his departure remains unclear. Perhaps he hoped that the government would continue the fight from North Africa. This hope proved to be false, if indeed it ever really existed. When he realized that France would not continue the struggle, especially after Petain's assumption of full powers, which he opposed, he reentered France and returned to the Dordogne to share the brunt of the occupation with his compatriots while remaining in complete sympathy with the Free French forces.[37] Like many others, such as Daladier, Reynaud, and Herriot, he was eventually arrested and deported in April, 1943. He remained imprisoned in solitary confinement in Germany at Oranienburg near Berlin for over two years. In the last tumultuous weeks of the Third Reich, in the face of the oncoming Soviets, he was evacuated south to a small camp near Plauen not far from the Czech border, where he was liberated by the United States Seventh Army on May 1, 1945. On May 7—his sixtieth birthday—he reentered France to begin life anew.[38]

Shortly after Delbos returned to France he was elected to the Constituent Assembly as a representative from the Dordogne. In January, 1946, he became Minister of State in the Paul Ramadier cabinet, the first government of the Fourth Republic. When the Ramadier government resigned in November, 1947, the President of the Republic asked Delbos to form a new government. But he declined on the grounds that his poor health, inherited no doubt from his wartime experiences, made it impossible for him to carry out this task. He later became Minister of National Education in the cabinet of André Marie (July, 1948), in the first government of Henri Queuille (September, 1948), and in the second Georges Bidault cabinet (October, 1949). One of a small group who tried to revitalize radicalism, he also reassumed his former position as President of the Radical Socialists in the National Assembly.[39]

In the postwar years Delbos enjoyed the status of an "elder statesman." While his efforts to regenerate the Radical party and his duties within the various cabinets on which he served were time consuming, his chief concern lay in rebuilding the French and European positions in international affairs. Except for the intervals when he was a member of the cabinet, he was a fixture on the Chamber's Foreign Affairs Committee throughout the entire period. Just as he had been an ardent supporter of the League of Nations, so, too, he championed the United Nations and served briefly as a French delegate in New York. He despaired at the rapidly widening gulf which separated the great powers and which made the intended function of that international organization impossible, although he may have been less surprised, given his prewar experiences with the League, than many others. As the Eastern and Central European states were dominated by and became pawns of the Soviet Union, his fear of further Communist expansion, as long as Europe remained in its weakened state, prompted him to become an "apostle of European Union," which would be propped up by the power of the United States and the Atlantic Alliance. He recognized that economic and strategic necessities dictated such a system of regional security. His friend Henri Bonnet maintained that "perhaps in all of his political life, Yvon Delbos had never held a more passionate conviction than to call for the union, in the economic, military, and political domains, of the six countries of continental Europe."[40] Undoubtedly, his strong support of the proposed European Defense Community (EDC) hurt his chances in his run for the presidency in 1953, but it was a principle on which he was unwilling to compromise.

The apogee of his postwar career, and a clear indication of the high regard with which he was held by his colleagues, came in 1953 when he was put forth as a candidate for the presidency of the Republic. The election, held amidst the continuing debate concerning the EDC, proved to be a pitifully humiliating spectacle for the Fourth Republic. The record-setting marathon balloting saw the deputies finally elect René Coty, perhaps out of exhaustion and bewilderment, on the thirteenth ballot. Delbos showed unexpected support in the early balloting, splitting the EDC vote with Georges Bidault. He peaked at 225 votes, a strong third, before withdrawing prior to the fourth ballot. As one keen observer subsequently lamented, however, even had he won, "he would have gathered little joy."[41]

Although politically secure in his seat in the Chamber of Deputies, he chose to run for the Senate in 1955 in order to preserve a seat for the Radicals, according to one commentator. Consequently, in the elections of June, 1955, in the twilight of a long and distinguished career, he won his last campaign. But at the age of seventy he was tired and discouraged. As the weight of the terrible humiliations at home and abroad mounted, the malaise of the Fourth Republic, of which the tragicomedy of the presidential elections of 1953 was merely a tiny symptom, had become painfully clear and had led him to doubt its ability to endure much longer. He had barely assumed his seat in the Senate when he became ill, and in early 1956 an operation disabled him for several months. Finally, at the height of the international crisis over Hungary and the Suez, he was stricken; and he died in Paris three days later, on November 15, 1956, at the age of seventy-one.[42]

It would be easy to conclude that Delbos' rapid ascent in politics was due at least as much to a shortage of capable men to whom the nation could turn as to any outstanding qualities of his own. One can point to the generation of leaders lost in World War I and a declining birth rate as causes of this dearth of qualified leaders. If forcefulness and creativity are the sole criteria for judgment, there is much to sustain this viewpoint. Yet upon further examination it becomes apparent that Delbos was a serviceable man whose attributes, skills, and character made him a highly valuable servant and a worthy defender of the Republic.

Considered to be "a good technician but not much of a theoretician,"[43] Delbos made a virtue out of a steady and enthusiastic exhibition of administrative proficiency. More importantly, he earned the deep respect and high esteem of his political colleagues by his honesty and integrity, attributes which when mixed with a good deal of modesty were frequently in short supply among politicians of the Third Republic. Moreover, he was generally considered to have a complete lack of high political ambitions.[44] For example, with the fall of the Laval government in January, 1936, before turning to Albert Sarraut, President Lebrun first asked Delbos, who had played a prominent role in Laval's defeat, to try to form a cabinet. Delbos is alleged to have told his advisor Henri Laugier that he could not be Premier because he had never been Premier before.[45] In his official refusal, however, he cited his opposition to Laval in the Chamber debates concerning sanctions against Italy. He argued that this would make it more difficult for him to form a government than for someone else from his party.[46] Naturally, his political modesty and integrity made him an attractive choice for cabinet posts by those Premiers who felt that their own positions might be threatened by more politically ambitious men. Many, of course, recognized that the unsettled times necessitated the stabilizing influence of such respectable, if less spectacular, men in positions of responsibility. In all likelihood, Premiers may have turned to him to fill posts in their cabinets because he was always ready to do his best, frequently in the less glamorous positions such as Minister of Education, to which few others aspired.

As Minister of Foreign Affairs he ably demonstrated his administrative talents. He gave his undersecretaries, such as Pierre Viénot, who was given charge of the French mandates and protectorates in the Middle East, a great degree of independence of action. Yet he never ceased to support them or to encourage them to seek new solutions and develop new policies. Given his rather informal training in foreign affairs, he found it desirable to surround himself with advisors, quickly arriving at an easy understanding and collaboration with the permanent career officials at the Foreign Office. He appreciated their devotion and seriously considered their proposals, although the fast-breaking events often did not permit the long debate and reflection that others had been afforded in less hectic times and from which he would have benefited greatly. On the whole, however, the Quai d'Orsay ran smoothly under his command; and one of his most able lieutenants and fellow *normalien*, René Massigli, later recalled: "I found the man of our common youth: the same honesty, the same sincere willingness to seek the solution most appropriate to conciliate the national and international interests, the same solicitude of understanding, the same scruples . . . loyalty called for loyalty and he was loyally served in these difficult months."[47]

Like many other eminent French politicians of the period, Delbos had easy access to at least one prominent journal of the Republican press. In his case it was the powerful Radical Socialist organ *La Dépêche de Toulouse,* which became the *Dépêche du Midi* after

World War II. His long and close relationship with the Sarraut brothers permitted him the opportunity of putting into practice his special training and interest in writing and education, only in a nonacademic capacity. Here again his record was one of respected and solid achievement. He was exacting in gathering information for his editorials and commentaries, utilizing every possible scrap of information, yet not forcing it into any preconceived notions that he might have concerning a topic. As Joseph Barsalou, Editor in Chief of the *Dépêche du Midi,* has recounted, Delbos developed his thoughts "with an enveloping force . . . but with always the most subtle nuances, as it was enriched by reflection."[48] His manuscripts were easily recognizable by the many alterations and marginal notations that spilled all over the pages, although without ruining the continuity or cohesion of thought, as he revised and refined the reasoning until the last possible moment before going to press. Much of this effort stemmed from "the fear of an error, even minor, or of an injustice" which weighed on his mind. His ultimate goal remained to persuade rather than to force recognition and adherence to his point of view, although he could denounce as vehemently and defend as arduously as any other journalist. His campaigns in *La Dépêche* against fascist totalitarianism (for which he was probably remembered by those who paid back old debts during the occupation and which undoubtedly had much bearing on the decision to have him deported to Germany), the dangers of which he understood earlier and more clearly than many others, rang loud and clear in the ears of those who cared to listen. His defense of and designs for the League of Nations and collective security were based on solid recommendations which might have worked had the times and the condition of that institution permitted their consideration. His cultural background permitted him to write and comment upon a wide variety of matters— from the character and temper of the Dordogne to the spirited and vivacious world of the theater and to the astute analysis of the Soviet Union's political, economic, and social structure. Invariably, however, he came back to his favorite topics of political, and especially foreign-affairs, commentary. His perspicacity and integrity were widely acknowledged, and he was accorded great esteem within the journalistic profession. He served for many years as President of the Association of Republican Journalists and as President of the Federation of the Press, the highest distinction within the profession.[49]

In domestic politics—unlike many of his Radical Socialist colleagues who were primarily concerned with protecting the frequently narrow interests of their constituents, realizing that if they did so their continued election would be assured regardless of their record on national issues—Delbos sought the active intervention of the state on behalf of human rights for all the people. The regionalism of his own constituents of southwestern France must have presented him with frequent dilemmas; but as a man of "liberal democratic" inclinations, due in large part no doubt to his family background and his training at the Ecole Normale, he was convinced that only by social progress could the unity and future of French republican institutions be assured.[50] For this principle he earned sympathy and recognition from those outside his party and from a wider constituency than his own. It was not unusual, therefore, that he got along well with the Socialists and frequently voted with them on issues of national importance.[51] Undoubtedly, this closeness of viewpoint with the Socialists helped to make him a highly acceptable member of the Popular Front cabinet. As his leading position among the Radicals in the Chamber suggests, however, he did not leave the fold often enough to damage his party standing. Perhaps his most obvious commitment to social progress came in the area of education. Here his own background and interests imbued him with a particular concern for the advancement of educational standards and easier accessibility to higher education in France, which he promoted during his frequent assignments to the Chamber's education committees and in his several terms as Minister of Education.[52]

In his personal life Delbos was a man of simple inclinations. He was typically middle class, although his "pure curiosity for things of the mind and of art" made him more culturally sophisticated than the ordinary Frenchman of that class.[53] In fact, he served briefly as Undersecretary of State for the Beaux Arts, and he moved about easily in the glamorous theatrical circles in Paris. But his roots remained in the region of Périgord and the Dordogne. The province provided the opportunity to get away from all of the glamor and responsibilities of public life in Paris, even if only for a Sunday. It was here in southwest France that Delbos' childhood and early training had imbued him with the characteristic capacity for enjoyment combined with the thrift that predominates among the people of that region.[54] Indeed, it has been pointed out that he remained quite "detached from the possessions of this world."[55] As a "genuine son of Périgord," he thoroughly enjoyed good food and fine wine. But as one observer noted, he was one of the few exceptions in an age when "it was almost proof of political importance to have liver trouble." The same observer added that Delbos "is a connoisseur, not a glutton, and when culinary matters are discussed, he opens up much more readily than if the discussion turns on foreign policy."[56] Like many Frenchmen in a country where the family stands supreme, he maintained intimate and longstanding ties with his family. Both of his parents—but especially his mother, who, as already indicated, influenced him profoundly—encouraged his entry into politics.[57] His regard for parental wishes, it has been said, led him to delay until quite late in his life—in 1953—marriage to his long-time mistress, Germaine Rouer, an actress at the Comédie-Française.[58]

After his brilliant career as a rugby player, he maintained a great interest in athletics. Achieving distinction in politics while remaining athletic was an unusual accomplishment in an era when sports were regarded as "irreconcilable with the dignity of a serious-minded, responsible person."[59]

Like so many other good Radical Socialist politicians, Delbos was not noted for his religious fervor, even though one of his uncles was a priest. He preferred to be considered a freethinker on the matter, although he "never professed a militant atheism."[60] Upon his death, of course, this created a ticklish question. A witness from the Dordogne, who wishes to remain unidentified, recounted the embarrassing situation that occurred when Madame Delbos inquired about the possibility of a religious burial. It was finally learned from the Jesuit Father who had tended to Delbos during his last moments at the hospital in Paris that the latter, fully conscious, had asked for and received the church's last sacraments and that he, therefore, could receive a religious burial (although the Bishop of Périgueux strongly intimated that the eulogies should be left to politicians). So, like many Radical Socialist leaders before and after him, Delbos made a deathbed repentance.

Delbos had little oratorical ability, which was probably a welcome relief from the polemical gymnastics of flowery words and smooth phrases utilized by many self-styled parliamentary debaters who surrounded him.[61] Perhaps this had much to do with his personal attractiveness. "An atmosphere of goodness and honesty emanated from his person and from his behavior." As a warm and personable man, his "natural cordiality" and his gracefulness earned him respect and affection, and put him on familiar terms with a wide range of people.[62] He never forgot his friends and comrades, and his simplicity remained untouched by arrogance or vanity.[63] He was a man who was indulgent of the mistakes of his subordinates and tolerant of the weaknesses of others.[64] Yet if this was ideally a desirable trait, it was also a source of weakness. Naively inclined to credit others with his own honest motivations and loyalties, it made him susceptible to the machinations of those of less pure intentions with whom he had to deal, both in domestic politics and in his negotiations abroad as Foreign Minister.

Delbos has been variously portrayed as "a good man, but not the type of man that could or would take any strong or decisive action" and as a rather "pale figure."[65] This, however, is to miss the point about the man's character, actions, and contributions to the Republic. It is undeniable that he had obvious shortcomings, and it is true that he never assumed the appearance of those imposing figures like Clemenceau, Churchill, and de Gaulle who, as "men of crisis," descended upon turbulent waters as if predestined to save their nations. But then such spectacular individuals are few and far between, and indeed, modern France has been singularly unlucky at producing them in crucial situations. There is, however, another rank of men upon whom the affairs of state most often depend: the Blums, the Herriots, the Monnets, and the Edens, who are most frequently the cement that holds their nations together in daily affairs in their own honest and conscientious, if unspectacular, ways. It is in this rank of men that Delbos must be cast.

Certainly, Delbos has had no lack of defenders. He has been characterized as "a man of strong conviction," and as "a man who really represented the mainstream of French thought on foreign affairs."[66] In a eulogy in 1956, Edouard Herriot recalled that his "unswerving *fidélité* made him the truest of friends. He lent our party the aura of his integrity [*sa caution morale*]." Guy Mollet echoed these sentiments: "His rectitude, his human compassion, and his intelligence made him one of the great servants of the land."[67] Jules Romains, a fellow *normalien* and long-time acquaintance, later described him as "one of the exemplary figures of the Third Republic."[68] On balance, however, perhaps the most astute estimate of the man came from a German contemporary, whose judgment was: "He is a creditable figure in the ranks of those under-estimated men with whom the Third Republic stands and falls—no more, no less."[69] He was indeed emblematic of those "men of good will" who were at once a source of strength and weakness for the Republic. Their strength assured the continued existence of the Republic until the collapse of 1940; their weakness stemmed from the fact that the Republic was forced to call on them for great actions in extraordinary times against incredible odds, and they, like most mortals, were found wanting. But to the end their attitude might be best summed up by a declaration made by Delbos during the dark days of 1940: "In the peril of the homeland [*la patrie*], there are no personal conveniences, there are only national conveniences."[70]

Although this brief summary of Delbos' career and character can only peripherally touch on his actions as Foreign Minister from 1936 to 1938, it does indicate his standing—founded above all upon a reputation for honesty, loyalty, and enthusiasm—among his constituents in the Dordogne, his fellow politicians in Paris, and his wide circle of friends. It also demonstrates that his conduct as Foreign Minister does not constitute the sum total of his record. Whatever may be the estimate of his ability and performance with regard to his conduct of foreign affairs, his contributions to other aspects of French political life make further study of the man worthwhile. Yet in spite of his record as a progressive and able journalist and as an administrator in French domestic politics, most will judge the place of Yvon Delbos in history by his actions as Foreign Minister during the period of the Popular Front.

2

Advent to the Quai d'Orsay

In order to understand how Delbos became Foreign Minister, one must briefly turn to an examination of the domestic situation in which France found herself in the spring of 1936. The period saw persistent internal political instability, deep divisions in public opinion, and an unremitting social crisis which diverted the attention of most Frenchmen from external problems. It has been said in a recent study that "the climate of France in 1936 was assuredly not a climate of civil war, but that the risks of civil war were not totally illusory."[1]

Since 1934, France had been undergoing an internal crisis promoted by the activity of the rightist *Ligues*, which had culminated in the riots of February 6, 1934. It has been observed that *"le 6 février* was neither a massacre of patriots nor a Fascist plot."[2] Nevertheless, the fact remains that the principal legacy of the 1934 disorders in Paris was a lingering fear among moderates and leftists that France was in danger of a fascist coup. Actually the danger was not as great as these groups imagined, but the continued growth of the Right, with its parades, uniforms, and storm-trooper tactics, seemed to confirm their fears.

Simultaneously, criticism mounted against the Laval government's deflationary financial policy, with its consequent increase in unemployment and decrease in production. Out of this discontent was born a countermovement among the parties of the Left. When the Communists proposed a united front, the Socialists quickly agreed. In the following year, 1935, the Radicals also joined; and the three parties united in an impressive display of solidarity on Bastille Day, July 14, 1935. The Socialist Léon Blum, the Radical Edouard Herriot, and the

Communist Maurice Thorez walked arm in arm at the head of three hundred thousand marchers.[3]

In January, 1936, Laval fell and Albert Sarraut formed a stopgap government to maintain order until the spring elections could determine the mood of the country. It was during this interval that Hitler took advantage of the continuing French malaise and paralysis to effectively tear away the last vestiges of the Versailles system with his reoccupation of the Rhineland. The bitterly fought campaign deeply aroused the passions of both the Left and Right. It has been estimated that "French prestige and French morale had never been so low as on that day in early May, 1936, when the people went to the polls to cast their votes for a new Chamber of Deputies."[4]

As a result of the vote, the Popular Front coalition gained an impressive victory in parliamentary representation. The Socialists became the largest party in the Chamber with 146 seats. The Radicals fell to a humiliating second with 116 seats. But the Communists benefited the most from the electoral cooperation among the parties. With a doubled popular vote, their representation in the Chamber climbed from 10 to 72. The Popular Front won 378 seats of 609 for its majority. Although the parliamentary majority was considerable, it was not matched by an equally imposing success in the popular vote. The actual vote for the parties of the Right declined only slightly. The Popular Front's margin of victory was due more to the cooperation among the three major parties than to any significant shift in voter sentiment. The precariousness of the electoral balance required that the parties of the Left coalition continue their close cooperation in the postelection period.[5]

As the largest party in the coalition, the Socialists were logically expected to provide the new Premier. Their leader, Léon Blum, had led them through some lean years since his assumption of leadership upon the death of Jean Jaurès on the eve of World War I. The tolerant and compassionate Blum had proved himself highly competent as a lawyer, journalist, and party leader. He energetically set to work constructing his cabinet and preparing innovative programs for the new government which was to take office in June.

One of the most important cabinet posts to be filled was that of Minister of Foreign Affairs, a position never considered appropriate for a political lightweight. Two questions arise at this point that are of major importance. First, why did Blum choose a Radical for such an important post in his government instead of a man from his own party? Second, why did he select Yvon Delbos as the Radical to fill the position?[6]

The answer to the first question appears to reside, at least partially, in the fact that the Communists, though agreeing to support Blum, ominously accepted no cabinet posts. Called "the first failure of the *Front Populaire*,"[7] it meant that the cabinet positions would have to be divided between the Radicals and Socialists. Since continued Radical support was necessary to keep the Popular Front in power, Radicals had to be given a fair share of the important cabinet posts. Inasmuch as the Socialists' greatest concern was the development of a French New Deal, Blum appointed fellow Socialists to positions that would afford them an opportunity to develop their domestic policies most effectively.[8] Therefore, of the important cabinet positions, the Ministries of Interior, Finance, Public Works, and National Economy and Industry went to Roger Salengro, Vincent Auriol, Albert Bedouce, and Charles Spinasse, all of whom were Socialists. The only important posts left for the Radicals to fill in the enlarged cabinet that Blum put together were those of Foreign Affairs, National Defense (and the defense-orientated ministries such as Aviation), and Vice-Premier. Consequently, in a cabinet which included sixteen Socialists and fourteen Radicals, Blum had virtually no choice but to distribute these posts among the most prominent Radicals he could coax into his ministry in an effort to make it as strong as possible. Thus, the political composition of the Popular Front, the lack of participation by the Communists in the government, and the deep social and economic dissatisfaction in the country explain why the portfolio of Foreign Minister went to a Radical.

There remains the question of why Yvon Delbos came to be chosen as the Radical to fill the post of Foreign Minister. Jules Moch, with whom Blum frequently conferred during the days of cabinet-making, has stated that he was surprised that the first man Blum chose for his cabinet was Yvon Delbos.[9] This is not verified, however, by other evidence collected on this matter. It appears certain that Blum first sought out Edouard Herriot for the post. This would appear to have been a logical choice. Herriot had been an important figure in the Radical party and in government circles for years. Former

President of the Radical party, he still led one of the important cliques within the party. He had been Premier himself and had served in many ministerial capacities in numerous cabinets during the inter-war period. Frequently an unofficial advisor on foreign affairs to various ministries, he had long had the privilege of access to confidential papers at the Quai d'Orsay. He had played a vital role in the direction of French foreign policy during the thirties. He had led the way in the rapprochement that ultimately resulted in the Franco-Soviet Pact of 1935. In London the *Times* commented that "for all of these reasons, and especially for the last, M. Herriot is the obvious candidate for the Quai d'Orsay."[10] On May 21 *Le Temps* reported that Herriot had met Blum at the house of a mutual friend on the evening of the nineteenth. In an effort to sweeten the offer, Blum evidently promised to give Herriot the maximum authority and freedom of action in his conduct of foreign affairs. Nevertheless, the newspaper reported that Herriot had declined Blum's offer, although assuring him of his continued support.[11] The *New York Times* speculated that Herriot had argued that he had been a strong partisan of sanctions against Italy and that probably the first action of the new Foreign Minister would be to lift the sanctions. Such an action could be more easily taken by one who had not been so closely identified with the sanctionist policy. It also reported that Herriot feared he had lost his hold on the Radical party. For these reasons Herriot preferred to remain outside the government, but he would accept the presidency of the Chamber of Deputies.[12] On May 23, after a meeting of the Radical Socialist Executive Committee, which passed a resolution providing for participation in the new government, Herriot privately said that he had declined Blum's invitation to a post in the new cabinet, but that he would not make his reasons public.[13] *Le Temps* reported on the twenty-fourth that Herriot had definitely told Blum he would not accept the proposed post.[14] In a speech at Lyon later in the week, Herriot emphasized that his refusal did not mean that there were any differences between the Socialists and himself. In addition, he was satisfied with the Radical decision to participate in the government.[15]

Thus it appears that in spite of Moch's statement that Delbos was the first man on Blum's list for the position of Foreign Minister, an offer was first made to Herriot. Even Henri Laugier, "the man who walked the closest with Delbos," has indicated that Blum asked Herriot before approaching Delbos.[16] It is quite possible, as Blum's son insists, that there was no formal written communiqué between the two men on the subject.[17] But Herriot could have easily made it known through intermediaries that he did not desire the post even before he talked with Blum on May 19.

One is still curious as to the real reasons for Herriot's refusal to assume the post at the Quai d'Orsay. A man of his stature would undoubtedly have strengthened the government, although it might have been difficult to have two domineering men conducting foreign affairs. Certainly he may have been tired of office after having served so many years in so many governments; he may have wished to remain out of the public eye while he reestablished his position in the Radical party; he assuredly felt that he could wield considerable power as President of the Chamber, a position he soon won over token opposition from the last-minute candidate of the extreme right wing, Xavier Vallat, by a vote of 377 to 150.[18] There is little doubt that Herriot had been a reluctant participant in the formative period of the Popular Front. His antagonism toward the Socialists had threatened to break up the coalition more than once.[19] One must wonder if Herriot had ever been really convinced of the ability of the Popular Front to sustain itself for very long. Conceivably, by remaining on the sidelines, he could step in as a savior to pick up the pieces after it had broken up.

Blum still needed to select a Foreign Minister. Among the press corps a good deal of speculation occurred about the suitability of various figures. But for all of the candidates considered, there were factors that made them unsuitable. Edouard Daladier was important enough in the ranks of the Radicals to obtain a place in the new cabinet. But objections to the "bull of the Vaucluse" as Foreign Minister centered upon his flirtation with Mussolini's Four Power Pact idea, which had aroused loud criticism. In some quarters he was not felt to be a wise negotiator. Moreover, his previous experience had been as Minister of Defense, and, indeed, he eventually assumed that post under Blum. Joseph Paul-Boncour had wide experience in foreign affairs as Foreign Minister and as the French delegate to the League of Nations. But Paul-Boncour had bolted from the ranks of the Socialist party and had formed his own Socialist group, the

Republican Socialist Union.[20] In matters of discipline the Socialist party had a long memory. More importantly, however, it was politically expedient to bestow such an important post upon a member of the other major party cooperating in the government. Consequently, Paul-Boncour remained the French delegate to the League. Other names that circulated, though not seriously considered, were Georges Bonnet and Camille Chautemps. Eventually the former went to Washington as Ambassador, while the latter entered the cabinet as Vice-Premier, where he could groom himself for taking command at a later date. It was even considered possible by some observers that Blum might take the post himself.[21] But Blum's conception of the premiership did not include the direction of any specific ministry. Instead, he envisioned his role to be that of supervision and policy guidance.[22]

It was not until May 25 that Delbos' activities began to attract some attention to him as a possible candidate for the post of Foreign Minister.[23] Le Temps reported that Blum had asked Delbos, "with insistence," to accept the post of Foreign Minister.[24] Delbos, however, remained very noncommittal in his reports to the press about his meeting with Blum, indicating only that they had reviewed the situation.[25] As of May 28, some quarters refused to take Delbos' candidacy seriously. The New York Times said, "He is without experience and without special competence in foreign affairs, and it may be said that Mr. Blum's choice is still not made."[26] Nevertheless, it would appear that Delbos had already decided to accept the position either at or shortly after his meeting with Blum on May 26. It has been asserted, however, that Delbos accepted only very hesitatingly.[27] Quite possibly he honestly recognized, at this early date, his own limitations and lack of experience in foreign affairs.[28]

The question remains: Why did Blum turn to Delbos as Foreign Minister after Herriot's refusal? A wide range of opinion on the probable reasons for this selection exists among Delbos' contemporaries. On the one hand, it is felt that Blum chose Delbos in the expectation that he could be easily manipulated. This would allow Blum to control foreign policy more directly. By bringing Delbos into the cabinet, he did not have to fear sharing the reins of power in foreign affairs with a more powerful Radical leader.[29] Perhaps, as Jules Moch observed, Blum felt that Delbos would not take any decisive action without first consulting the Premier. The latter could in this way exercise more effective control over the decision-making process at the Quai d'Orsay.[30] The rightist *Je suis partout* reported Blum as saying, "It is necessary for me to have a docile man, who may not have any ideas."[31]

This explanation has been rejected in most other quarters. Henri Bonnet has noted that no Premier ever chooses a man who is likely to disagree strongly with his own position, especially in such an important post as Minister of Foreign Affairs.[32] Indeed, it is in this direction that one must look to find the reasons for Blum's selection of Delbos. The fact is that the two men agreed very closely in their basic conceptions of foreign policy.[33] Even on domestic issues the moderate but slightly leftist Delbos had frequently sided with the Socialists. In addition, it has been said that Blum "had a great feeling for Delbos."[34] In return, Delbos held a great admiration for Blum, even though he was less pacifistic and more nationalistic than the latter.[35] Consequently, there is no doubt that a close friendship existed between the two men. Blum testified before the postwar Parliamentary Commission that "a great confidence existed between the two of us."[36] Their intimate personal relationship, as well as their closeness of views on foreign and domestic issues, was further enhanced by the fact that they lived in the same building on the Ile St. Louis. During the election campaign and while they controlled the reins of government, the two men frequently talked on the staircase from one floor to the next as they discussed the problems of the day.[37] As Blum said later, "When we had not been able to exchange our information or impressions during the day, we did it in the evening or early in the morning."[38] This fact must be kept in mind later when assigning responsibility for the formulation of French foreign policy while Blum and Delbos were in the same cabinet. It is quite likely that in this manner they made tentative policy decisions that never became part of the public record. This has rendered it virtually impossible firmly to establish who was the originator of various ideas that were ultimately implemented, if indeed it was ever clear to the principals themselves.

Perhaps as important as this friendship and similarity of viewpoint was the trust that Blum felt he could place in Delbos. As has been previously indicated, many of Delbos' contemporaries feel that he was basically a man without high political ambition. Robert Blum has surmised that his father knew that he could rely upon Delbos' cooperation without the latter becoming involved in political intrigue and maneuvering within the government.[39] This type of loyalty had a particular attraction for Blum as he teetered in his precarious position at the head of the Popular Front coalition.

In a more tangible sense, Delbos had taken an active interest in foreign affairs. He had taken strong stands beside the Socialists on various issues in the Chamber. He had been an ardent supporter of Herriot and had helped him carry the issue of the Franco-Soviet Pact to the public. He had presented detailed justifications of the fact in *La Dépêche de Toulouse.*[40] In fact, as has already been indicated, he had become convinced of the need for such an agreement during his trip to Russia in 1932. This position accorded closely with that of Léon Blum and the Socialists, although Blum, after opposing the pact for a considerable time, never shared Delbos' or Herriot's enthusiasm for it.[41]

In a debate on December 27 and 28, 1935, Delbos had taken the lead, along with Paul Reynaud and Blum, in attacking Laval's policy toward Italy as symbolized by the Hoare-Laval Plan. Some considered that the attack delivered by Delbos ranked with that of Reynaud as decisive in the eventual fall of the Laval government.[42] Delbos exclaimed, "Your plan is dead and buried. . . . Two lessons emerge. The first is that you were in a dead end because you upset everyone without satisfying Italy. The second is that we must return to the spirit of the Covenant by preserving the agreement with the nations gathered at Geneva."[43] Coming on top of the speeches by Reynaud and Blum, Delbos' motion of censure might have toppled Laval had the vote been taken that day. But passions cooled overnight. The vote on the following day, taken in a calmer atmosphere, maintained Laval by the narrow margin of 296 to 276. But "it was only a stay of execution; within six weeks the government was down."[44] This stand by Delbos is considered by some to have been a significant factor when Blum began forming his cabinet.[45]

It is possible that Delbos favored a strong action against the German reoccupation of the Rhineland, although this is not entirely clear. It is evident, however, that he had earned the reputation of being a staunch supporter of collective security through the League, as his speech against Laval indicates, and of complete cooperation with Great Britain.[46] These views were remarkably close to those held by Blum.

Others have pointed to Delbos' important position in the Radical party. As a long-time deputy, former president of the parliamentary Radical Group, Vice-President of the Chamber, and former minister, he had developed considerable support and influence in the party.[47] After Herriot had decided to run for the presidency of the Chamber and Daladier had accepted the post of Minister of Defense and Chautemps that of Vice-Premier, who else remained among the qualified Radicals? Assuming that Blum recognized the usefulness of having a Radical at the Quai d'Orsay, his choice of candidates had become quite limited.

René Massigli, a long-time diplomat and official at the Quai d'Orsay, has suggested that the popularity of Delbos among his constituents was another possible reason for his selection.[48] It is doubtful, however, that this swayed Blum. Delbos did not, after all, have much of a following outside of southwestern France and, therefore, would not bring significant national backing to the government.

The precise reason for Blum's selection of Delbos as his Foreign Minister is not clear. Indeed, as is usual in such instances, the probable explanation must be found in some combination of all of these factors: The close personal relationship between the two men; their similar attitudes in matters of foreign affairs; Delbos' activity in foreign affairs, particularly with regard to the Hoare-Laval Plan and the Franco-Soviet Pact; his high rank and influence within the Radical party; and his lack of any obvious high political ambition, all must be weighed when analyzing Blum's motivations. With the benefit of hindsight, however, it is clear that the selection of Delbos should not have been too surprising, inasmuch as the logic of this wide variety of factors increasingly pointed to him as the Foreign Minister of the Popular Front.

3

Spain: The Decision
for Nonintervention

For the first few weeks after the Popular Front's ascent to power in June, 1936, the foreign policy of the Blum government was dominated by the consequences of the Abyssinian War and the reoccupation of the Rhineland. But *un clou chasse l'autre,* says the French proverb, and, indeed, events in Spain soon drove all other considerations from the attention of the Blum government. There is little doubt that the Spanish Civil War became the central foreign-policy problem of the Popular Front era. Scarcely a day passed during the remainder of 1936 and throughout 1937 that did not bring discussions in the cabinet or at the Quai d'Orsay over the many problems raised by the Spanish question. Some indication of the importance of the insurrection for France is reflected in the comment of Pierre Cot, who considers that "we lost the first battle of the world war in Spain, in allowing the crushing of the Spanish Republic."[1]

In 1936 a general election in Spain gave power to a coalition of Radicals, Socialists, and Communists similar to that formed in France. This new Frente Popular provoked fear among the conservative elements in Spain—the monarchists, the military, and the fascists. Never noted for its democratic tradition, Spain had precariously maintained a democratic republic since 1931. Now, however, it appeared to many Spaniards that the uncertain balance between the rightists and leftists was in danger of being upset. Public order began to break down as acts of terrorism by one side evoked retaliation by the other. Ultimately, the murder of one of the rightist leaders, Calvo Sotelo, provided the pretext for a full-scale military rebellion in Spanish Morocco

31

on July 17, 1936. The revolt had been planned for some time and had "received a vague blessing from Mussolini."[2] On July 18 General Francisco Franco flew from the Canary Islands to Morocco to take over the revolt as it spread to many of the garrisons in Spain. On the same day Moroccan troops began crossing to the mainland. Such an event was hardly novel to Spain. It might have been a mere passing incident without any implications for the rest of the continent had it been either quickly triumphant or promptly suppressed. But this was not to be. Within a short time a situation developed that found the country split into two halves. On the one hand, there were the rebels, or Nationalists, led by the rebellious army. On the other hand, there were the Loyalists, led by the existing government and supported by the workers. Rather than a quick victory or defeat, a long civil war ensued. In the uncertain situation in which Europe found itself in 1936, the Spanish Civil War was not allowed to unfold as a purely localized affair. Instead, Spain became the battleground of competing ideologies and interests.[3]

From the first days of the Spanish Civil War the great European powers began taking sides. Italian and German assistance to the Nationalists was immediate. Their ships helped to transport Franco's troops from Morocco to Andalusia on July 18. Russian aid to the Loyalists was announced on July 28.[4]

In view of the ideological and strategic interests that the totalitarian states had in the Spanish conflict, the question arose—What would France do? France had taken advantage of the decline of Spain in the nineteenth and twentieth centuries to obtain greater freedom of action in the Mediterranean, and therefore did not wish to see a strong government installed in Madrid which might want to resume an active foreign policy and seek to modify the status quo. The French were anxious to safeguard the security of communications between North Africa and metropolitan France. Consequently, they feared an Italo-Spanish collaboration which might result in an Italian presence in the Balearic Islands.[5] A rebel victory might mean that Spanish Morocco would be thrown open to Italian or German penetration, with inevitable repercussions in French Morocco and in the Mediterranean in general.[6] In 1905 France had gone to the brink of war to prevent such a penetration. Would she do so again?

The case for supporting the Spanish government seemed overwhelming. Not only was it an ideological friend of the French Popular Front, but Spain was vital for French strategic interests in the Mediterranean. Yet in spite of these arguments, within a few weeks France had cut off aid in arms and volunteers, and the government had formulated and adopted a policy of nonintervention by the great powers.

The history of international affairs during the interwar period witnessed few actions more significant than the French decision to pursue a policy of nonintervention towards Spain. Yet few decisions are as difficult for the historian to reconstruct. The sequel is easy enough to describe. But the how and why of the final decision have remained most puzzling to students of the problem. The influences and motivation that dominated the men involved in developing the policy cannot be ascertained with any great degree of certainty. With the availability of new source materials, however, it has become possible to take another look at the circumstances that determined the decisions made and the actions taken in late July and early August, 1936.[7]

The problem of ascertaining the full story has been compounded by the fact that many of the individuals closely connected with the decision have revealed few of the intimate details that are so important for a complete reconstruction of the course of events. There is certainly no dearth of memoirs existing for the interwar years, but few members of the inner circle of Blum's government who wrote their autobiographies reminisced about the "inside story" of the Spanish decision.[8] Even those who testified before the postwar commission inquiring into the interwar years shed little new light on the problem.[9]

Consequently, there are a number of vital questions that remain to be answered. It is uncertain which segment of the cabinet was represented by the policy ultimately decided upon. But more importantly, what induced the members of the government to act as they did? Why did caution become the better part of valor? Was it a reaction to the pressure of public opinion? Was it a response dictated by the intangible psychological and emotional factors residing in a very human process? Or perhaps one should just chalk it up to a loss of nerve and cowardice. More significantly, how much did foreign pressures, particularly that of Britain, influence the French resolve? At any rate, there is little agreement among the contemporaries concerning these questions.[10] Moreover, it would be presumptuous to state with any degree of finality which were the determining factors. But by studying the new evidence as well as the old, valuable insight into the process may be gained by evaluating the role played by the Foreign Minister of the Popular Front, Yvon Delbos.

Although he must not be held totally responsible for what has often been described as the worst foreign policy error of the Popular Front,[11] there can be little doubt that Delbos played a crucial, if not decisive, role in the formulation of the French policy towards the Spanish Civil War.

Sotelo's murder had served to increase fears of an impending rightist military coup d'etat. Rumors of such an uprising had been circulating throughout Madrid for some time.[12] Yet Blum later maintained that when the revolt of the military broke out, it came with "startling suddenness." In fact he had been assured on July 18, by the Vice-President of the Spanish Cortes, that the political situation was "excellent."[13] On the afternoon of the eighteenth the first word of the rebellion arrived from Jean Herbette, the French Ambassador in Madrid. In the first note no particular urgency appeared to be attached to the affair.[14] But on the following day he reported that "the situation is appreciably aggravated."[15] Indeed, the situation had become quite grave as military uprisings broke out in Barcelona, Cadiz, Seville, and Malaga. Blum had predicted that complications would arise when he learned of the outbreak.[16] On Monday, the twentieth, as he arrived at his office, Blum's prediction came true. Three dramatic weeks of frantic meetings, negotiations, and consultations followed as the Blum government sought to formulate its policy toward the Spanish conflict. On the twentieth, Blum received from José Giral, the Spanish Premier, a telegram *en clair*—by-passing the usual diplomatic channels through the Spanish Embassy—requesting permission to procure arms and planes in France in order to suppress the Nationalist rebellion. There was little doubt about the legality of the Spanish appeal. Under international law a legal government has the right to purchase war materials when confronted with a rebellion. In December, 1935, this general principle had been supplemented by a specific commercial agreement signed between France and Spain. A *note confidentielle* provided for Spanish purchase of armaments in France up to the amount of twenty million francs.[17]

Upon receiving Giral's request, Blum moved quickly. On July 21 he met with Delbos, Edouard Daladier, Minister of Defense, and Pierre Cot, Minister of Aviation. The legality of Giral's government and the Franco-Spanish Commercial Pact of 1935 were important considerations in the decision to send arms. In addition, however, they felt that the Spanish government was a friendly one, and they recognized that a fascist victory in Spain would permit Italy and Germany to establish bases in the Balearics and Canaries. Nevertheless, the ministers decided to keep the transaction as secret as possible to prevent adding new fuel to the rightist press in France.[18] Daladier and Cot were instructed to determine how France could best satisfy the Spanish requirements.[19] The Spanish Ambassador, Juan F. de Cárdenas, was informed; and the Spanish government sent Fernando de los Ríos, their representative at the League of Nations, to Paris to settle the technical problems concerning the arms shipments.[20]

But any hopes of maintaining secrecy about the intended arms shipments were immediately shattered. The rebels had friends in the Spanish Embassy. Giral's awareness of that fact had led him to go directly to Blum with his first appeal. But when arrangements for the delivery of arms were made, they had to pass through the hands of the Military Attaché at the Embassy. The latter was a supporter of Franco who resigned shortly thereafter and leaked the details to the rightist press.[21] L'Action Française and L'Echo de Paris promptly unleashed a vigorous campaign to prevent the delivery of arms to Spain.[22] On July 23 Henri de Kerillis published the complete details in L'Echo de Paris and asked, "Will the French Popular Front dare to arm the Spanish Popular Front?"[23] In L'Action Française, Maurice Pujo demanded to know if Blum and Cot "have the right to launch France upon this disgraceful adventure which will furnish a legal precedent and an example to other nations who would be tempted to intervene one day in our own affairs." He concluded by asking, "Yes or no, has this treason been committed?"[24] Both denounced the role of de los Ríos in the transaction and called the shipment of the arms despicable. As they grasped for straws, they invoked fears of weakening France's national defenses and rejected any interference in the internal affairs of a foreign state. If France sent arms to the Republicans, the fascist powers would be provoked into sending aid to the Nationalists. Besides, they added, Delbos did not entirely agree with the position of Blum and Cot. Pierre Renouvin believes this information to be correct. He cites a communiqué of the twenty-fourth: "Any delivery of arms cannot be made to a foreign power without the Quai d'Orsay being consulted." But the note further indicated that the Foreign Minister had not acknowledged any demands of that type.[25] Blum's son has suggested that this was typical of Delbos' behavior. He did not directly oppose arms shipments to Spain, but he made haste slowly in sending aid. On the other hand, he acted with dispatch on anything that would encourage nonintervention.[26]

In the meantime, however, Blum, Delbos, and Alexis Léger, Secretary General at the Quai d'Orsay, had gone to England to meet with the Prime Ministers and Foreign Ministers of Britain and Belgium. A standard interpretation of this meeting is that on July 21 Charles Corbin, the French Ambassador in London, telephoned Blum to indicate the grave concern felt by the British. The Baldwin government felt that the French might become embroiled in the Spanish conflict as a result of their decision to send arms to the Republicans. He urged Blum and Delbos to come to London at once to confer with Baldwin and Eden on the matter. Supporters of this interpretation add that Eden then impressed upon them the great danger to European peace that might result from continued French support of the Madrid government. This interpretation stems mainly from Cordell Hull's memoirs. His source was the report of the American Ambassador in Paris, Jesse Isidor Straus.[27] A more recent interpretation, however, casts doubt upon the validity of this explanation.[28]

Indeed, Blum gave no indication in his postwar testimony that the meeting had been called for the purpose of discussing the Spanish affair.[29] In fact, Pierre Cot appears to be nearer the truth when he states that the "trip had been planned long before the revolt of the Spanish generals" and that Blum "wished to establish personal contacts with the British leaders, and was going to join Yvon Delbos, . . . who was representing us in London at a conference of England, France and Belgium." The object of the meeting was to examine the consequences of Germany's remilitarization of the Rhineland.[30]

As early as July 3 Delbos had reached agreement at Geneva with Eden and Van Zeeland, the Belgian Prime Minister, about the necessity for the three signatory powers of the arrangement of March 19 to meet and reexamine the Rhineland situation.[31] By July 8 it had been established that the meeting between the three Locarno powers would take place on July 22.[32] Clearly, then, the British did not call Blum to London as a reaction to the French policy toward Spain. In fact, it is highly unlikely that the Spanish problem even entered into the formal discussions except in a most incidental fashion. On July 17 Delbos indicated that "the first order of business should be that of regulating the situation created by the German intiative of March 7 and of negotiating afterwards, on an equal footing, a new accord intended to take the place of the Rhineland Pact made at Locarno."[33] There is little to lead one to believe that this did not remain the primary item of business among the ministers. It was hoped that an agreement between the three powers would pave the way for a later meeting which would include Germany and Italy.[34] The French *Procès-verbal* of the two sessions of July 23, during which Delbos carried the main burden of discussion, does not include any mention of the Spanish problem.[35] The official communiqué emphasized that the main intention of the powers was "to consolidate peace by means of a general settlement." It added that "nothing would be more fatal to the hope of such a settlement than the division of Europe, apparent or real, into opposing blocs."[36]

Thus, the London Conference of July 23, 1936, was not called to debate the Spanish question; nor was the topic formally raised during the meetings. This does not mean, however, that the conflict was not discussed at all among the participants. Given the increasingly difficult position in which France found itself in its relationship with Spain, it would have been foolish to neglect the opportunity to sound out the British position. In reality, Blum was very anxious to find out where the British stood with regard to Spain.[37]

Indications of the British attitude were not long in coming. Shortly after his arrival in London, Blum was approached by the French journalist Pertinax (André Géraud). Blum confirmed to him the government's intentions of supplying arms to the Republicans. Pertinax then warned, "You know that it is not very well seen here."[38] Blum subsequently learned from Corbin that considerable prorebel sympathy existed in the Baldwin cabinet. The cabinet reflected the opinion of British Conservatives who had social and financial interests in their Spanish counterparts. Fearing a peasant takeover of the

Spanish landed estates, even those British Conservatives most aware of the fascist menace preferred Franco to the Loyalists.[39]

Blum and Delbos soon had direct confirmation of this feeling among governing circles. On the twenty-third, before and between sessions of the three-power meeting, various members of the British cabinet expressed "great apprehension" over French aid to Republican Spain. According to Joel Colton, "Blum, Delbos, and Léger were clearly made to understand the negative attitude of the British Conservatives, who did not wish to take sides in the 'faction fight' in Spain."[40] Before the French ministers left London, Eden paid Blum a visit at his hotel. After Blum confirmed his desire to send arms to the Republicans, Eden said, "It is your affair, but I ask of you one thing: I beg you, be prudent."[41]

If these words of caution weighed heavily upon Blum, as Colton indicates,[42] there can be little doubt that they impressed Delbos as well. The atmosphere in London put Delbos in a serious dilemma. Born and raised in southwestern France, Delbos felt a certain sympathy for the Spanish people. He had been especially impressed by some of the Republicans such as Juan Negrín. In addition, he knew well many of the leading Socialists in the Frente Popular. Undoubtedly this sentiment had inspired him to respond favorably to the first Spanish appeals for assistance. But the overriding issue in his mind was the restoration of a close relationship with Britain.[43] During his flight back to Paris on the twenty-fourth, he pondered the cautious words that he had heard in London. They must have given him considerable cause to reflect about his position and the path that France should pursue towards Spain.

If the situation in London appeared grave to Blum and Delbos, the imbroglio they found in Paris upon their return to Le Bourget airfield hardly encouraged them to take vigorous action on behalf of the Madrid government. While Blum and Delbos had been in London, the rightist press had whipped itself into a frenzy condemning French interference in Spain. Therefore, Jules Moch, André Blumel, and Marx Dormoy, Blum's closest confidants in the government, sought to warn them of the press campaign before they returned to Paris. One is struck by the drama as the three men dashed out to Le Bourget only to find that Camille Chautemps, the Vice-Premier, had arrived ahead of them.[44]

Chautemps had come to tell the returning ministers of the "grave" situation in Paris. He recounted the resounding press campaign initiated by *L'Echo de Paris*, in which the full details of the arrangements with the Spanish had been made public. He indicated that considerable emotion had been aroused in the Assembly. One domestic consequence of the policy could be the dissolution of the government due to Radical Socialist hostility to the anticipated arms shipments. He raised the specter of increased international tensions and possible conflict.[45] Only later, during the ride into Paris, did Moch and Blumel have the opportunity to pull Blum aside and attempt to relieve the sense of impending doom conveyed by Chautemps.[46]

Blum immediately set about trying to determine the extent of the opposition aroused by the government's policy. He found Jules Jeanneney, President of the Senate, extremely upset over the fact that Blum "could at this moment engage [himself] in an enterprise of which one cannot exactly measure the consequences, the idea that perhaps we could be led to war for the affairs of Spain." He reminded Blum that France had not acted when the Rhineland crisis had confronted it with a direct threat to its security. It would be difficult to understand why France should then go to war over Spain. Once again the fear of acting alone was brought home to Blum as Jeanneney declared, "We are all certain that if there were European complications provoked by an intervention in the Spanish affair, England would not follow us."[47] Edouard Herriot, then President of the Chamber, added to the gloom by begging Blum not to become involved in the Spanish business. In the meantime, Delbos had been having meetings as well, particularly with various Radical leaders who expressed fears over the government's initiative in sending arms to Spain.[48] The difficulties of the policy became increasingly clear in Delbos' mind.

Later that night Blum called together at his home the ministers most involved with delivering the Spanish requests. The Minister of Finance, Vincent Auriol, joined the group that had made the initial decision to make the shipment on the twenty-first—Delbos, Daladier, and Cot. De los Ríos, the special Spanish representative, also attended and made the Spanish position clear, emphasizing the need for planes. Of the four ministers present, only Delbos hesitated. Impressed, no doubt, by his conversations in London, he had returned to Paris only to find a frenzied press attack being carried on against the government's decision and increasing opposition among leaders of his own party. Nevertheless, he asked only that precautions be taken in order not to alarm public opinion unnecessarily. After de los Ríos departed, Delbos again repeated his advice to be cautious, but agreed that the Spanish arms request should be met.[49] In retrospect, Delbos' wavering at this meeting is indicative of the change of heart that he was undergoing. Ultimately, his revised position would lead him to aid in developing a policy of strict nonintervention in Spain. Once committed to the policy, he would press vigorously for its adoption by the cabinet.

On the following day Blum held the first of three full cabinet meetings devoted to the Spanish problem. Out of these sessions, held over a period of two weeks, the Popular Front's policy of nonintervention unfolded. The rightist press campaign had become increasingly vigorous. Henri de Kerillis asked in *L'Echo de Paris*, "Will the French airplanes handed over by Pierre Cot go to Madrid?" He declared that "the government's act is criminal and abominable. . . . Germany and Italy are showing nervousness and anger. . . . Neither of them has any interest in seeing Communism triumph in the Mediterranean area and in the west of Europe. The interference of France is such as to provoke their own."[50] *L'Action Française* wanted to know, "Is it on account of the affairs of Spain that . . . Blum will lead us to war?"[51]

This was the atmosphere that prevailed when the cabinet met on the evening of July 25 to examine the Spanish situation. Chautemps told of the effect of the rightist press campaign upon the conservative senators. Delbos again reported the attitude of the British Ministers during the London Conference. Although Cot recorded that "the possibility of denouncing the treaty which allowed the Spanish government to buy arms in France was never considered for a moment,"[52] this seems unlikely in view of the communiqué released to the press, which stated:

> The French government, after having deliberated in the Council of Ministers this afternoon, has been unanimous in deciding not to intervene in any manner in the internal conflict of Spain. This thesis supported by M. Yvon Delbos, Minister of Foreign Affairs, has been unanimously approved. Finally, on the

subject of furnishing materials of war that the Spanish government had solicited, they declared, in the official sphere, at the end of the meeting of the Council of Ministers: it is not true that the French government affirmed itself resolved to practice a policy of intervention.[53]

Indeed, it appears that the caution and wavering that Delbos had displayed the night before had turned into bona-fide support of partial nonintervention. On the following day Delbos sent a telegram to Auriol, telling him that the exportation of all war material to Spain must be prohibited. Planes without armaments, however, would be authorized for shipment to the Spanish government by private industry. On the twenty-seventh a circular to the most important diplomatic posts confirmed the decision.[54] As can be seen, the policy was not yet a full-scale, all-inclusive policy of nonintervention, but the first step in that direction had been taken. Others were to follow with increasing rapidity.

At this point Blum felt that the decision made on the twenty-fifth would allow more time during which the pressure of public opinion could be brought to support those who desired to aid Spain.[55] In the meantime, plans were pushed ahead to ship certain war materials to Mexico, for reshipment to Spain.[56]

The press reaction to the decision of July 25 showed an exultant Right and a deeply aroused Left. The press of the extreme Left equated the decision with giving "direct aid to the Spanish fascists." *Le Peuple* predicted a series of abdications by the government. *L'Humanité* said, "It is not indifferent to us that France might have tomorrow a frontier to defend on the southwest."[57] In addition, a majority of articles in the British press seemed to sympathize with France's problem, and similar reactions were noted in Poland and Belgium. Foreign support would, of course, be of vital importance should a general war break out over Spain.[58]

On July 30 a telegram came from Rabat to the Quai d'Orsay which almost changed the march of events. Two Italian airplanes, heading for Spanish Morocco, were forced to land in French territory in North Africa. Although carrying civilian passports, the pilots appeared to be members of the Italian air force.[59] The ensuing investigation firmly established that the Italian government had sent the planes and pilots to aid Franco.[60] "We felt ourselves a lot more

at ease," said Blum in 1947. This proof of intervention freed Blum
from the rightist warnings of Italian action being provoked by French
aid to the Republicans. Italy had already intervened.[61] Perhaps Blum
could now act as he had desired in the first place. Before the Senate
Foreign Affairs Committee on July 30, he flatly denied all the rumors
of French shipments of arms to Spain. But he added that if Germany
and Italy openly armed Franco, the government would consider
itself completely released from the precautions that it had imposed.
In other words, it would resume its freedom of action.[62] On the
following day, July 31, Delbos stated in the Chamber debate on
foreign policy that

> the Spanish Government is a regular government, whose
> legitimacy no one can contest . . . and, moreover, a government
> friendly to France. By furnishing arms to this government,
> France will in no way violate the principle of nonintervention in
> the affairs of another country. Such an action would not be a
> violation of international law, for it would be made to a regular
> de jure and de facto government.[63]

He added that France had avoided shipping arms "in order not to
give even the appearance of a pretext to those who might be tempted to
support the insurgents with arms."[64] Although he alluded only briefly
to the landing of the Italian planes in North Africa on the preceding day, he, like Blum, seemed to be holding open the possibility that
France could alter its position should the situation warrant it. Delbos
had refused to commit himself to any unqualified policy of nonintervention. The determining factor appeared to be the actions of Germany and Italy. Unfortunately, however, French policy increasingly
emphasized reaction rather than the taking of bold initiatives. It
was not a trend that could be easily reversed.

The sense of relief among those in the government proved to be
only temporary. New fears of an ideological conflict between the
great powers swept over them.[65] The rightist newspapers became
particularly aroused over the possible consequences of France resum-
ing the freedom of action to which Blum and Delbos had alluded.
Wladimir d'Ormesson, writing in *Le Figaro,* warned of the possibility
of an international *fugue* between the reds and whites, and that an
incident could throw Europe into the situation in which it found

itself in 1914.[66] In *L'Action Française,* Charles Maurras argued that the intervention of others in Spain did not give France the right to intervene also. He, too, warned of the possibility of war and drew attention to France's unpreparedness for any conflict. "Those who would want to compel us to engage [the sword] . . . are scoundrels or fools."[67]

This was the situation at home on August 1, when Blum decided to convoke the cabinet to analyze the possibilities and consequences of French action. The government was split, the country was divided, and the Italian intervention had evoked widespread fear and anger. Debate had developed between those who saw the impudent Italian intervention as justification for full French aid to the Republicans and those who feared that any additional intervention by the European powers might lead to a general conflict.[68]

At the cabinet meeting on the morning of August 1, Delbos again explained the position of the British government. He pointed out that the British Conservatives continued to prefer the rebels to the Republicans. In the name of Anglo-French amity, France had been unofficially advised that she should not become involved and should observe strict neutrality. Discussion continued as President Lebrun advised the cabinet to be "prudent," and Blum declared, "Our duty requires that we aid our Spanish friends, whatever the consequences of this support may be." Ultimately, Delbos made a proposal to send out an appeal to the Great Powers "which would lead to the adoption of 'common rules of nonintervention.' "[69] The suggestion was not accepted without considerable debate in the long meeting and during the afternoon after the meeting.[70]

The plan that Delbos presented to the cabinet had first been formulated in the mind of Léger in the Foreign Office. Léger felt that it was "the best available insurance against the spread of conflict."[71] On the day after the meeting, Delbos revealed the main points of the new French scheme in a communiqué to the French representatives in London, Rome, and Brussels. France would "address an urgent appeal to the principal interested governments for the immediate adoption and strict observance with Spain of common rules of nonintervention." France had strictly observed its decision not to authorize any exportation of arms to Spain, even in execution of contracts made before the beginning of the civil war. But while awaiting the establishment of a common viewpoint on this subject, "the fact that war material is now being furnished from abroad to the insurgents obliges the French government to reserve its freedom of judgment as to the application of the decision taken."[72] It was only this last provision that made the proposal agreeable to the proponents of unqualified support for the Republicans.[73] Nevertheless, the communiqué was conditional, as it announced that the French intended to deliver arms, but that they would renounce their intentions if the Italian government ceased its own shipments. "It transformed the Italian government's violation of a no less unquestionable rule of international law—the furnishing of arms to rebels."[74]

On August 4 Britain replied favorably, asking only that the proposal be extended to Germany, Italy, and Portugal in order that all of those powers most directly interested in the Spanish question be subjected to the same limitations from the beginning. In addition, it offered to support the French proposal by a declaration of its own.[75] Delbos accepted the offer of the British and asked them to use their influence in Rome and Lisbon to secure the favorable response of those two governments.[76] On the following day, August 5, after France had received only a vague response from Germany and Italy had remained silent, Delbos addressed a new note to Britain in which he included the text of the declaration he hoped would induce the adherence of the two powers to the cause of nonintervention. The statement called for the powers to prohibit "the exportation, direct or indirect, the reexportation and the transit, destined for Spain, Spanish possessions, or the zone of Spanish Morocco, of all arms, munitions and war materials, as well as all aircraft, assembled or dismantled, and all warships."[77]

In the meantime, Cot, Daladier, and Moch accelerated their efforts to make shipments of arms and planes to Spain. Moch has indicated to this writer that Delbos opposed the sale of these arms to Spain. Moch was in charge of liaison with Spain and, therefore, shipment of arms to that country. Consequently, behind Delbos' back, he and Cot arranged for Mexico and Lithuania to buy arms. As soon as these arms left French territorial waters, they were redirected toward Republican Spanish ports such as Santander.[78]

During this interval Blum attempted to determine more clearly the position of the British on Spain. He sought to enlist their aid for the Republican cause. On July 30, on the pretext of making a personal visit, Moch was sent to London to attempt to change the British attitude. But the resultant meetings, the nature of which remain unclear, served no purpose except to disclose the hostility of some British politicians to sending aid to Spain.[79]

Meanwhile, Blum was pursuing another course. At a meeting with Philip Noel Baker, the British Labor Party leader, Blum suggested that the British Admiralty, if it could be convinced of the need to aid the Spanish Republic, might be able to change the attitude of the British cabinet. Sir Maurice Hankey was mentioned as one who would take the initiative if the Admiralty recommended it.[80] Although it is unclear whether Delbos was informed of this new initiative, Daladier was consulted, and it was decided that Admiral Darlan should attempt to convince Admiral Chatfield of the possible consequences of a rebel victory. Darlan was on confidential terms with Chatfield; and as a man slightly to the Left at the time, Darlan did not want an additional fascist regime on France's borders.[81]

The mission was a failure.[82] At their meeting on August 5, Darlan sought in vain to convince Chatfield of the dangers that would result from concessions to Germany and Italy should the rebels become victorious. Chatfield agreed that it would be a grave situation, but he had no clear evidence of German and Italian ambitions in the area. He recalled that his government had responded favorably to the French suggestion of nonintervention and that the French and British had identical points of view on the matter. He rejected Darlan's proposal that an effort be made to mediate between the two sides in the Spanish Civil War. They had rejected earlier attempts at mediation, and they had "apparently decided to exterminate one another." By intervening, even to mediate, the European powers would rapidly find themselves "between the hammer and the anvil." Chatfield expressed surprise at Darlan's suggestion to seek Hankey's views, and turned aside the suggestion by indicating that the latter would probably be absent from London for the parliamentary holiday. Besides, he said, the British cabinet was convinced that it must not interfere in any manner in the Spanish Civil War.[83] Darlan returned to Paris very disillusioned about the prospects of persuading the British to aid Spain.[84]

Thus, the reports of Moch and Darlan confirmed the impression

Blum had received in his earlier meetings with the British: England would not act if war broke out over Spain. This feeling was further supported by a statement attributed to Neville Chamberlain: "We British hate fascism. But we also hate Bolshevism. Therefore, if there is a country where the two kill off each other, it is a great good for humanity."[85] The fact that the British identified the Republicans with the Bolshevists—even though at this early stage of the Spanish Civil War nothing could have been further from the truth—clearly indicated their train of thought.

Blum later recalled that "the failure of the Darlan mission had a considerable influence on the decision which had then finally been made in Paris at the third Council of Ministers" on August 8.[86] This is true, but it must be seen as part of a total situation. The French felt isolated in Europe. Only the Soviets and Czechs sympathized with the Spanish Republicans to the point where they would actively aid them. As the press campaigns showed, French public opinion had become increasingly divided and vocal. The division among the populace also was reflected in Chamber and cabinet rifts. Blum, thoroughly discouraged, was "strongly tempted" to resign in order to avoid supporting a policy that he did not approve. Most of his legislative program had been passed, and he felt certain that the cabinet and Chamber would not support a policy of direct aid to Spain. It was only the Spanish emissaries, de los Ríos and Ximines de Asua, who persuaded him to remain. They reasoned that a friendly Blum government, even with its hands tied by a policy of nonintervention, could render more support to the Republicans' cause than another government which probably would be more conservative.[87] All of these factors were building to a head for the meeting of August 8. But one other incident, which has been totally neglected by historians, may have applied the *coup de grâce* to any further French initiative in aiding Republican Spain.

On the afternoon of August 7 Sir George Clerk, the British Ambassador to France, paid a visit to Delbos to receive "some comfort" about Spain.[88] Delbos reviewed the latest information about the progress that the French plan for nonintervention was making in various capitals. He indicated that Italy had not responded since its note of the sixth,[89] concerning which he refused to be drawn into polemics. Von Neurath had expressed personal agreement in principle, but Delbos had received no official German reply.[90] Clerk then brought up the question of French aid to Spain. Delbos admitted that although the French government would continue to refuse to deliver ammunition or war material to the Madrid government, it felt that it could not refuse to allow five aircraft ordered before the war to be delivered. He said that in view of the facts that Italian aircraft were being supplied to the rebels and twenty-eight German aircraft had been dispatched to the same forces, the French government felt that it was impossible to maintain its embargo. But this showed the urgent need for agreement on the French proposal. Clerk asked how Delbos could be certain that the Madrid government was the real government and not a screen for anarchists. Delbos replied that the government was not hampered by extremists. Clerk reported:

> I concluded the interview by expressing the hope that the French Government, even though, pending an agreement of nonintervention, they might feel themselves precluded from stopping private commercial transactions with Spain, would do what it could to limit and retard such transactions as much as possible. I asked M. Delbos to forgive me for speaking so frankly and I repeated that all I had said was entirely personal and on my own responsibility but I felt that in so critical a situation I must put before him the danger of any action which might definitely commit the French Government to one side of the conflict and make more difficult the close co-operation between our two countries which was called for by this crisis.[91]

One can well imagine the effect that Clerk's grave warning must have had on Delbos. It came just a few short hours before the cabinet meeting that was finally to decide French policy.[92] The increasing public division, the possibility of Blum's resignation, and his opposition to "ideological crusading" weighed on Delbos' mind. But from the first he had considered that the entente with England must be the keystone of French policy. Added to the meetings and conversations in London on July 24 and the failure of the Darlan mission, Clerk's warning had a significant impact upon Delbos.

In the cabinet meeting that followed, Delbos left the ranks of the wavering and took the lead in promoting strict adherence to a policy of nonintervention. At the third meeting in a fortnight, on

August 8, amid feverish activity at the Quai d'Orsay to determine the positions of the various powers, the Blum government made its final decision. Blum, with encouragement from his Spanish friends, had decided against resigning and had now fully rationalized within himself the need for a policy of nonintervention in Spain. He now argued that the fascist states would be able to intervene more frequently and more decisively than the democratic states.[93] During the stormy meeting Cot continued to urge that in view of the aid supplied to the rebels by Germany and Italy, French war materials must be dispatched to the Spanish government. But Delbos was now firmly committed to a policy of total nonintervention. He informed the cabinet of the progress of the negotiations involving the French proposals of August 1. Delbos stretched the truth a bit when he pointed out that all responses received from Italy, Germany, and Russia had been "favorable in principle."[94] Delbos insisted that France must take the lead by living up to the obligations of nonintervention if its proposal was to have any chance of success. No longer could France rationalize sending aid to Spain under the guise of maintaining its "freedom of action." He evoked the fear of a general European conflict should these negotiations break down. He reviewed the assistance Britain was willing to render by making contacts in various capitals, such as Berlin, where France lacked influence. But with his meeting with Clerk and the failure of the Darlan mission fresh in his mind, Delbos left no illusions about British support for France should it become involved in a conflict over Spain. He then proposed that the cabinet agree on the suspension of all exports of war material to Spain, including commercial as well as military aircraft. It has been suggested by a number of sources that Delbos had become so firmly committed to this line of action that he threatened to resign and provoke a ministerial crisis if the plan was not adopted.[95] Pierre Cot has stated that the cabinet was divided into three unequal camps over the proposal. The proponents of nonintervention started with a weak minority. The opponents of nonintervention were more numerous, but still not a majority. A third group comprised those who were undecided.[96] Ultimately, the bulk of the vacillating third group became convinced of the need for pursuing Delbos' proposal, and the final cabinet division was made along the following lines:[97]

Against Nonintervention	*For Nonintervention*
SOCIALISTS	SOCIALISTS
Auriol	Spinasse
Salengro	Rivière
Monnet	Bedouce
Moutet	Blum
Lebas	Faure
	Jardillier
RADICALS	RADICALS
Cot	Delbos
Viollette	Chautemps
Zay	Bastid
Gasnier Duparc	Daladier

Two others—Léo Lagrange and Pierre Viénot—supported Cot and the opposition, but they were undersecretaries and did not carry decisive weight in the cabinet. Of course some, like Daladier, vacillated a great deal and are hard to categorize. The position of others, such as the Radical Marc Rucart, remains uncertain; but the significant fact remains that the almost complete tally above makes it plainly evident that the issue transcended party lines. Moreover, it clearly reveals that the policy hardly commanded an overwhelming majority, although admittedly many of those who supported nonintervention, including Blum, Faure, Daladier, and Delbos, wielded considerably more political influence than those in the opposing faction.

In any event, the die was cast. On the following day, August 9, the Quai d'Orsay sent out the order that "the exportation of war material destined for Spain and its possessions, until a new order is issued, must be prohibited without exception."[98] During his tenure as Foreign Minister, Delbos never rescinded this directive.

Thus began what one observer has called "one of the most outrageous diplomatic farces perpetrated in Europe between the wars."[99] The story of the tragicomedy of Delbos' plan of nonintervention and the London Committee has been well told in other works.[100] It is not the objective of this study to examine it again. The fact is that once France started the ball rolling, its momentum kept leading the democracies to one concession after another. It can only be seen as one of the most important milestones along the road to their unfortunate attempt to appease the dictators. Today it is clear that the policy of nonintervention in Spain was disastrous. It was intended to preserve the peace, but it only allowed Hitler greater freedom in preparing for war.[101] Yet it is important to review and understand the dominant forces and factors that led Delbos, and ultimately Blum, to adopt this policy.

In June, 1937, Eleanor Rathbone, a Labor M.P. in the House of Commons, wrote to Eden, telling him of comments made by Delbos, Pertinax, and Alexander Werth which implied that the British government had brought pressure to bear on the French to induce them to ban arms shipments to Spain. She suggested that the British had even gone so far as to intimate that the Locarno guarantee would not operate if such a ban were not applied. Eden wrote back that these assertions were untrue. C. A. Shuckburgh, of the Foreign Office, added his marginal comment that it was "entirely untrue that the British Government intimated to the French Government at the beginning of August that we would not support France against an aggression arising out of her sending arms to Spain, or that we were responsible for the unilateral decision of the French Government on August 8th, to ban arms to Spain. These statements are typical of the slapdash historians and journalists from whom they are quoted."[102] In the cabinet, Eden later denied any such British pressure, and he publicly denied it in the House of Commons and in his memoirs.[103]

Yet the fact remains that the British position was the single most important factor in Delbos' decision to pursue a policy of nonintervention in Spain. Both Delbos and Blum agreed upon the need for close Franco-British relations. In fact, this Franco-British solidarity became the cornerstone of their policy for restructuring the French security system. Pierre Laval's reluctance to employ effective sanctions against Italy with regard to Abyssinia had irritated the British, just as the latter's refusal to agree to sanctions against Germany when it reoccupied the Rhineland had aggravated some Frenchmen. In addition, Britain had signed a naval agreement with Germany without even consulting France. With the coming of the Popular Front, it was rumored that many in Conservative circles preferred an Anglo-German entente rather than one with a leftist France. Consequently, the deterioration of relations between the two countries had been uppermost in the minds of Delbos and Blum. They had set out to rectify the situation, but when the Spanish Civil War broke out in July, the policy had not yet reached fruition. Delbos and Blum were convinced that French actions with regard to Spain required the utmost discretion.

It has been said that Britain's position was well known in France and that there was no need for any official intervention by the Baldwin government to make its general position known.[104] Indeed, the conversations held in London on July 23—including Eden's advice to Blum to be prudent—the failure of Darlan's mission on the fifth, and the dispatches that flowed into the Quai d'Orsay during the entire period from French representatives in London, all left little doubt as to British feelings. Delbos and Blum could not avoid being swayed by these "unofficial" contacts. But the most unmistakable statement of British viewpoint, and possibly the most impressive to Delbos' mind, was Clerk's warning of August 7. Although it must be classified as "unofficial," it received the full support of the Foreign Office and Anthony Eden and therefore verged on being very "official." Delbos felt France was in no position to ruin its political and psychological ties with Britain, and he had said so as early as the meeting of August 1. Clerk's message confirmed this opinion.

Perhaps one can gain a clearer view of Delbos' motivations from his speeches and writings after the event. In a speech quoted in Le Temps on September 14, 1936, Delbos said, "Finally, we knew that there were friendly nations that would not have approved a policy of intervention by supplying arms and, consequently, would not have supported us in facing the possible consequence of such a policy."[105] It seems clear that he could only be referring to Britain. In an article that he wrote three months after leaving office, Delbos said that it was "known that the British government, which had hardly initiated its gigantic rearmament program, was determined to pursue a policy of strictest neutrality. But although determined neither to follow nor support France by furnishing arms, it was prepared to join with her in the enforcement of nonintervention." Under these circumstances, he concluded that there were only two alternatives. France could enter into competition for Spain by sending arms and equipment to the Loyalists. But this could produce a general conflict with Germany and Italy in which the French treaties of collective security might not be effective. France's isolation, her internal difficulties, which he considered highly exaggerated, and the highly developed armaments of the totalitarian countries would have to be considered. The alternative was to maintain and reinforce Franco-British solidarity and redouble efforts to bring about a nonintervention agreement that would include a majority of countries involved.[106] For a man who could not see beyond two alternatives, the second seemed to be the safest, so he seized it.

Nevertheless, other factors undoubtedly figured in Delbos' decision to make a determined effort to formulate a nonintervention policy. Certainly the fear of a general European war did not seem wholly unfounded. Delbos later maintained that Europe stood on the brink of an ideological war.[107] Two days after the communiqué of August 2, Delbos showed his fear of any such war: "There must be no ideological crusade in Europe"; such a crusade would inevitably end in war.[108] He must have felt, as did Blum, that "neither England, nor the United States, nor Poland, nor Belgium would follow us" in a war emanating from the Spanish conflict.[109]

Neither can domestic circumstances be neglected. At the Radical Party Congress at Lille in October, 1937, Delbos pointed to the divided public opinion that faced the government in its decision.[110] The division became apparent to Delbos on his return to Paris from London on July 25. From the first, when information that arms were going to be sent to Spain was received from the Spanish Embassy, and continuing through the crisis, the rightist press became increasingly aggressive. As it screamed predictions of an impending Communist coup and an international conflict, the leftist papers retaliated with their own absurdities. Delbos felt that the hour of national disunion would only be hastened by calling on the government to take sides for or against the Spanish Loyalists.[111]

In government circles the opposition and division was no less evident. Increasingly, the people occupying posts of importance sounded their warnings. Herriot, President of the Chamber; Jeanneney, President of the Senate; Lebrun, President of the Republic; and Chautemps, Vice-Premier, all advised caution and compromise. This was a formidable array of opposition to any positive action in Spain. As can be seen by the cabinet vote on August 8, the parties were split over the policy to be pursued. It is clear, moreover, that the majority of Radicals were opposed to becoming involved in Spain.[112] Delbos' public support of nonintervention in a speech on August 3 brought a chorus of praise by the Radical press. It was evident that the majority of the Radical party would not tolerate any meddling in the Spanish affair.[113] Delbos did not wish to disregard the will of his party.

Blum's ambivalent attitude must also be considered. The Premier, subjected to most of the same influences as Delbos, was forced to calculate some of the same unpleasant alternatives to nonintervention: he was fearful of impairing efforts to rejuvenate the entente with Britain; he was apprehensive that domestic division might inspire a right-wing revolt, perhaps leading to a civil war in France itself; and he was particularly alarmed about the possibility of the Spanish war degenerating into a general European conflict, thereby demolishing any likelihood of negotiating a general settlement that would open the door to the pacification of Europe, which was so dear to him.[114] It is difficult to know with any certainty how much Blum's hesitation, given the admonitions from other important political quarters, encouraged Delbos to press for nonintervention. For that matter, it is interesting to speculate—for that is all the sources will permit—about the degree to which Blum and Delbos helped to propel each other in the same direction, feeding upon their respective anxieties as they chatted informally at the Quai d'Bourbon. It is certain, in any case, that Blum made little concerted effort to dissuade his Foreign Minister; and thereby, indirectly to be sure, he apparently further prompted Delbos to pursue a policy of nonintervention. Admittedly though, this can be regarded as merely a small point among the myriad of larger considerations.

The effects of other motivations, such as the influence exercised by Léger and other career officials of the Quai d'Orsay, and the workers' strikes of June, 1936, are more difficult to gauge. Léger, like Delbos, held a high regard for the British tie, and he knew that they viewed with alarm the workers' agitation in France.[115] Perhaps the workers' strikes were more than Delbos had bargained for when he joined the Popular Front. Conceivably it would not hurt to have the Left put in its place by the sobering effects of a defeat of the Frente Popular in Spain. But documentation is too sparse at this point to clarify either of these considerations with any degree of assurance.

In any event, the fact remains that British pressure was the decisive factor in Delbos' decision to champion the policy of nonintervention in Spain. It was through his ardent defense that the government eventually came to adopt the policy. Yet it must not be seen entirely as one of weakness and decadence. Rather, as René Massigli has said, "It was the policy of a people who wished to avoid war."[116] Delbos was in the mainstream of French thought as he pointed out that the policy had been inspired by the humane wish to prevent the prolongation of the horrors of war and by the desire to prevent it from spreading in Europe. The peace of Europe had been maintained. Although some might say that the peril had only been postponed, he felt that time gained for peace was never gained in vain.[117]

4

Nyon: A Flicker of Opposition

For the better part of three years subsequent to the feverish diplomatic activity of July and August, 1936, the drama of the Spanish Civil War played itself out. Until the spring of 1938, it remained potentially the most dangerous problem that confronted Europe. In an attempt to localize the conflict, a European Nonintervention Committee was established in London, where it hastily set about its task of devising schemes for supervising an arms embargo on Spain that could be observed by all interested powers. But the deliberations, which began in September and continued spasmodically until the end of the conflict, proved to be painfully unproductive and need not be detailed here. It will suffice to say that the committee merely served as a useful diplomatic safety valve and a smoke screen behind which massive intervention occurred. While Hitler sent assistance to the Nationalists, and while Russia aided the Republicans, Italy became the most flagrant offender of the Nonintervention Agreement. Mussolini scarcely made a secret of the enormous quantities of arms and increasingly larger number of regular-army units sent under the guise of "volunteers," complete with arms, uniforms, and officers. Committed to the ultimate triumph of Franco's forces, Mussolini sank deeper and deeper into a quagmire from which he would not retreat regardless of the circumstances.

The failure of the Nonintervention Committee to enforce its solemn decrees contributed to the lack of agreement over policy in France. The complexities of the domestic and international situation tended to obscure all perception of national interests. Traditional antagonism between the Right and the Left was magnified by divisions

55

within political parties and among Catholics and intellectuals. Indeed, Frenchmen found themselves embroiled in their own undeclared quasi war. Supporters and enemies of the Popular Front found the Spanish conflict to be an extension of their own domestic quarrels, and they arrayed themselves accordingly. Confronted with such enmity and discord in the country, it was difficult for the Popular Front government to take decisive action in order to reorient its policy, even if its leaders desired such a change.

Blum was quite aware of the rising tide of criticism directed against him, the government, and the policy of nonintervention. He found himself constantly harassed with cries of *"Des avions pour Espagne!"* and *"Blum à l'action!"*[1] Yet he also heard the shrieks of *"Blum-la-guerre."*[2] It was a nasty dilemma for such a sincere and humane man. In addition, British opposition to abandoning the policy convinced him that any other policy would not preserve peace any better than the Nonintervention Agreement, and the thought of losing the British entente was anathema to him. The closest Blum came to reorienting his government's policy came during the spring of 1937. A plan of relaxed nonintervention (*nonintervention relâchée*) was developed. The government systematically closed its eyes to arms shipments to Spain. Eventually governmental officials—Vincent Auriol as "organizer in chief," along with Pierre Cot and Jules Moch—organized the transportation of arms to Spain.[3] Although such semiclandestine aid to Spain may have helped to ease some French consciences, the trickle of arms from France did very little to strengthen the Republicans in comparison to what the massive flow of men and arms from Italy and Germany was doing to strengthen Franco.

Yvon Delbos did little to induce Blum to act in a stronger manner. As the man most responsible for French formulation and patronage of the policy of nonintervention, Delbos was convinced that once adopted, the policy must be strictly applied. Consequently, he pressed for scrupluous adherence to nonintervention, frowned upon all efforts to send surreptitious aid to the Spanish Republic, discouraged all efforts to accord belligerent rights to either side, and pushed for legislation that would prevent French ships or personnel from being involved in carrying war materials to Spain.[4] Yet, curiously enough, one of the most positive and resolute actions taken by the Western powers during the decade prior to the war—the Nyon Accords—came at the instigation and promotion of Delbos. Again the contradictory character of the man became evident. It is worthwhile to investigate the circumstances surrounding this abrupt, brief, but unmistakable, about-face in Delbos' formulation of French policy.

Shortly after the Nonintervention Committee began meeting in London, it became quite evident that the committee had failed to prevent Axis aid from reaching the Spanish rebels. Mussolini even boasted openly of the aid Italy had contributed to Franco. In October, 1936, the Soviets announced that they would keep their promise of nonintervention only to the extent that Germany and Italy kept theirs. Indeed, Russian tanks, artillery, planes, and technicians soon began to flow to the Spanish Republic. In November the German and Italian governments notified the committee that they intended to recognize the Franco regime. This inevitably meant that more military aid would be sent to the rebels. The French and British governments reacted to each of these new acts with calls for strict observance of the Nonintervention Agreement. But it was clear that some effective form of regulation had to be instituted.[5]

During the winter and spring of 1936–1937, France and Britain made several efforts to increase the effectiveness of the London Committee by establishing an effective control system to prevent infringements of the Nonintervention Agreement. But the difficult task of working out the technical details of such a scheme proved laborious and time consuming.[6] Meanwhile, Italy continued to pour additional troops into Spain.

It was not long, however, before the issue of foreign troops was overshadowed by a more serious crisis in the Mediterranean. On May 24, 1937, Republican planes bombed the German battleship *Deutschland*, killing twenty and wounding seventy-three men. This incident generated a series of circumstances that paralyzed the Nonintervention Committee and led the French, who had taken a back seat to the British after the initial Nonintervention Agreement had been signed, to lead the way again in taking decisive action. The Germans immediately retaliated for the attack on the *Deutschland* by bombarding the Republican city of Almeria. The same day Joachim von Ribbentrop, the German Ambassador in London, announced that

Germany would withdraw from the nonintervention discussions, and Count Grandi said that Italy would do the same. Furthermore, they indicated that they would no longer participate in the naval control scheme. For the next two weeks France and Britain made every effort to bring the Axis powers back into the committee by trying to convince them that similar incidents would not recur. Delbos told Count von Welczeck, the German Ambassador, that France also had been provoked on several occasions by the Nationalists, but had taken no reprisals. He pointed out that it was impossible for the committee to prevent such incidents as the attack on the *Deutschland*. Delbos felt that now that the Germans had "spat out their venom," perhaps an agreement could be reached. At the same time Eden held a similar meeting with Ribbentrop.[7]

Ultimately, Delbos and Eden secured the return of the Axis powers to the control scheme and to the London Committee. But the meetings had no sooner been resumed than Germany declared on June 18 that a submarine attack had occurred against the German patrol cruiser *Leipzig*. Von Neurath, the German Foreign Minister, cancelled a proposed visit to London; and on June 22, Ribbentrop, also the German delegate to the Nonintervention Committee, insisted that the nonintervention powers should confront the Republican government with a demonstration of solidarity. But the French were unwilling to consider any demonstration unless it was made simultaneously to both sides. Ribbentrop then informed them that the Axis ships would withdraw from the naval patrol, although Germany would not withdraw from the Nonintervention Committee.[8] There was considerable concern among the French that Germany might take some arbitrary action even after its decision to withdraw from the patrol.[9] But the only other action taken by Germany and Italy was a proposal on July 2 that recognition of belligerent status should be accorded both combatants. Since this would serve to strengthen the position of Franco, Delbos and the Quai d'Orsay still opposed such a move.

There can be little doubt that the events of May and June, 1937, increased the tension between the major European powers to its highest level since the outbreak of the conflict and further paralyzed the feeble efforts of the London Committee. Yet if the situation seemed serious in the early summer, the events of midsummer 1937 led to a further deterioration of the international situation and heightened the possibility of open conflict between two or more of the powers.

In August, Mussolini agreed to a Nationalist request that the Italian fleet strike against shipping in the Mediterranean in an effort to limit the aid being sent to the Republicans.[10] Submarine and aircraft attacks began to occur against Spanish, Russian, British, French, and other neutral shipping. Between July 27 and September 3, eighteen ships were attacked. Although the Nonintervention Committee, France, and Britain labeled the submarines "unknown," journalist Louis Fischer wrote that "everybody in the world knew that the 'unknown' submarines were Italian." He added that foreign correspondents in Rome referred to Mussolini as the "unknown" statesman and jokingly said that Mussolini proposed to erect a monument to the "unknown" submarine next to the monument for the "unknown" soldier.[11] Alexander Werth wrote that "it was suggested in Paris that the Boulevard des Italiens be rechristened the Boulevard des Inconnus."[12]

As the attacks continued to mount throughout August, considerable concern, if not anger, became evident in Paris. Concern for maintaining communications links with Algeria had been one of the strongest arguments of those who had favored intervention in Spain during the previous summer. Indeed, it now appeared that Italy was bent upon developing the Mediterranean into a *mare nostrum.* This fact, combined with the Axis withdrawal from the naval patrol system, the Axis proposal of belligerency status for Franco, and the feebleness of the deadlocked Nonintervention Committee, pointed the way to a serious reconsideration of French foreign policy.

In France, the period that has been described as "the most beautiful, the most glorious epoch for this government and for French democracy" had ended.[13] Shortly after the beginning of 1937, the Popular Front began to lose its momentum. In January, Blum announced a "pause" in the government's social and economic program. The situation presented a curious paradox. On the one hand, the decisions and reforms of June, 1936, had been quickly adopted, the economy had begun to rebound, unemployment had declined, and production had increased. On the other hand, the budget and treasury had not recovered their equilibrium, and the franc had failed to regain its stability. The capital that had fled the country during the first months of the Blum government had failed to return. During the "pause," the absence of important social reforms was in distinct contrast to the activity and programs of 1936.[14] In the spring, a renewal of strikes and violence, added to the agitation created by the Spanish Civil War, increased the widespread disillusionment with the Popular Front. On June 22, 1937, confronted with a new financial crisis, Blum resigned, to be succeeded by Camille Chautemps. No great revamping occurred in the cabinet. Many of the same faces remained, and the appearance of a Popular Front government was maintained.[15] Blum returned as Vice-Premier, and Delbos remained at the Quai d'Orsay.

This change in governments appears to have brought about an alteration in Delbos' attitude on French foreign policy, at least for a brief time. His revised position had implications for French policy towards Spain. Although one can only speculate about the reasons, Delbos began to be more and more assertive in the government—both personally and with regard to his ideas.[16]

As the summer wore on, French policy makers, including Delbos, began to doubt the efficacy of blind compliance with the policy of nonintervention in Spain. Violations by the Axis never ceased, and piracy in the Mediterranean increased. Even though the French had refused to intervene actively in Spain, they were bound to be concerned about maintaining the status quo in the Mediterranean. Delbos and Alexis Léger at the Quai d'Orsay began to realize that the appeasement policy, particularly as it developed after Neville Chamberlain assumed leadership in England, might undermine the entire French position on the continent. The events of the summer of 1937 convinced them that France must reassert itself and terminate a policy that could ultimately lead to catastrophe. Unhappily, powerful elements in the cabinet such as Chautemps and the new Minister of Finance, Georges Bonnet, desired to continue the policy of appeasement. Consequently, during July and August, debate over the future course of French foreign policy delayed any positive action. Delbos, however, increasingly displayed his dissatisfaction with the flow of events. He expressed his profound displeasure over the German retaliation for the *Deutschland* episode; and on July 2 he told Sir Eric Phipps, the British Ambassador in Paris, that Britain and France should act to defend their interests in the Mediterranean, whether the Axis powers liked it or not. It is possible that he even threatened to open the Franco-Spanish frontier for shipments of arms to the Republicans and perhaps to dissolve the Anglo-French entente.[17]

The question of granting belligerent status to Franco's forces added to Delbos' irritation. Although the British were leaning towards such a status for Franco, Delbos was only willing to recognize Franco as a belligerent after all foreign volunteers had been withdrawn from Spain and effective control instituted to prevent their return.[18] When Britain presented a plan on July 14 calling for the recognition of the two sides in Spain and granting them belligerent rights at sea,[19] Delbos severely criticized the proposal. He was convinced that the British overture would not only lead to qualified recognition of Franco, but that it had also seriously compromised the Franco-British common front. The dictatorships would be greatly encouraged by this obvious withdrawal of England from close cooperation with France. The plan had been formulated and presented without even consulting the French officials.[20] He was still angry a month later when he confided to Ambassador Bullitt that "he was furious with Eden and Chamberlain for having inaugurated a *rapprochement* with Italy."[21] Delbos then vowed to the Nonintervention Committee that France would not discuss belligerent rights until Axis volunteers had been withdrawn.[22] The French need not have worried about the British plan being accepted by the Axis. Léger had predicted that any British proposal would be rejected, and this proved to be the case.[23] During the committee meetings of July and August, the Axis powers procrastinated, and the usual deadlock occurred.

In the meantime, Delbos still felt great apprehension about the possibility of a general European war should the committee fail to reach any prompt agreement. Therefore, he dropped feelers to the Pope and President Roosevelt, hoping for their effective mediation. But Delbos correctly estimated that the papal appeal would fail due to Republican as well as German hostility toward the Vatican.[24] The Americans, engrossed in developing more neutrality legislation, were determined to avoid any European entanglements. Faced with the breakdown of the Nonintervention Committee, Delbos indicated that

France would be obliged to support the Republicans by supplying munitions and permitting the passage of troops through and from France. He maintained that Italy must not be allowed to control Spain, regardless of the dangers of French action.[25]

Even the German Ambassador in Paris, Welczeck, warned Berlin that Delbos had become convinced that "Mussolini can be kept within bounds only by firmness." Welczeck also indicated that French public opinion was increasingly convinced that some action, even opening the Franco-Spanish frontier, would be more tolerable than the continued uncertainty of the committee.[26] Yet Delbos' position was not overwhelmingly endorsed by the cabinet. Chautemps argued that French diplomatic relations with Germany and Italy made it difficult for France to control the course of events.[27] It seems clear that while Delbos wanted to pick up the ball and run with it, Chautemps hoped that he would fumble it back to the British. Bitter debate ensued in the cabinet over the suitable policy to be followed in Spain.[28]

Ultimately, however, Delbos did manage to win sufficient support for taking action against the naval attacks in the Mediterranean. The assaults had continued to grow in number during August. The increase in aggressive activity by the Italians had forced both the French and the British into taking unilateral measures for the protection of their shipping. The French organized a system of patrols and convoys along the North African coast. Britain ordered all of its men-of-war to fire upon submarines attacking British merchant ships.[29] But Delbos had been irritated beyond the point of mere unilateral patrolling. His hostility was intensified by the declarations of solidarity exchanged between Mussolini and Franco and the publicizing of the Italian contribution to the rebel victory at Santander.[30]

On August 26 the French Chargé d'Affaires in London, Roger Cambon, made a "feeler" to Eden. He had been directed by René Massigli, Deputy Director of Political Affairs at the Quai d'Orsay, to indicate the French inclination to initiate diplomatic conversations between France, Britain, and Italy before the upcoming League meeting in order to ease relations between the powers. Eden replied favorably to the "feeler," although he admitted that he was not clear as to the nature of the conversations. Cambon admitted that he too was unsure and that he would ask the Quai d'Orsay to explain its proposal more fully.[31]

Cambon called again at the Foreign Office on August 30. After conferring with Delbos about the British response, he brought a more detailed communiqué. The proposal called for British and French delegations to "arrange" a meeting of the Mediterranean powers (France, Britain, Greece, Yugoslavia, Turkey, and Egypt) to review the best means of assuring the protection of navigation and air lanes in the Mediterranean. Moreover, the note proposed that participation of the Black Sea states of Rumania, Bulgaria, and the Soviet Union be considered. After noting the belligerent activity of Italy, the communication made it clear that the French Council of Ministers had closely examined the situation. The Council considered notification of the London Committee as necessary, and it hoped that Britain would associate itself with the action. Delbos considered that "only common action by France and England would serve to bring about a modification in the Italian attitude." If it proved impossible to secure this result without delay, "the French government would examine the basis on which rests the Nonintervention Agreement and redeem its right of complete freedom of action."[32]

"This was the germ of the Nyon Conference," acknowledged Eden, who immediately sent the French note to Chamberlain.[33] Eden called a cabinet meeting for September 2 to discuss the French proposal. It was agreed that a meeting limited to the Mediterranean powers, including Italy, would be desirable. In the meantime, Britain would increase its destroyer strength in the Mediterranean.[34] (The British decision was probably influenced by the submarine attacks on the *Havock* and *Woodford*, the latter occurring on the same day as the meeting.)

On September 2 Eden called in Cambon and gave his government's reply to the French proposal. The British cabinet was inclined to the view that, initially, the discussions should be limited to the Mediterranean powers, although they felt that Turkish attendance would be of doubtful utility at the moment. Eden indicated that the Foreign Office had already spoken to the Italians on the subject of submarine activity in the Mediterranean. Although definitive proof of Italian activity was lacking, perhaps it might be of value for the French to approach the Italians through diplomatic channels. In addition, Eden sought to sound out the French position on nonintervention. Perhaps Delbos' veiled threat of a reconsideration of the French position disturbed Eden. In any event, he inquired whether the French wished to bring nonintervention to an end and, if so, what alternative policy they had in mind.[35]

It soon became apparent, however, that the British and French governments had differing opinions on the powers to be invited to the suggested conference, and "acrimonious controversy" soon developed over the problem. Initially, in telephone discussions with Eden, Delbos suggested that the Spanish Republican government at Valencia be invited, but not the Italian government. Eden argued, however, that neither of the two Spanish governments should attend the conference. On the other hand, the conference should be attended by all the Mediterranean powers, including Italy.[36] Ultimately, Delbos agreed that the Valencia government should be excluded and that Italy should be included. But he then insisted that the Black Sea powers also be invited. This meant inviting the Soviet Union, which, after all, had also lost ships through submarine attacks in the Mediterranean. Eden replied that he opposed extension of the list of those to be invited. He felt that the powers most directly concerned, and those most able to take action, were the Mediterranean powers. Eden did his utmost to modify Delbos' demand for Soviet attendance and warned that if Russia was included, Germany would also have to be invited. But Delbos firmly replied that the matter had been considered by the French cabinet and that if Britain insisted upon excluding the Soviets, the situation in the French government would become extremely grave. Delbos himself might be swept from office. Faced with Delbos' adamant stand, Eden agreed that Russia would be invited provided that Germany was also asked.[37] On September 5, with this problem resolved, the French and British governments issued invitations to the conference to be held on September 10, at the small town of Nyon near Geneva, Switzerland.[38]

Complications soon arose with regard to Italy. The invitation was delivered to Count Ciano by the French and British representatives on the evening of September 6.[39] The Italian Chargé d'Affaires in London had indicated to Eden his government's apprehension about attending a conference that included the Soviets. He feared that they would merely use it to repeat accusations about Italian submarines sinking Russian vessels. The Italians hoped that Britain could promise that any such outburst would not occur. Eden quite obviously could not make such a commitment. Nevertheless, the British Ambassador in Rome indicated that Italy would probably attend the conference.[40] When the formal invitation was delivered on the evening of the sixth, Ciano admitted that his government, although skeptical about certain issues that might be raised, had been prepared to attend the meeting. Unfortunately, that same afternoon an incident had occurred that made it impossible to sit at the same table with the Soviets.[41]

The incident referred to by Ciano came in the form of a note delivered by the Soviets to the Italian government on the afternoon of the sixth. The note charged that the Soviet government had indisputable proof that two Soviet steamers had been torpedoed by vessels of the Italian government. "These gestures," charged the Soviets, "are in contradiction with the principles of humanity and international law." The note went on to demand cessation of the Italian acts of aggression and reparation for damages incurred.[42] On the following day *Pravda* published the note, further adding to the embarrassment and anger of the Italians.[43]

Italy immediately denied the Russian charges and denounced the demands as a "new Soviet torpedo against European peace." The message said that the object of the Soviets was to wreck the impending Mediterranean conference. It openly hinted at reconsidering the Italian attitude toward the conference and added that it would be senseless for Italy to attend the conference as an accused party. On the other hand, any Mediterranean conference without Italy being present would be absurd.[44]

When Delbos had persuaded the British that the Soviets be included in the conference, it had been impressed upon him that "if things went wrong and Russia tried to torpedo the Conference it would be the French Government's responsibility."[45] They made it clear to the French that the Soviets would try something. The Russian bombshell made the British warning appear quite prophetic. The French admitted that the note to Italy was singularly ill-timed, but Delbos maintained that the Soviets stood to lose more than any other government by cancellation of the conference. Moreover, the French still felt that the Soviets were likely to give less trouble inside the conference than if they were further isolated from the other powers. The precipitous Soviet broadside fired at the Italians was due to stupidity and nothing else.[46]

It is clear, however, that the Russian action cannot be entirely charged to stupidity. In fact, the Soviets did desire to dissuade Italy from attending the conference. They undoubtedly saw the possibility of real action being taken and sought to remove the usual Axis delaying tactics which had so hampered the Nonintervention Committee. How else can one explain the delay of nearly a week (coming so close to the formal invitations to the conference), before protesting the Italian attacks? The Soviets were hardly in a position to follow up on their solemn warnings and demands, particularly if the possibility of a conflict with a major power would be involved. The Soviets' geographical location precluded that. On the other hand, their denunciation made the conference table an unlikely place for the two powers to meet. The Italians fell headlong into the Soviet trap. By refusing to go to Nyon the Italians would be playing the Russians' game.[47] Yet that is exactly what they chose to do. On September 9 they handed their reply to the French and British representatives in Rome. It said, in part, that the Italian government must postpone any affirmative decision to go to Nyon until the incident created by the Russian note had been satisfactorily settled. Germany also chose to find the "unproved accusations" a convenient excuse for refusing to attend.[48] Consequently, the two supporters of Franco's forces eliminated themselves. Although Delbos and the French were jolted by the Russian note, it cannot be said that they were disappointed in its results.[49] After all, Delbos had not desired the attendance of Italy or Germany in the first place.

In the meantime, France and Britain both moved ahead with proposals that would form the basis of discussion at the conference. The French advocated that the conference should be mainly of a technical nature and that arrangements should be made between the French and British navies for effective action to combat piracy in the Mediterranean.[50] In notes of September 6 and 8 Delbos proposed that all aggressors, whether aircraft, submarines, or surface vessels, be attacked. He proposed that a convoy system be established for the protection of commerce and that zones be established and patrolled by the interested powers. Areas would be left for the Mediterranean powers, in which naval exercises could be carried out. The movements of submarine fleets would take place only with forewarning and would be made on the surface.[51] Basically the British proposals communicated to the French on September 3 closely paralleled those of Delbos.[52] The Admiralty, however, held that defensive measures should be limited to submarine attacks, whereas the French argued that aircraft and surface vessels be included. The British insisted, in spite of anticipated French opposition, that it had been submarine attacks that had led to the crisis. Therefore, agreement should first be reached with regard to submarines. The other points raised by the French, however, could be considered at a subsequent meeting. In addition, the Admiralty expressed doubt about the French desire to divide the Mediterranean into national areas for patrol purposes. Each power should remain free to operate throughout the Mediterranean.[53]

On September 9, upon the invitation of Delbos, Eden dined with the French Foreign Minister in Paris on his way to Geneva and Nyon. During the evening and at a meeting on the following morning, they decided upon a common policy for the meetings at Nyon. The aim of the conference, which should be brief, would be to organize the naval forces available in the Mediterranean to deal promptly with the unlawful attacks on commerce. They would go ahead with or without Italy's cooperation, although they would keep the Axis powers informed of their progress. In the interest of speed, with Eden winning acceptance of the British viewpoint on this matter, the conference would deal with the submarine attacks exclusively. Other considerations, such as attacks by aircraft and surface vessels, would be examined later.[54]

During the entire period of August and early September, the French press took an active interest in the Mediterranean crisis. After Franco's capture of Santander and Mussolini's subsequent gloating over Italy's contribution, the leftist papers became particularly vocal against the "nonintervention farce." When rumors of the French approach to Britain calling for a meeting of the Mediterranean powers were circulated, all sections of the press became interested. The news of the attack on the *Havock* elicited further comment. They correctly presumed that the French government was determined to make some sort of stand at that point and hoped that Britain would support them.[55] *Le Temps,* which enjoyed a close relationship with the Quai d'Orsay, cut to the heart of the matter when it asked if the policy of nonintervention remained a reality, or if the system was bankrupt and must be abandoned. If it were to be established that nonintervention could no longer function, all the interested powers would have to reconsider their positions.[56] Even the rightist *L'Echo de Paris* expressed the opinion that Mussolini's message to Franco made it very difficult to maintain the fiction of nonintervention. It warned that if Paris was forced by Rome to reconsider its attitude, Europe would find itself in a dangerous position.[57]

Preparations for the conference attracted headlines in most of the newspapers. The complete agreement between Paris and London (which was not really so complete after all) was stressed. The question as to which powers were to be invited inevitably gave rise to comment by both the Left and the Right. *L'Humanité* protested that Germany should not be included, since Republican Spain was not. *L'Oeuvre* criticized England for insisting on Germany's inclusion merely to satisfy Italy. It suggested that the conference could fulfill its essential task if the torpedoings stopped, no matter who attended. The papers of the Right remained fairly objective and satisfied with the conference as it took shape.[58] On September 7 *Le Temps* warned against allowing the conference to lower itself to ideological polemics and therefore encounter the same vexations as the Nonintervention Committee. The conference would have a limited objective; the situation, which recalled the worst days of barbarian piracy, had to be ameliorated. It admitted that Italy had considerable interests in the Mediterranean; but France and Britain had at least equal interests, which they could not allow to be compromised.[59]

The Soviet indictment of Italy, of course, provoked considerable comment from both sides. The Communist *L'Humanité* charged, "Italy insolently rejects the Soviet government's representations and thus creates a grave diplomatic incident." The newspapers of the Right, such as *L'Action Française,* accused the Soviets of trying to torpedo the proposed conference, but *Le Temps* appealed for calm. It expressed the hope that the incident would be cleared up and that Italy and Germany would attend the conference. The newspaper concluded that it was hard to see what practical result the Soviet initiative could have, because there was no obligation for any other power to intervene in an Italo-Russian dispute.[60]

Generally, approval by the papers of the Left, Center, and Right accompanied the French decision to call a conference of the Mediterranean powers, and this support remained rather steadfast for the ensuing fortnight. The popular enthusiasm for the conference undoubtedly strengthened the resolve of Delbos and other members of the French delegation as they arrived in Geneva.

On the afternoon of September 10, 1937, Delbos, Eden, and their delegations moved to the village of Nyon, about fifteen miles from Geneva on the shores of the lake. It was here that the nine governments formulated and adopted measures to stop the attacks of the "unknown" submarines.[61] After the opening formalities, Eden rose and nominated Delbos for the presidency of the conference. After the selection had been made unanimously, Delbos ascended to the chair and delivered his charge to the delegates:

> The present state of insecurity which exists in the Mediterranean cannot be allowed to continue without grave risk. It is not possible that shipping should remain at the mercy of piratical undertakings which do not respect any flag and which torpedo merchant ships without warning and without consideration either of cargo or of destination, according to methods which we might have thought had been abolished, and which are directly contrary to the Protocol of 1936 on the humanization of submarine warfare.
>
> We regret that for reasons which are peculiar to them, two Governments should have seen fit to decline the invitation which has been extended to them and that they have added that in their view the problem could have been dealt with in another place. We have not thought it possible to accept that situation. We must act quickly and settle a definite question which, in many respects, is foreign to the problems which are before the Non-Intervention Committee.
>
> In asking that this Conference be summoned, the French and British Governments have looked for a two-fold result. We expect a rapid agreement which will put an end to the state of piracy, and an immediate lessening of the intolerable tension which involves the risk of new and graver incidents. But we also

hope for more. We hope that rapid success, due to the collaboration of all, will clear the atmosphere which for many weeks we have felt to be too heavy, and will thus create a favourable atmosphere in which we can approach, in a spirit of conciliation, the new European tasks.[62]

Delbos' insistence upon speed and his vigorous call for positive action, with or without the Axis powers, set the mood of the conference.[63]

Maxim Litvinov, the Soviet delegate, who was present at the insistence of Delbos, could not let the occasion pass without throwing a few barbs in Italy's direction. "Everyone knows the object of this piracy, and what State is pursuing that object; its name is on everyone's lips, even though it may not be pronounced in this hall." He probed deeper by adding:

> Only those States can avoid participating in such a conference if, while possessing a commercial fleet and utilizing the Mediterranean, they consider themselves guaranteed against piracy, either because they organise it themselves as an instrument of their national policy or because of their extreme intimacy with the pirates and ability to come to an understanding with them. It is only such States which can be interested in the torpedoing and sabotaging of the Conference by refusing to take part in it, or in some other way.[64]

Although less judicious than Delbos, Litvinov certainly cut to the core of what was on most minds.

Eden, too, made a plea for urgency, and called for the conference to keep the absent powers informed of its progress. The delegates then formed a standing committee and set to work in private sessions.[65]

The Franco-British plan was accepted by the delegates as a basis for discussion. The plan called for the Mediterranean to be divided into patrol zones, one of which would be offered to Italy. Since it was impossible to patrol the entire sea, the plan called for concentrating upon areas where the attacks had been most frequent. France and Britain would patrol the western end of the Mediterranean, while the Aegean would be patrolled by Russia and Turkey in the north and Greece and Yugoslavia in the south. France and Britain would aid the smaller powers as much as possible in carrying out their responsibilities. But certain aspects of the plan created the only serious logjam of the conference. During an informal discussion, which included "an altercation with the Russians," it became clear that the small eastern Mediterranean countries were unwilling to cooperate with the Soviets in patrol duties.[66] Eden was quite "surprised at the strength of this feeling." The Turks, who would share a patrol area with Russia under the plan, were quite adamant. In a meeting on the night of the tenth, no progress was made, and it appeared that the whole conference might collapse before agreement could be reached.[67] Such a failure could have dire consequences for all of Europe. Italy would continue its attacks, France would be forced to reconsider its position, and the cold war between the two could quickly heat up.

Fortunately, on the following morning, the delegates devised a satisfactory solution. As leader of the French delegation, Delbos played an important role in formulating a new proposal. Eden has indicated that the bottleneck was removed due to the vigorous attitude of the French, who offered more destroyers. This meant that France and Britain could take on the additional burden of patrolling the Aegean, thus making Russian vessels unnecessary. This satisfied the small powers, who feared that Russia would take advantage of its patrol duties to extend its influence southward. "The splendid contribution the French were prepared to make . . . gave fresh impetus to our plans," wrote Eden.[68] France and Britain would perform the bulk of patrolling in the western Mediterranean as well as the Aegean. Rather than helping the small powers to patrol the Aegean, the French and British would have the right to call upon Russia and the smaller powers for assistance. The Soviets would have no reason for being in the Aegean unless called upon. Eden recalled the delegates' surprise at Litvinov's acceptance of the plan. But it must be remembered, as Litvinov later reminded the powers, that the Soviets had already voluntarily renounced the part in the Mediterranean naval control that had been accorded to them by the London Committee. At Nyon, Litvinov remained opposed to committing Soviet naval forces for patrol purposes.[69] Perhaps he was, as Eden speculates, taken aback by Soviet unpopularity among the small states.[70]

Before midnight on September 11, scarcely more than twenty-four hours after the opening session, the delegates reached full agreement. The text of the agreement released to the press that evening provided:

1. Any submarine which attacks [a neutral merchant] ship in a manner contrary to the Rules of International Law referred to in the Treaty for the Limitation and Reduction of Naval Armaments signed in London on April 22, 1930 and confirmed in the Protocol signed in London November 6th, 1936, shall be counter-attacked and if possible destroyed.

2. The instruction mentioned in the preceding paragraph shall extend to any submarine encountered in the vicinity of a position where a ship not belonging to either of the conflicting Spanish parties has recently been attacked in violation of the rules referred to in the preceding paragraph in circumstances which give valid grounds for the belief that the submarine was guilty of the attack.

It was stated that all submarines could proceed in the Mediterranean only after notification of the other participating powers. In addition, they must proceed on the surface and must be accompanied by a surface vessel.[71]

In order to enforce the plan, France and Britain would patrol the main Mediterranean trade routes from Suez to Gibraltar, from the Dardanelles to Gibraltar, and from North Africa to Marseilles. The smaller eastern Mediterranean states would patrol their own territorial waters and would assist, upon request, in patrolling the main arteries. The proposal also left the door open for Italy. If the powers gave Italy an area to patrol in the central Mediterranean, this would leave a gap where Italian submarines could safely continue their attacks. The powers hit upon the idea of allowing the Tyrrhenian Sea to "form the subject of special arrangements." It would be a large enough area to suit Mussolini's ego, but it was not vital to the patrol scheme.[72] Mussolini "could then send his warships to hunt his own submarines where it mattered least."[73]

The formal signing of the Nyon Arrangement came on September 14.[74] Delbos closed the conference by praising the dispatch with which the powers had acted and promising that the measures would be carried out without delay. He warned that "we have reserved our right to consider reinforcing those measures, if necessary." He added that "we are protecting one of the most valuable attributes

of civilisation, namely, the existence of an international morality."
He further vowed that "the times when only the law of might prevailed will no longer be tolerated or allowed to go unpunished." After
giving notice of the powers' determination to enforce the accord,
Delbos held out the carrot to Italy by inviting her "to participate in
the work we have undertaken. . . . Italy's help . . . will favourably
complete the work of pacification which we are so desirous of carrying out."[75]

Three days later, on September 17, the nine powers met again.
At the Hôtel des Bergues in Geneva, the delegates formulated the
Supplementary Agreement to the Nyon Arrangement. It had been
understood when the Nyon Arrangement had been signed on the
fourteenth that subsequent agreement would be reached on other
measures. The delegations had utilized the brief intervening period
to formulate a draft for the protection of commercial shipping from
attacks by surface vessels and aircraft.[76] After considerable argument,[77] the Supplementary Agreement was adopted, which provided:

> Any surface war vessel, engaged in the protection of mer-
> chant shipping in conformity with the Nyon Arrangement . . .
> shall
> (a) if the attack is committed by an aircraft, open fire on the
> aircraft.
> (b) if the attack is committed by a surface vessel, intervene
> to resist it within the limits of its powers.[78]

The French public response to the Nyon Arrangement and the
ensuing Supplementary Agreement was one of satisfaction. With the
exception of the extremist papers such as *L'Humanité* on the Left
and *L'Action Française* on the Right, the French press was virtually
unanimous in its approval of the agreement reached at Nyon. The
Left was pleased at what it considered to be a triumph for collective
security, while the Right was happy that Soviet warships would have
no cause to move into the Mediterranean.[79] In fact, one observer
noted:

> It is considered specially satisfactory that this has been
> achieved by an agreement which is directed against nobody, and
> which has been concluded . . . with scrupulous respect for the
> susceptibilities of all Powers concerned. Opinion is unanimous

in approving the decision to sign the agreement without waiting further and to admit of no delay in putting it into operation.[80]

Le Temps on September 12 congratulated France and Britain on the results of the conference. It remarked that everything had been done to avoid giving offense to Germany, and that the exclusion of Russia from the Mediterranean would make the adhesion of Italy to the arrangement much easier.[81] In fact, the Italian attitude and reaction was on most minds during the next few days. On September 13, the day before the formal signing, the French and British representatives in Rome delivered a note containing the provisions of the Nyon Arrangement. Particular attention was drawn to the clause providing for Italian participation in patrolling the Tyrrhenian Sea. The note expressed the hope that the Italians would take part in the plan.[82] Italy had been watching the proceedings at Nyon with mixed feelings. The fact that France and Britain plunged ahead with the conference without the Axis powers and the rapidity with which agreement was reached probably shocked the Italians. The attitude of Count Ciano upon receiving the joint Franco-British note was one of deeply injured pride. He felt Italy was being presented with a *fait accompli.* The Italians had been sufficiently hurt to refuse the offer of participation in spite of the openings provided by the Nyon signatories. There was some fear that the Italian reaction would be so quick and uncompromising that there would be neither time nor opportunity for diplomatic maneuvering.[83]

But the Italians quickly recovered their composure. Delbos believed that the reversal was due to a message from Berlin urging moderation, although he had no direct evidence to support his view other than the "logic of the situation."[84] Of course, it is possible that Mussolini may have restrained Ciano.[85] On September 15 Renato Bova-Scoppa, the Italian representative in Geneva, visited M. Spitzmuller, First Secretary of the French Delegation. Bova-Scoppa was anxious to learn what the French and British were expecting from Italy. Spitzmuller consulted Delbos, who said that he could inform the Italians that the French and British had invited, and even urged, the Italian government to attend the Nyon Conference. They had kept the Italian government informed of the result of the negotiations and had invited them to participate in the agreement. Under the circumstances, the French government was quite ready to listen to any further observations that the Italians could make, but they were not asking for anything. If the Italian government had anything to say, it would certainly be listened to with due consideration. Delbos made it quite clear, however, that any change in the Italian policy would be left up to the Italian government. The French viewpoint was to be expressed privately and unofficially to Bova-Scoppa. The latter inquired about the British position and was told that it coincided exactly with that of the French.[86]

On September 16 Bova-Scoppa again approached Spitzmuller. He had communicated Delbos' reply to Rome. This had been received by Count Ciano with surprise and disappointment. He felt that Italy "had left the door open for the Nyon Powers, and the latter would not even touch the door handle." The claim for absolute parity in any antipiracy arrangement was the Italian counterproposal. Spitzmuller informed Delbos of the Italian attitude. The latter retorted that the Italian reply made it exceedingly difficult for the French government to regard it as an encouragement to continue negotiations with Italy. He again indicated a willingness to consider any Italian observations, provided that they were made through diplomatic channels.[87] Although it is difficult to assess how much Bova-Scoppa's anxiety about ascertaining the French attitude was indicative of general Italian attitudes, it is clear that the Italians were nervous about the Franco-British determination to stand firm.

Faced with the Franco-British resolve to prevent any negotiations that would weaken the effect of the Nyon Arrangement, the Italians backed off. On September 19 Mussolini hinted to the French and British representatives in Rome that once the principle of Italian parity with the French and British fleets, tasks, and zones had been accepted, Italy was only too anxious to cooperate.[88] By the twenty-first the French and British assured the Italians that they had never intended to refuse recognition of the position due to Italy as a great Mediterranean power. They would be happy to obtain Italy's cooperation in the application of the Nyon Arrangement. This, of course, allowed the Italians to save face and satisfied their desire for prestige without France and Britain having to make any concessions on the basic plan laid out at Nyon. Shortly thereafter, it was decided that experts from the three countries would meet in Paris in the near future to establish Italian participation in the plan.[89] Finally, representatives met in Paris from September 27 to 30. At the final meeting the Italians agreed to adhere to the Nyon agreements and to take part in the control of piracy, beginning on November 11, 1937. Although the text of the agreement was not made public, the Italians were evidently made responsible for zones in the central and eastern Mediterranean, a zone between the Balearic Islands and Sardinia as well as the Tyrrhenian Sea.[90] Thus the Nyon Arrangement was adjusted to accommodate the Italians.

The Nyon Conference has been described as the only achievement of French and British diplomacy during 1937.[91] One could go further. It proved to be one of the rare successes, fleeting to be sure, of Western diplomacy in the entire Hitlerian era. The conference was one of the few occasions during the interwar period when the Western powers made a resolute stand against totalitarian aggression. When the piracy immediately stopped, it became clear that determined resistance could be effective. "Here was a demonstration, never repeated, that Mussolini would respect a show of strength."[92] As Louis Fischer put it, "Mussolini understood the smoke of British cruisers better than the perfumed notes of the British Foreign Office. . . . Nyon pointed the way to a method of checking Fascist aggression. It was a stinging answer to those who maintained that to halt the totalitarian dictatorships it was necessary to go to war. Nyon was not war. Yet Mussolini pulled in his horns. . . . Nyon was a moment of sanity, a burst of realism."[93]

France took the lead in the Nyon negotiations, and the events surrounding the conference increased considerably the prestige of both France and England. Italy suffered a serious diplomatic defeat. Mussolini fell into a Soviet trap and absented himself from the conference. Consequently, he had to look on as France and England dominated Mediterranean policy.

Yvon Delbos, the man who did the most to promote and ensure the success of the conference,[94] called Nyon "a striking example of [French] determination and of the fortunate results that might have ensued if it had prevailed."[95] At Geneva, two weeks after the Nyon Conference, he showed more of the spirit that had motivated him to

push for the conference when he declared, "Encouraged by the success of the Nyon Conference, we have the will, in the days ahead,
to employ all our power for making truly real the application of the
engagements contracted."[96] In October, at the Radical Party Congress
in Lille, he warned that French policy must avoid two kinds of imprudent action. One form might be the utterance of threats, while
failing to measure all the consequences of such words or actions.
France should not embark upon a policy, however, without knowing
that it could be carried through. Another form of imprudence would
be to push conciliatory caution to the point that it might become an
actual temptation to others. France would never employ threats, but
it would never bow its head where the dignity and security of France
were at stake. "[France] does not dream of victory and conquests.
It finds its glory in preventing war. But it knows also that in order
to prevent war, it must be in a position to win a war if it is imposed
upon her."[97]

There can be little doubt that the results achieved at the Nyon
Conference strengthened the internal position of Delbos and the
Chautemps government. The fact is that Delbos, rather than irreso-
lutely following along in the wake of British policy, as standard
accounts of the period most often allege, clearly seized the initiative
and confronted the Axis powers with a resolve that reasserted Western
preeminence in the Mediterranean. Yet the truth of the matter is that
"Nyon proved to be only a flashlight, not a fixed beacon."[98] The
British sought to end the Spanish Civil War by negotiation through
the normal diplomatic channels. They realized that Nyon had placed
a heavy strain upon Anglo-Italian relations, and consequently, they
set about trying to instill new vigor into the "Gentleman's Agreement"
of 1937. In doing so, however, the British "destroyed the moral and
practical advantages which had accrued to the Western democracies
from their forthright stand in the Mediterranean and permitted the
diplomatic initiative to pass once more to the fascist powers."[99] Delbos
and the French, after the brief flurry of opposition concerning the
Mediterranean, did not have the strength or will to put up much
more than token resistance to Chamberlain's plan to initiate a rapprochement with Mussolini. Ultimately, after the temporary success
at Nyon, the farce of the London Committee was resumed.[100]

Perhaps Winston Churchill best summed up the long-range effect of the Nyon Conference when he wrote:

The Nyon Conference, although an incident, is a proof of how powerful the combined influence of Britain and France, if expressed with conviction and a readiness to use force, would have been upon the mood and policy of the Dictators. That such a policy would have prevented war at this stage cannot be asserted. It might easily have delayed it.[101]

Eden, in a letter to Churchill, pointed out that "the really important political fact is that we have emphasised that co-operation between Britain and France can be effective, and that the two Western Democracies can still play a decisive part in European affairs."[102]

The fact is that Nyon assisted elements in France and Britain that were working for a close alliance between the two powers. It was an alliance that Delbos consistently sought to achieve as the cornerstone of French foreign policy. It is the rocky road toward this goal that will be explored next.

5

The Entente Cordiale:
Keystone of
Popular Front Foreign Policy

"For me a new and much happier era of relations with France now opened up. From this moment [the ascent to office of Léon Blum and Yvon Delbos] until my resignation in February 1938, French Ministers and I worked together without even a momentary breach of an understanding which grew increasingly confident."[1] This statement, made by Sir Anthony Eden, points to the chief concern of those responsible for the formulation of the foreign policy of the Popular Front. The development of closer relations with Britain was to be the foundation of French policy. Yvon Delbos, as Foreign Minister, was instrumental in the efforts to recement the Entente Cordiale. Here again, due to their close personal relationship, it is very difficult to determine whether Blum or Delbos was primarily responsible for this rapprochement. The fact that they lived in the same building meant that a great deal was exchanged between them on the subject of foreign policy which never became part of the public record. There can be little doubt, however, that both men—and one can probably add Alexis Léger, the Secretary General at the Quai d'Orsay—considered that the reestablishment of close relations with Britain had to be the keystone of the government's foreign policy.

In view of past relations, however, such a policy was bound to be beset with tremendous obstacles. Although the two countries had been allies in war and peace for the past twenty-five years, it must be said that the two nationalities had proved themselves quite incompatible. Sir Harold Nicolson once observed that the average Englishman regarded Frenchmen as

> vivacious, and therefore volatile; as nimble-witted, and therefore unreliable; as hedonistic, and therefore profligate. He mistrusts their politicians, whom he regards as treacherous and corrupt. He is irritated by their press polemics, which he attributes, and not without reason, to foreign subventions. And he dislikes their foreign policy, which jars on his isolationist feelings and makes him dread lest we be dragged into trouble "at the coat-tails of France."[2]

Sir Robert Vansittart, Permanent Undersecretary of State for Foreign Affairs during most of the period under consideration, sought to explain the British attitude toward the French by going back to Victorian England for its roots:

> Victorian England was vaguely convinced that nineteenth century France had too good a time; that France laughed too much and cooked too well. . . . More serious still, Victorian England suspected that the French put more into, and got more out of, sex than the English. Victorian England had not the vaguest idea how this was done, but was fairly sure that the advantage was not fair, and quite sure that it was not nice. There was a song in Noel Coward's early nineteenth century "Conversation Piece," in which he acted with Yvonne Printemps: 'There's always something fishy about the French.'[3]

Vansittart considered this outlook to be typical of the England of Baldwin and Chamberlain as well. "The English always spoke of the place as 'Gay Parree' and were profoundly unhappy when they got there."[4]

Conversely, Frenchmen reciprocated the English distaste in kind. The expression "*Albion perfide*" undoubtedly dates from an early period and maintained its currency among average Frenchmen during the interwar years. The journalist André Géraud (Pertinax) once sought to establish the mixed emotions that the English aroused in Frenchmen. They admired the English independence of thought and their disregard for others' judgments of their actions, and they delighted in Voltaire's quip that "the Englishman, like a free man, goes to heaven by the way which pleases him." Yet the French regarded the English as selfish, despised their air of social superiority, and scorned their humanitarianism as superficial. Many, in fact, cherished the rebuke addressed to Gladstone by one of his adversaries as a fitting admonition of the English in general: "I do not mind your playing with a card up your sleeve. What I object to is your pretending that God put it there." Moreover, the British habit of "muddling through" was very exasperating to the French, especially in view of past British successes. There was resentment that the English took it for granted "that the French Army alone should man the forts and trenches while the noble tasks on land and sea are reserved for them."[5] It all leads one to agree with Samuel M. Osgood's observation about the complexity of the French attitude toward the English: "John Bull's eating habits may have been disgusting, and his sex life a fit object of ridicule, yet there was something about the man that incited in Monsieur Prudhomme feelings of awe, suspicion, puzzlement, jealousy, and reluctant admiration."[6] But when all is said and done, Nicolson was correct in observing that "the fact remains that most Englishmen dislike the French and most Frenchmen dislike the English."[7]

One of the most important factors in European affairs following World War I was the relationship between France and England. Peace on the remapped continent required that the two Western powers cooperate in administering the Treaty of Versailles. The treaty provisions would constantly call for decisions to be made by the allies. Yet it quickly became evident that the two powers held widely divergent views on how the peace could be best maintained. The conflict between their policies was to become a major source of Europe's catastrophe. The basic issue in the Franco-British controversy was the problem of Germany's power and position. The two powers disagreed on how strong Germany should be permitted to become without threatening their vital interests. Herein lay the source of the discord that existed between them.[8]

As the neighbor of a traditional enemy that was potentially stronger than France itself, France kept an eye fixed on "the blue line of the Vosges." France assumed that its own security could not allow any increase in German strength above the limits imposed at Versailles. In order to insure itself against any German resurgence, France continuously sought security through the development of an elaborate alliance system. These *garanties de sécurité* would dissuade Germany by making the defenders of the status quo invincible.[9]

But Britain was opposed to any idea that a need existed for an organized system of mutual assistance against aggression. Such a system implied coercion by the threat of military force against any aggressor. Instead, hostility should be dissipated through reconciliation and the development of good will. Trust in the League was therefore widely advocated by the British.[10] The French, however, felt that the League could be an effective guarantee of security only if it could be transformed into a superstate, which would have its own effective police force. Of course, the British rejected such arguments. The League could settle disputes through the "peaceable methods of arbitration and discussion."[11]

Moreover, the British argued that armaments provoked fear and suspicion, which helped to cause war. Nations should first disarm, then security would follow. The French disagreed. The fear of war, they said, makes nations arm for their own defense. Once the fear of attack is removed, armaments will be reduced. In other words, once security had been assured, the nations would feel safe in disarming.[12] It was the old story of the chicken or the egg. Both powers recognized the value of the League and disarmament for maintaining the peace, but they differed in their fundamental approaches to each.

The fact remained that while France wanted to organize a superior force for carrying out coercive measures, Britain was engaged in applying methods of conciliation and appeasement. France tried to prevent a German revolt against the new European alignment by emphasizing the irrevocability of the treaty and the strength of the defenders of the status quo. Britain sought to ward off the danger by removing what she considered to be its main causes. To the French the British inclination to beat swords into plowshares appeared fraught with danger. It would merely promote German resistance to the settlement.[13] But whereas Britain pursued its policy with perseverance, even to the point of unilateral disarmament, France, after the departure of Poincaré and Briand, was inconsistent and irresolute in carrying out its policy. Perhaps, as J. W. Wheeler-Bennett has said, "behind a crumbling facade of bluster the dry rot of moral decay had entered the body politic of France."[14]

As a result of these fundamental divergences in policy, the interwar years were laden with issues over which the two democracies clashed. Disagreement which began over differing concepts of security at the peace conference continued through the Ruhr occupation, the Chanak episode, reparations and interallied debts, military and naval disarmament, and relations with the Soviets. But if relations between the two were unsatisfactory during the twenties and early thirties, events of 1935 and 1936 made them even more acrimonious.

In June, 1935, the Anglo-German Naval Agreement was signed, which permitted Germany to build up to thirty-five percent of Britain's naval force and forty-five percent of its submarine strength. Exasperated by what has been termed "perhaps the most senseless piece of diplomacy of the time,"[15] the French found it increasingly difficult to discount Lord Tyrrell's epigram: "The real defect in English policy since 1918 has been to mistake the Germans for Englishmen and the French for Germans."[16]

Conversely, when the Italian attack on Abyssinia occurred, French public and military opinion was hostile toward the adoption of effective sanctions against Italy, as Britain proposed. When sanctions had clearly failed, an alternative scheme—the Hoare-Laval Plan— was developed. When a premature leak of the details to the French press made the plan inoperative, irritation with the French among British governing circles became quite vociferous. English opinion was convinced that Italian success had been due to the French reluctance to support more rigorous efforts at restraining Mussolini.[17] Lord Cecil, the League's most prominent enthusiast in Britain, expressed the widespread resentment:

> I am deeply grieved at the attitude of France. If we are to be asked to defend France in the event of treaties being broken, France must realize . . . that what applies to the German goose applies equally to the Abyssinian gander. The half-hearted action of France about the Italian-Abyssinian war has gravely chilled our friendship. We do not like the way the French treat the League as a sort of particular umbrella, valuable for keeping France out of the wet, but when not so needed to be rolled up and used only for gesticulation. . . . We shall keep our word to France; yet keeping faith is something different from friendship.[18]

Cecil also wondered what particular interest Britain had on the

Rhine. Perhaps even the time when Britain had a special interest in the Low Countries was long past.[19]

Thus, relations between the two powers were quite unpleasant when Hitler reoccupied the Rhineland in March, 1936. Again they were not prepared to cooperate effectively in the face of the newest act of Nazi defiance. Confronted with Britain's advice to be prudent, cool-headed, and conciliatory, France did not have the will to act alone. Therefore, while the two Western democracies conferred and procrastinated, they probably missed their last chance to halt Nazi Germany without the risk of a serious war.[20] The episode opened new fissures in Franco-British relations. The failure to act was quickly blamed on the British. The French, it was said, were eager to act, but the British threatened a rupture and held them back. The fact is, regardless of assessing relative degrees of blame, France and Britain were partners in disgrace. It was not the kind of basis upon which a new entente could be easily forged. In fact, Emile Mireaux, Editor of Le Temps, observed that in both countries "public opinion has been convinced that the action of its own Government has been paralysed by the hesitation, the reserve, the suspicion, and the lack of understanding—if not actually by the ill-will—of the Government of the other."[21] Indeed, there can be little doubt that the events of 1935 and 1936 had brought Franco-British relations to a new low. This was the situation that faced the Popular Front government when it took office in June, 1936.

Confronted with the consequences of the Abyssinian War and the reoccupation of the Rhineland, "above all, Léon Blum wanted to reestablish the Franco-English Entente." Delbos also desired to revive a close diplomatic relationship with the British. On December 5, 1936, Blum told the Chamber that "Yvon Delbos has given first priority to the close cordiality of our relations with England, and he is right. For our other friends are unanimous in recognizing and declaring that the Franco-English accord affects the whole realm of international relations."[22]

The orientation of the Popular Front's foreign policy became quite clear in the ministerial declaration read by Delbos in the Chamber, and by Blum in the Senate, on June 23. The government emphasized its "will for peace." It promised to support collective security backed by military force and the use of League financial and economic sanctions. In the process of reconstructing the collective security system, France could be sure of the "unconditional support of the great English democracy, whom so many memories and common efforts united to the French democracy." The government declared that "the close and confident cooperation between the two countries is the essential guarantee of peace in Europe."[23]

In order to effectuate their plan of reestablishing closer relations with England, the French began to put out "feelers" through Charles Corbin, the French Ambasador in London, for a meeting of the Locarno powers.[24] At Geneva on July 3, Delbos, Blum, Eden, and Van Zeeland, the Belgian Prime Minister, agreed upon the necessity for a meeting of the three Locarno signatories to reexamine the Rhineland situation in the light of Germany's refusal to answer the British questionnaire of May 7.[25] The British attributed the French eagerness to hold a three-power meeting to considerations of domestic policy. Eden told the cabinet that "the [Blum] Government was weak and wanted to show that they counted for something at any rate with the United Kingdom and Belgium."[26] The British feared that the Germans would consider the conference as an attempt to impose a program on them. Therefore, they proposed to invite Germany in the hopes of obtaining "a general amelioration of the international situation." They asked the Belgians to obtain French acceptance of German participation.[27] Delbos refused to consider the British proposal. Since the Rhineland coup the Germans had refused to give any satisfaction to the legitimate demands of the powers that were affected by the German action. Therefore, to invite Germany would be "publicly to consecrate the final success of the method of the *fait accompli*." Corbin was told to express the French surprise at an "initiative which is in contradiction with the precise assurances given at Geneva by Mr. Eden himself."[28]

Delbos won his point. He partially agreed, however, with Eden's suggestion that the conference should not confine itself to the Locarno question, but should aim at a general settlement of all European problems. Still, Delbos maintained that "the first order of business must be to settle the situation created by the German initiative of March 7 and to negotiate afterwards . . . a new accord destined to replace the Rhineland clauses of the Pact of Locarno." Only if satisfactory solutions resulted in these areas would other general European questions be posed.[29]

On July 23, as the Spanish crisis burst forth about them, representatives of the three powers met in London in order to draft plans for a new Locarno Conference.[30] At the morning session Delbos led the French delegation. The session went smoothly, although some disagreement occurred over the text of a communiqué distributed to the powers on July 20.[31] The preliminary communiqué called for "an eventual extension of the scope of the discussion." Delbos feared that the expansion would merely include Italy and Germany in a five-power conference. He felt that the next round of discussions should include "the participation of all interested powers." This could be interpreted to involve Czechoslovakia and Poland. It became quite apparent that the British did not desire to become involved in providing guarantees for an Eastern Locarno. During the afternoon session, Van Zeeland ultimately proposed a compromise that proved satisfactory to both Delbos and the British. The three powers envisaged "the extension of the scope of the discussion in a manner to facilitate, with the collaboration of other interested powers, the settlement of problems the solution of which was essential for the peace of Europe."[32] The vagueness of the statement allowed each power to interpret it as it pleased.

After a formal luncheon, Blum assumed leadership of the French delegation. He spoke of the willingness of the French to talk with the Germans on an equal footing about all subjects. But he warned the delegates that "the perils which exist today are not peculiar to France and Germany." Eden commended the French and Belgians for their spirit of conciliation and reaffirmed Britain's willingness to aid the two countries, should they become the object of an unprovoked aggression. Delbos thanked Eden for this declaration of support and added that France had "full confidence in the loyalty of the British Government." He continued that "an affirmation of solidarity constitutes the best guarantee of the peace of Europe, and he hoped that this solidarity . . . might come to include later five powers, and then all of Europe." Delbos, however, remained skeptical that a five-power conference would produce results and was anxious to consider Britain's attitude should this occur. But Eden felt that such an effort would undermine the work of the preliminary three-power conference.

Blum also warned that should the five-power conference fail, France would be forced to "give its reaction the most firm character."[33]

The official communiqué, issued at the conclusion of the conference that evening, underlined the importance of reaching a general settlement. "Such a settlement can only be achieved by the free cooperation of all the powers concerned, and nothing would be more fatal for the hopes of such a settlement than the division, apparent or real, of Europe into opposing blocks." The three powers proposed a new five-power conference. "The first task must be, in their opinion, the negotiating of a new agreement designed to replace the Rhineland Pact of Locarno and settling, through the collaboration of all concerned, the situation created by the German initiative of March 7." Invitations to participate would be sent to the Germans and Italians. "If progress can be realized at this meeting, other questions concerning the peace of Europe will come under consideration."[34]

Delbos and Blum made an excellent impression in London. "People at the Foreign Office said that they had never yet met any French Ministers who were 'so easy to get on with.' "[35] The conference, of course, was an important step in the efforts of Blum and Delbos to establish closer ties with Britain. It must be admitted, however, that not much else came out of the London Conference. Delbos' fears of a lack of progress towards a new settlement proved quite justified. The British delayed until September 17 before delivering the invitations to Germany and Italy which had been agreed upon in London. The notes suggested that the powers meet at the "most appropriate date." The British note recalled the recommendation put forth in the communiqué of July 23 and offered suggestions as to the problems to be discussed at the five-power meeting.[36] The Germans, typically, did not reply to the British note until October 12. Obviously the Germans had no intention of entering into the system of regional pacts called for by the British proposal. On the other hand, they indicated their willingness to conclude a new Locarno agreement and to renounce aggression against France and Belgium—a position which had not changed since the promises they had made following the Rhineland episode. Thus, the Germans continued to do little more than express their pious desire for peace. "By the beginning of November . . . the Blum Government was no longer under any illusions regarding the possibility of achieving a general settlement within the revised

European balance of power arising from the Rhineland crisis."[37] The tragedy is that Delbos and Blum, in spite of the willingness they had expressed in London to take action in the case of a breakdown in negotiations, failed to take any decisive steps to resist the Axis aggression.

In the meantime, of course, attention had been drawn to the Spanish problem, which was exploding even as the London Conference met. Although the conference can be seen as an important first step in the French plan to breathe new life into the entente, Delbos and eventually Blum saw that the Spanish war could nullify the progress made in that direction. Consequently, as we have seen in an earlier chapter, the French, under considerable "unofficial" British pressure, decided to formulate and adopt a policy of nonintervention in Spain. When the farcical Nonintervention Committee began meeting in London, France allowed the British to assume the leading role.

Thus, it is clear that in their initial efforts to establish a closer relationship with Britain, the French were willing to follow in Britain's wake. The London Conference of July 23 need not have been a surrender to Britain's leadership. But when France took no action in the face of Germany's dilatory tactics while the Rhineland coup faded from the world's attention, it became quite evident that Spain would not be the only place where France would follow British wishes.

As a result of French willingness to take a back seat to Britain during the late summer and fall of 1936, relations between the two nations improved considerably. Toward the end of the year Eden admitted to the cabinet that their relations were "close and cordial and had never been better in recent times."[38] Perhaps the most spectacular, although not the most substantial, confirmation of this détente came in late November and early December. In a speech to his constituents at Leamington on November 20, Eden, while speaking on the need for British rearmament, declared: "Our arms may, and if the occasion arose they would, be used in the defence of France and Belgium against unprovoked aggression in accordance with our existing obligations."[39] Naturally, Eden's pledge was enthusiastically received in Paris. Geneviève Tabouis in *L'Oeuvre* wrote that after years of vague promises of collaboration from Britain, the fact had now been put down in black and white that Great Britain would defend France and Belgium in the event of unprovoked aggression.[40] *Le*

Temps assured its readers that Eden had stated Britain's position in a manner so formal and categorical that there could be no misunderstanding about an attitude that had hitherto given rise to contradictory interpretations.[41]

On December 4, Delbos spoke before the Chamber and reciprocated Eden's pledge. He said:

> These words are in no way unexpected since they are in accordance with our mutual engagements. But their tone, the echo which they have evoked in England, and the circumstances in which they were pronounced, give them a particular value. I wish to declare, in the name of the government, that, likewise, all the forces of France, on land, on sea, and in the air, would be spontaneously and immediately used for the defense of Great Britain in the event of an unprovoked aggression.[42]

Delbos added that "Parliament, the government, and the whole country are attached to Great Britain by the most solid ties of reason and of heart. They know that Franco-British friendship is the keystone of European peace." He warned that "their [the democracies'] pacifism does not mean that they are resigned, as some seem to think, to submit to anything in order to prevent war, but it does mean that in offering peace to all they do not intend to offer a reward to aggression, but to be in a position to defend themselves victoriously if attacked. Such is the essential object of Franco-British solidarity."[43] He sought to defend himself and the government against the attacks of those who criticized the apparently increasing French dependency upon Britain.[44]

> I am surprised at the insinuations which have been made here in France, as well as in England, . . . accusing the one government of allowing itself to be influenced to too great an extent by the other. No, gentlemen! It is a case of constant and confident collaboration that is the basis of our agreement, which is itself the result of a previously established harmony and of our will to understand each other, an agreement which covers the different problems which are raised and which we are examining in a common desire to defend peace and to face the dangers which might threaten us both. . . . In the meanwhile the best pledge of our security is . . . the reality and efficacy of the tightening of Franco-British friendship.[45]

It was a strong defense of the policy upon which the government had embarked. Indeed, at the end of 1936 relations between the two countries had become closer than they had been for several years. Nevertheless, the French government had gone a long way down the path of abdicating its independence in foreign policy. Its critics had a telling point.

On January 2, 1937, the British signed a "Gentleman's Agreement" with Italy. In spite of the fact that Franco-Italian relations had steadily deteriorated since the beginning of the Spanish Civil War, the agreement does not seem to have bothered Delbos too greatly. When rumors began circulating in November that Anglo-Italian talks were about to begin, Delbos ordered Corbin to express France's concern about the position it would be put in by a Mediterranean agreement between the two powers.[46] Eden and Sir Orme Sargent, British Undersecretary of State at the Foreign Office, sought to dispel French fears. Sargent observed that the resolution of Anglo-Italian difficulties in the Mediterranean would also benefit France's interests there.[47] The British informed the French that they had desired French participation in the negotiations. They feared, however, that the state of relations between France and Italy would merely hamper progress toward an agreement.[48] But the British promised to keep the French informed on the development of the conversations.[49] Eden later wrote: "I was most anxious to remain in step with the French Government. The more so because Delbos had shown us many acts of friendship recently, not least in using his influence, during the Abdication crisis, to restrain his country's press. I therefore asked Sir George Clerk to give the Foreign Minister a full account of the negotiations."[50] On December 12, Clerk saw Delbos and explained the British position. They felt that an Anglo-Italian accord could be "a means of detaching Italy from Germany and of preventing Mediterranean complications." Delbos replied with a summary of the French position: "(1) We see no objection . . . to an Italo-English rapprochement, (2) we desire likewise a Franco-Italian rapprochement." He feared, however, that "Italy and Germany will not fail to exploit the fact that France's absence is a sign that its general position and its good relations with England have weakened."[51]

Ultimately, the British did keep the French informed of the state of the negotiations. In fact, they apprised the French of the text of the agreement before releasing it to the press.[52] The "Gentleman's Agreement" of January 2, 1937, disclaimed any desire by the two countries to modify the status quo in the Mediterranean. They promised to discourage any activities that would impair relations between the two nations.[53] Eden wrote in his diary that "the French Government have behaved very well, and I have been repaid for keeping Delbos informed and making the Italians wait for forty-eight hours before the publication of the Exchange of Assurances by an excellent message of good-will which Delbos gave the French press."[54]

The statement released by Delbos on the evening of January 2 expressed his satisfaction with the Anglo-Italian Agreement. "Good understanding between these two European Powers, both attached to France by traditional friendship and by community of interests, has always been regarded in France as an element of order in the Mediterranean."[55] Delbos did not encourage the British to fish in the troubled waters of the Mediterranean. Once again, however, his desire to maintain a close relationship with England discouraged him from actively exerting pressure to the contrary. He satisfied himself by merely noting the dangers that could accrue from dealing with Mussolini. The British willingness to keep him informed of the progress of the negotiations, which they publicly acknowledged in their announcement, made the action somewhat easier to swallow. Moreover, the French press, with the exception of the extreme Left, welcomed the agreement. Geneviève Tabouis, writing in L'Oeuvre, speculated that it would bring an element of moderation into the Italian activities in Spain, and it would give London more influence in Rome. She hoped that it would lead to similar Franco-Italian negotiation, although she recognized that this would be more difficult for France than it had been for England.[56] Le Temps also expressed the hope that a Franco-Italian rapprochement could be developed. The "Gentleman's Agreement" would create again the favorable moral conditions for France, Britain, and Italy to cooperate in maintaining peace.[57] L'Humanité, however, declared that "France is duped by the Anglo-Italian Accord." The agreement meant Italian acceptance of English predominance in the Eastern Mediterranean, but in return England recognized Italy as predominant in the Western Mediterranean. This could not suit France. Moreover, Italo-German cooperation was not affected, nor was the attitude of Italy towards Spain.[58]

The "Gentleman's Agreement" did not pave the way for four-power talks leading to a general European settlement as the Baldwin government had hoped. Indeed, as *L'Humanité* predicted, the agreement failed to modify Italian policy in Spain. Italian assistance continued to increase until Mussolini even threw away the pretense of "volunteers" and acknowledged and even boasted of the presence of regular army units in Spain. It also became clear that the talks between Blum and Schacht would be fruitless in improving Franco-German relations. Consequently, Delbos began making efforts to strengthen the French system of alliances in Eastern Europe, a topic which will be dealt with later.

In the meantime, Delbos continued his efforts during the spring of 1937 to maintain the close relationship with England. If possible, he hoped to obtain a British commitment to support the French alliances in Eastern Europe.[59] In a speech at Châteauroux at the end of January, on the occasion of the unveiling of a World War I memorial, Delbos called for courage, prudence, and obedience to the dictates of reason rather than of passion. He declared that "our close intimacy with England, the solidity of our agreements with the Little Entente, Poland, and the U.S.S.R., constitute for us so many guarantees in our struggle against war."[60] But Delbos' efforts had to surmount considerable English opposition. He correctly assumed that closer Franco-British ties would encourage the support of many of those who felt that the entente threatened no one and represented the best possible guarantee for peace. On the other hand, there were those who feared that France's eastern alliances would merely lead to its involvement in the quarrels of that area.[61]

The latter attitude became more pronounced in British governing circles with the accession of Neville Chamberlain to the post of Prime Minister in May, 1937. Chamberlain realized that cooperation with France was inescapable, but he was convinced that the defense of Britain did not necessarily depend upon the existence of Austria and Czechoslovakia. This attitude, of course, differed greatly from French conceptions about its responsibilities in Eastern Europe. In fact, as Arthur Furnia correctly concludes, "relations with France within the *'Entente Cordiale,'* suddenly became less cordial. The basis of the Anglo-French relationship now became one of cold geopolitics."[62]

Simultaneously with Chamberlain's new approach in Britain, a new resistance to the British policy of appeasement arose in France. This resistance, spurred on to a great extent by the Axis intervention in Spain, received a large boost from the submarine sinkings in the Mediterranean in the late summer of 1937. As we have seen, a combination of factors led Delbos to reassert the French leadership in the Entente Cordiale. The Nyon Conference, which he initiated, promoted, and directed, resulted in one of the most notable testimonials displayed by the democracies during the entire decade prior to World War II to what determined action could achieve in the face of aggression. The success of the conference strengthened Delbos' hand in the Franco-British partnership, and it undoubtedly strengthened the antiappeasement, pro-French elements in England which were working for a closer alliance between the two powers.

Perhaps Delbos sought to utilize the momentum of renewed Franco-British cooperation and success at Nyon, limited and momentary though it may have been, for a move towards a general strengthening of the French position in Europe, particularly among the states of Eastern Europe. In any event, Delbos had not abandoned his plan to close the widening fissures in the French Eastern European alliance system. In his speech before the Radical Party Congress at Lille on October 29, he reiterated his view that the continuation of Franco-British friendship and solidarity was one of the surest guarantees of world peace. But he also made it a point of referring to the French ties in Eastern Europe. He noted, "We have tightened our alliance with Poland." He believed that "the Franco-Soviet pact of friendship —in spite of the attacks against it . . . —preserves all its peaceful value." Moreover, the visits and statements by the leaders of Yugoslavia and Rumania had attested to "the solidarity that unites [France] to the Little Entente."[63]

Early in November Delbos began to formulate plans for a tour through the Eastern European capitals. He undoubtedly hoped to breathe new life into the decaying French alliance system in that area, just as Louis Barthou had done in 1934. But it appeared that Delbos and Chamberlain were working at cross purposes. Just as Delbos sought to renew ties in Eastern and Central Europe, the British were engaged in an act of diplomacy which revealed to Hitler that the Western powers would not vigorously defend that area.

After the events of the summer and fall of 1937 had made a détente with Mussolini unlikely for the moment, Chamberlain eagerly sought to approach the Germans. His opportunity came in November when Lord Halifax, Lord President of the Council and Master of the Middleton Foxhounds, was invited by Hermann Göring, head of the *Luftwaffe* and Chief Huntsman of the Reich, to an international hunting exhibition in Berlin. Chamberlain seized upon the opportunity to establish personal contact with the Germans. Eden hesitantly agreed to the Halifax trip, but upon learning that in order to talk with Hitler, Halifax would have to pursue him to his "eyrie" at Berchtesgaden, he thought that the visit did not justify such a concession to Hitler. Chamberlain, however, had made up his mind that it was possible "to do business with Hitler." During the third week of November, Halifax made his trip to Germany.[64]

France had not been told of the deliberations in Britain or of the final decision to send Halifax. News of the impending visit soon leaked to the London press, and on November 13 Delbos called Eden to express his "anxiety" about the reported trip. Delbos said it was unfortunate that the French government had not been informed beforehand. Eden later wrote:

> Delbos . . . was not opposed to the journey, though he anticipated that Lord Halifax would be asked some awkward questions. It was, however, imperative to do nothing at this time to weaken the good relations between our two countries. . . .
> . . . Delbos begged that we should be very careful to give no encouragement to anything in the nature of a Nazi adventure in Czechoslovakia. In these days, he said, it was not enough to warn against war and invasion; there was a new technique. This was the reason why, in a recent speech, he had referred to France's guarantee to Czechoslovakia as being operative in general terms, and had not limited it only to invasion. He had wished specifically to make it plain that intervention in the internal affairs of Czechoslovakia, in order to facilitate aggression, would be as serious as a direct attack.[65]

Yet the discussions that Halifax had with Hitler at Berchtesgaden had precisely the effect of accomplishing what Delbos had hoped to avoid.

On November 22 word reached the Foreign Office that French

Premier Chautemps was seriously thinking of proposing a meeting in London or Paris. Chautemps and Delbos would meet with Chamberlain and Eden prior to Delbos' departure on his eastern tour. William Strang, Undersecretary of State, advised that the meeting would be advantageous. Apart from the opportunity for personal contact with the French, it would be a particularly good occasion to give the French an account of what had passed between Halifax and Hitler. It would allow the two governments to discuss European affairs generally, with special attention being paid to Delbos' forthcoming series of visits.[66] Two days later Eden informed the cabinet that it had been arranged that Chautemps and Delbos would visit London on November 29 and 30.[67]

The conversations between the French and British Ministers began with a report by Halifax of his discussions with Hitler. The topics which held the most interest for the Frenchmen were those dealing with Central and Eastern Europe as well as the colonial question. With regard to the first problem, Halifax told them that he had stressed to Hitler the importance of doing nothing that might provoke dangerous reactions.[68] But, as Eden noted later, Halifax had also told Hitler of

> possible alterations in the European order which might be destined to come about with the passage of time. Amongst these questions were Danzig, Austria and Czechoslovakia. England was interested to see that any alterations should come through the course of peaceful evolution and that methods should be avoided which might cause far-reaching disturbances, which neither the Chancellor nor other countries desired.[69]

Hitler had replied that Germany had agreements with Austria which were being respected. "He hoped that reasonable elements in Czechoslovakia would make it possible for the Sudeten Germans to enjoy a status which would safeguard their position."[70]

Chautemps later told Ambassador Bullitt that he considered Halifax's statements on Central Europe to be a great blunder.[71] Delbos cautioned that the Germans had been extremely noncommittal in their remarks to Halifax about Austria and Czechoslovakia. They had acted as if they felt the British should have little interest in Central Europe.[72] Chamberlain confirmed that a strong feeling persisted in Britain that the government should not become entangled in a war on account of Czechoslovakia, a country which was a long way off and with which Britain did not have a great deal in common. Chamberlain did feel, however, that support could be gained for a reasonable and peaceful settlement between Germany and Czechoslovakia. Delbos replied firmly that efforts should be directed toward both sides. He warned that Germany was really aiming at the absorption of Austria and part of Czechoslovakia. Such actions would have dire consequences for Europe. Germany would achieve hegemony over all of Central and Eastern Europe, which would merely whet its appetite for further conquest. He asserted that treaties should be respected because they formed the basis of the law of nations. France had a treaty with Czechoslovakia and, therefore, could not abandon its ally.[73]

Chamberlain later admitted to his cabinet that it had appeared that the French would press the British to adopt "a more forthcoming attitude in Central Europe." The British did not encourage them to persist in their stand. Eden said that Britain would not ask France to reconsider its obligations to Central Europe. But, he indicated, there was a feeling in Britain that the Sudeten Germans had certain grievances that should be redressed. Chamberlain added that he did not believe that the Germans would go so far as to ask for the autonomy of the Sudeten Germans. Faced with British indolence, the French were not sufficiently resolute to demand a firm British commitment in Central Europe. They finally suggested that two policies were possible: (1) to disinterest themselves, and (2) to interest themselves in a spirit of conciliation. The Frenchmen agreed that appropriate concessions might be made by Czechoslovakia and that an effort should be made to reach a general settlement with Germany. But they pointed out the difficulty of pressing the Czechs too far. Delbos was asked to ascertain, during his forthcoming visit to Prague, what concessions the Czechs might be willing to make. The French doubted that there would be an immediate German intervention in Austria or Czechoslovakia, but felt that the Germans expected to get what they wanted in due course. Perhaps if the issue could be postponed, it would settle itself or not even arise.[74]

Halifax informed the French of his discussion concerning the question of a colonial readjustment. Hitler had argued that it was unreasonable to consider Germany unworthy of colonies. He looked

upon the question as the only important direct issue existing between
Germany and Britain. Britain and France should examine the problem together and propose a solution. Halifax had repeatedly explained to Hitler that it was out of the question to discuss the colonial
issue except in the context of a general settlement. Chamberlain later
complained that this had been the most difficult item in the discussion
with the French. He felt that "with France it was only a question of
whether they could cede Togoland and the Cameroons. In our case
exchanges of territory . . . [entailed] strategical difficulties."[75] Nevertheless, French concerns did not really differ greatly from those of the
British. Both governments felt that any discussion of the question must
be in the context of a general settlement and not as a separate problem. Chamberlain said that France would not be asked to make a
sacrifice if Britain was not prepared to do likewise. Chautemps made
it clear that his government would be willing to make some sacrifice
as part of a general settlement, although he doubted whether French
public opinion had reached that stage as yet.[76] The Ministers agreed
that the Germans should be informed that the question of colonies
would need prolonged study and could only be solved within the
framework of a general agreement. Delbos later explained, "We
agreed that we should both be ready to make concessions to produce
peace but that we should make no concessions whatsoever of any
nature that would strengthen Germany for another war. We agreed
to remain for the moment completely in our present positions, making
no concessions whatsoever, but informing the Germans that we were
ready to discuss constructive proposals for the maintaining of peace."
He added that any specific proposals would have to come from the
German side.[77] As Geneviève Tabouis correctly noted, the lack of
enthusiasm by both governments for redressing German colonial
grievances was the diplomatic way of abandoning the question.

The remainder of the conversations, Eden later recalled, "was
in the main notable for an admirable definition by Delbos of his
country's attitude to the Spanish civil war."[78] Other topics included
the possibility of bilateral English discussions with Germany and
Italy, to which the French raised no objections, providing that they
were included at the appropriate time in any discussions involving
disarmament, the League of Nations, and the Far Eastern situation.[79]

Before concluding the meetings, the Ministers devoted time to planning the strategy of Delbos' forthcoming trip. They decided that he should not only press Benes to consider concessions on the matter of German minorities, but that he should also express to the Poles the Franco-British concern over the actions of the League High Commissioner in Danzig. In fact, Chamberlain asked Delbos to represent the British as well as the French on his trip through Central Europe.[80]

After having lunch with the King and Queen, Delbos and Chautemps were seen off at Victoria Station by Chamberlain and Eden. The outcome of the London discussions evoked widespread satisfaction. Bullitt found Delbos "for the first time in the past year extremely satisfied with himself and full of confidence." Before going to London, Delbos had been concerned about a report that real disagreement existed between Chamberlain and Eden. He now felt certain that the report was unfounded. He had been told that Chamberlain desired to give Germany a free hand in Central Europe in return for a promise by Germany not to ask for British colonies. But he had found Chamberlain in full agreement with Chautemps and himself.[81]

Eden also believed that the talks had been very useful for several reasons. They had halted rumors of a divergence of views between the two governments about policy towards Germany and the colonial question. There had been no sign that the French Ministers desired to line up with the Left bloc in Europe. "Neither did they appear to be in any way under Russian influence." He also felt that the "conversations had enabled them to take an indispensible first step in the direction of some dealings with Germany over colonies, and the views of the two Governments had proved to be identical."[82]

Although the final communiqué at the end of the conference had been carefully worded to prevent arousing exaggerated hopes of concrete results in the immediate future, the French press greeted the London conversations with considerable satisfaction. There had been doubts about whether the cooperation between France and England would be strong enough to withstand the international pressures of the period.[83] On the Left, L'Humanité was disturbed at the imprecision of the communiqué and at the omission of references to the League and collective security. But it remained less critical than usual.[84] Le Populaire enthusiastically praised Franco-British efforts to move towards "the goal of determining a program of common action."[85] *L'Oeuvre* noted that colonial concessions had been refused and that England had declared itself not disinterested in Central Europe.[86] *Le Temps* emphasized areas of agreement between the two governments.[87] On the Right, Charles Maurras, in *L'Action Française*, remained critical of the government. He particularly condemned the optimistic, vague, and blind *"habituel communiqué"* which failed to reveal the actual divisions between France and Britain.[88] *16 0048*

There is little doubt that the London conversations helped to smooth over the frequent Franco-British disagreements that had developed during the summer and fall of 1937. The countries of Central and Eastern Europe must have received a certain reassurance from the apparently solidified entente. It could have been of particular importance, since in the final communiqué the French had managed to evoke some expression of interest in Central Europe from the British. This certainly gave added prestige to Delbos' trip through that region, which was to start on the following day. The fact that Delbos had been empowered to speak for the British also added to his authority when explaining the general ideas developed at the London discussions. Yet Bullitt may have been correct when he indicated that Delbos "will leave Paris tomorrow very confident, and more under British influence than ever."[89] The fact that Delbos was determined to travel to Central and Eastern Europe to revitalize French ties showed his continued desire for an independent French policy and a rejection of the policy of appeasement. But the fact that he first visited London had the effect of compromising his efforts even before he left. His failure to gain a firm commitment from Britain on behalf of Austria and Czechoslovakia meant the distinct possibility that France would have to act alone in the face of German aggression against those countries. Still convinced of France's inability to act alone, he had agreed that the French could only "interest themselves in a spirit of conciliation." It would be a difficult stance from which to kindle a renewed spirit in the French alliance system.

Franco-British relations had grown increasingly intimate during the closing months of 1937, although it appeared that the French had become increasingly reliant upon British leadership. During the early weeks of 1938, however, an event occurred which further compromised the possibility of a concerted Franco-British resistance to new

Axis aggression. Chamberlain had decided that the time was right
to pursue his policy of appeasement.[90] Always distrustful of the
permanent officials at the Foreign Office, he sought to by-pass them
with his own style of personal diplomacy. It was difficult, however,
to circumvent his own Foreign Secretary. Eden had become increasingly suspicious of Hitler and Mussolini. He particularly regretted
Chamberlain's efforts to appease Mussolini. Consequently, in the
cabinet and in public speeches, he became increasingly critical of
Chamberlain's policy. His promotion of the Nyon Conference, his
speeches at Leamington and Birmingham, and his general support of
closer Franco-British relations naturally made Chamberlain's efforts
at reestablishing a rapprochement with Italy increasingly difficult.[91]
Although Delbos, after the London Conference, professed to discount
rumors of dissension between Eden and Chamberlain, one must
wonder if he was sincere in his belief.[92] In any event, when Chamberlain decided to initiate new conversations with Italy in January, 1938,
the tension between Eden and Chamberlain increased noticeably.
Eden believed that Chamberlain was pursuing Mussolini, while
Chamberlain felt that the Foreign Secretary was throwing up road-
blocks to meaningful negotiations. The divergence of views smoldered
beneath the surface for some time before a combination of incidents
brought about a complete rupture.[93]

In January, 1938, President Roosevelt proposed a world conference to draft a plan for the reduction of international tensions. During
the absence of Eden, who was in France on a holiday, Chamberlain
spurned the offer. He replied that such a proposal might hinder his
own efforts at approaching Germany and Italy. Such a rebuff clearly
conflicted with Eden's own judgment. He tried to rectify the situation, but it was too late. In February, Chamberlain made his approach
to Italy, aiming at another "gentleman's agreement." Since Eden
considered the previous effort worthless, he would agree to support
this proposal only on the condition that Italy give assurances in
advance of a withdrawal from Spain. At a meeting with Count Grandi
on February 18, the two men heatedly argued over the policy to be
pursued. On the following day, during a cabinet debate over negotiations with Italy, Eden offered to resign. The next day, February 20,
after much cabinet discussion and attempts to find a solution, he
officially resigned. The fundamental difference of attitude between

the two men could not be reconciled, and Eden made this clear in his resignation speech.[94]

Eden's resignation had a tremendous impact upon France, particularly since Hitler had delivered a violent speech to the Reichstag on the same day, and the Austrian problem had begun to heat up.[95] The Chautemps government was gravely upset by the new crisis. Delbos and Chautemps begged Sir Eric Phipps to remind Chamberlain of their agreement at the London talks to consult each other before embarking upon any new policy. They clearly feared a change in British policy and desired assurances that the agreement would be observed. If a radical change in policy should occur, the effect in France would be quite serious.[96] Chamberlain sought to soothe the qualms of the French by instructing Phipps to assure them that the event "must in no way be interpreted as indicating any weakening of the bonds that hold our two countries together."[97] Chautemps feared that, given the international situation, Eden's resignation would be regarded as a German and Italian victory. He thought that it might even necessitate a change in the French government in order to gain a broader base of support.[98]

Eden's resignation came as a shocking personal blow to Delbos. His relationship with the pro-French Eden had become quite cordial during the previous twenty months. Their frequent correspondence, their meetings, and their common recognition of the need for a revitalized Entente Cordiale had led to an increased understanding between the two men. To Delbos it appeared as if his policy of reestablishing close Franco-British cooperation as the cornerstone of French security, a policy which he had clung to through great adversity, was disintegrating.[99] It was rumored that he had even tried to resign several times, but that Chautemps had rejected his resignation.[100] By the morning of February 26, on the occasion of a Chamber debate on foreign affairs, Delbos had regained his composure. After paying tribute to Eden, he said that he had not forgotten the complete agreement that had always existed between Chamberlain and the French government. He stated that the French had agreed that negotiations with Italy were desirable if the outstanding problems could be solved. He informed the Deputies that the negotiations would be carried on with the knowledge of the French, and nothing would be discussed or concluded without French agreement. He concluded his remarks on Franco-British relations by affirming his complete confidence in the close solidarity that united the two countries.[101]

One cannot deny that Delbos' decision to pursue a policy of close association with Britain was a wise one.[102] Indeed, no guarantee equaled that which Britain could offer. The difficulty remained, however, that as the relationship spasmodically blew hot and cold, Delbos' determination to maintain the policy ultimately led to an abject surrender to British leadership. Therefore, the bankrupt policy of appeasing the dictators continued. In a world of the blind, the one-eyed man is king! There is every indication that Delbos saw the dangers that confronted Europe more clearly than did the British. But he suffered all the infirmities of half vision. He did not see clearly enough the corollary to the necessity of British support for France. As R. W. Seton-Watson wrote at the time, "Britain stands as much in need of French co-operation as France of British."[103] Another writer, Charles Micaud, correctly asserts that "the fate of England was linked to that of France, and whatever the latter undertook, the former was bound to support. A determined France could have taken along a reluctant Britain in crushing Pan-Germanism."[104] If "peace and security" were Britain's foremost aims, did not France have the same aims?[105] In other words, the two powers had fundamental common interests. As nations with equal interests and responsibilities, they should have been equal partners. It should have been made clear to the British that although France needed their diplomatic and military support, Britain equally needed the French army, which was still an important factor in the European balance. In an era of increased aerial warfare Britain could no longer afford the luxury of "spendid isolation." Neither could it be the "honest broker" of Europe. Delbos should have impressed these points upon the British. He did not. Instead he alternated between meekly following the British lead in appeasement, as seen by the decision for nonintervention in Spain, and gallant defiance and independence, as indicated by Nyon and his eastern tour. Torn between an inclination to resist the Axis aggression and the desire to avoid irritating the British lest irreparable damage be done to the entente, Delbos was not the man who could resolutely pursue an independent policy. Consequently, when Delbos departed from the Quai d'Orsay less than a month after Eden's resignation, the total French capitulation to British leadership, which became so evident at Munich, had already begun. In the meantime, the alternative to the British alliance, a revitalized Eastern European alliance network, had failed to materialize. Delbos' efforts in Eastern Europe, the failure of which would have serious consequences for that area as well as for France, will be examined next.

6

Reluctance to Strengthen the Franco-Soviet Alliance

In August and September of 1932, Yvon Delbos traveled throughout the Soviet Union. Although he was primarily interested in observing economic and social conditions, the journey gave him an opportunity to formulate his thoughts on what should be the nature of Franco-Soviet relations. While he rejected the Soviet economic and social system, he felt that it would be a mistake, for the purposes of French security and national defense, to ignore completely the potential usefulness of the Soviet Union. He believed that France was becoming increasingly isolated as England tried to withdraw from Continental affairs and Italy drew closer to Germany. But Russia, which until recently had made a common front with France's enemies, was in the process of reconsidering its position. The Soviet Union "realized that it would be placed in a dangerous position should France become the vassal of Germany or of Italy." Consequently, Delbos became convinced that the Soviet Union sought a rapprochement with France.[1]

In his book *L'Expérience rouge*, Delbos developed his thoughts more fully. He warned of German efforts at deception:

> The double maneuver attempted by the imperialists of Germany and Italy must be definitely thwarted. While they propose to the U.S.S.R. the formation of an anti-French front, certain German leaders offer us participation in a great anti-Bolshevist crusade.
>
> In the second instance, it would be the course to an arma-

ments race with war at the end; which must suffice to dispel these propositions. This would be for France, as for the U.S.S.R., a fool's game. Should we permit Germany to rearm, under the pretext of combating Bolshevism, this would not delay it from turning its arms against us. As for the U.S.S.R., if it made itself the accomplice to a policy aiming at crushing France, the realization of this objective would be the prelude to its own defeat. It is clear in effect that the fascists and pan-Germans, once masters of the rest of Europe, would immediately hurl themselves against it. They would be prompted to aggression by their imperialist ambitions and by their hatred of Bolshevism.

A common peril, the progress of the fascist leprosy in Europe, must therefore suffice to bring together France and the U.S.S.R.[2]

Delbos believed that one of the most important causes of the disequilibrium in Europe had been the failure to reintegrate Russia into the activities of the powers. He admitted that Soviet propaganda and its promotion of social and colonial strife had created antagonisms. But recent actions such as bilateral nonaggression pacts, like that signed with France in 1932, and Russian participation in the League of Nations indicated its desire for cooperation against the fascist threat. He noted that improved Franco-Soviet relations "are however only a step towards genuine peace which must not be only a passive state of 'non-guerre,' but an active state of rapprochement and collaboration."[3] "The question of life or death thus posed evidently prevails over the others. It must array on the same side all those who understand that it is above all a matter of saving humanity in danger."[4]

Indeed, in the face of France's deteriorating position vis-à-vis Germany and Italy, Delbos was quite correct in recognizing, long before many others, the need for a Franco-Soviet agreement. For the next three years he worked vigorously to negotiate an effective alliance between the two countries. He helped Edouard Herriot, the pact's chief supporter, take the issue to the public. He wrote detailed justifications for such a pact in *La Dépêche de Toulouse*. On May 20, 1933, basing his argument almost entirely on the need for security, Delbos wrote that France could not ignore a growing industrial and military power of 160 million people. He observed, "Our present relationship with the Soviet Union is analogous to that which brought us together with Tsarist Russia, so it is true that geography and history govern policy."[5] On April 29 and May 23, 1935, both before and after ratification of the pact, Delbos again wrote editorials defending the alliance.[6] The search for an effective military ally in the east to threaten Germany with a second front in the event of open warfare was a historic tradition of French diplomacy, and it made eminently good sense geographically.[7]

A reorientation in Franco-Soviet relations had become evident in 1932, when the two countries signed a Nonaggression Pact. This pact, which Delbos enthusiastically supported in *L'Expérience rouge,* was a reciprocal agreement not to join any coalition directed against the other country.[8] In May, 1933, the Chamber, in a "rare manifestation of national unity," ratified it by a vote of 520 to 0.[9] During most of 1934, France, confronted with a mounting Nazi peril, continued toward a general rapprochement with Russia. Louis Barthou sponsored the Soviet entrance into the League of Nations as a first step towards making Russia, as in 1914, France's great eastern ally against Germany.[10] Under Barthou's direction, French diplomats proceeded to start negotiations for a more comprehensive Franco-Soviet agreement. Pierre Laval continued the negotiations after Barthou's assassination, although with considerably less enthusiasm. Ultimately, Laval and Litvinov concluded the final negotiations in April, 1935, and in May a Franco-Soviet Pact was signed. But Laval watered down the pact to the point that it held little of value. As he told the Supreme Military Committee: "I have extracted the most dangerous things from it. I do not trust the Russians."[11] The two nations agreed to come to each other's aid in case of aggression by another European power. But the aggression would first have to be certified by both the League and the Locarno Powers. The pact was so encumbered with provisions that would lead to delay, that any aggressor nation would have had considerable time to carry out its attack before the two powers could have acted. Perhaps more importantly, the pact had no real teeth due to the French reluctance to conclude a supplementary military convention.[12] Consequently, the pact hardly fit Delbos' description of an "active state of rapprochement and collaboration."

Although the Popular Front's first foreign-policy statement made only passing reference to the Franco-Soviet Pact,[13] Blum envisaged reviving the agreement, which had become a dead letter since its signing.[14] Confronted with the German-Polish rapprochement of 1934, Blum recognized the need for closer relations with the Soviets. Moreover, although he had only reluctantly endorsed the pact, he recognized its value as a counterweight to the Rome-Berlin Axis. After relations with England had been improved, the government would then pursue closer relations with Russia. He believed that "the rapprochement between France and Britain, on the one hand, and with the U.S.S.R., on the other hand, must lead to a later rapprochement between Britain and the U.S.S.R., that it to say, a combination recreating the Triple Entente of 1914."[15]

The Soviets, of course, were eager to transform the Pact of 1935 into an effective military alliance. Indeed, relations between the two countries during the period of the Popular Front centered around Soviet attempts to initiate negotiations for a military convention. They even offered to inform the French of the complete status of their military and industrial resources, as well as the arms that they would put at the disposal of the French in the event of a general European conflict.[16] But the French consistently procrastinated and frustrated these efforts. Given Delbos' vigorous support for the pact prior to 1936, one might justifiably assume that he would take the lead in promoting such military cooperation. He did not. Therefore, he must share a large portion of the responsibility for the Popular Front's failure to conclude an effective military agreement with the Soviet Union.

The first indication of Delbos' revised attitude toward the Soviet Pact came in the fall of 1936. Before departing for Moscow to take up his post as Ambassador, Robert Coulondre made a *"tour d'horizon"* among important officials and politicians to ascertain their views on Franco-Soviet relations. The instructions he received from Delbos indicated a substantial transformation in the latter's attitude towards the Soviets. Coulondre recalled that "the presentation of his statement was made completely in a negative sense."[17] Delbos told Coulondre that the Soviets' attitude at Geneva during the Ethiopian Affair and in London at the meetings of the Nonintervention Committee, as well as the activities of the French Communist Party, "led him to wonder whether they were not looking to push us into a conflict with Germany."[18] Given this doubt, Delbos made it clear that Coulondre should emphasize three French concerns to the Soviets: No preventive war would be undertaken against Germany; the question of the extent of Soviet military aid in case of a conflict must be clarified; and there must be an end to Russian interference in French domestic affairs.[19]

Obviously, Delbos early recognized what many others only came to realize quite belatedly: in a preventive war against Germany, France would lose in two ways. "If defeated it would be Nazified. If victorious, it must, due to the destruction of German power, submit, with the rest of Europe, to the overwhelming weight of the Slavic world, armed with the communist flamethrower." If, however, war could not be avoided, France had to know the plans of the Kremlin and the nature of its aid. In other words, before negotiating, France would have to first ascertain the Soviet intention. In addition, Delbos made it clear that "it is necessary above all that the Soviets understand that they are choosing between the pact and the continuation of their interference."[20] He intimated that if Russia continued to use the pact as a cover for Communist propaganda, public opinion would force the government to reconsider its position. "The future of this agreement is more in [Soviet] hands than in ours." He warned, "France wants external as well as internal peace, and the French government does not expect the Franco-Soviet Pact to perform in a manner contrary to this desire."[21] Such antipathy on the part of one of the pact's earliest and foremost supporters did not augur well for its future.

At about the same time, Delbos assured Eden that there would be no possibility of staff conversations with Russia in the immediate future. The whole question would have at least to await the outcome of the Five-Power meeting scheduled for November.[22] Of course, as the British Foreign Office correctly noted, Delbos' assurances referred only to military conversations. They did not preclude political attempts to consolidate Franco-Soviet relations.[23]

Indeed, Coulondre, shortly after assuming his post in Moscow in November, 1936, emphasized the need for arriving at some sort of agreement with the Soviets. He warned Delbos that "in order to pose . . . the problem of Franco-Soviet relations, it is not only necessary to ask if the U.S.S.R. will be with us or not, *but with whom will she be?*" He added, "Russia's feet are not of clay, as it is currently said, but rest solidly on the Russian land, which serves to nourish its steel muscles which I see growing stronger month by month."[24]

But Delbos, as well as Blum, was under adverse pressure from the French General Staff. The reticence of the General Staff became quite apparent when General Schweisguth, Deputy Chief of the General Staff, after observing the annual maneuvers of the Red Army, submitted his report on October 5, 1936.[25] Blum found that the report fundamentally disagreed with all that had been established by General Lucien Loizeau in a similar communication the previous year. Blum asked for Loizeau's report, and after "a certain delay," the General Staff produced it for him. The two reports differed on nearly every line.[26] While recognizing various deficiencies in the Red Army, Loizeau had judged that it was a well-trained and capably led force, imbued with a high morale and supported by abundant modern equipment. He concluded that "this army appeared to me therefore to be capable of a great initial effort which would permit it to retain on the eastern front, during the period so critical as the beginning of a conflict, important opposing forces."[27] Schweisguth, however, after his conversations with Marshal Voroshilov, the Soviet Minister of War, concluded that "the Soviet army appeared strong, endowed with abundant and modern matériel, animated with a good offensive spirit, at least in the cadres, but insufficiently prepared for a war against a Great European Power. The circumstances of its employment against Germany remain very problematical." Although Russia would be loyal to France in the event of a German attack, he warned that the Soviets much preferred that "the storm burst first upon France." In a Franco-German conflict the lack of a common frontier with Germany meant that all Soviet forces would remain outside the conflict, allowing Russia "to arbitrate the situation in the face of a Europe exhausted by battle."[28]

As Blum told the postwar Parliamentary Investigating Commission, it was clear that the "General Staff did not consider Soviet military aid to be a fact of prime importance."[29] In fact, from the very beginning of the secret negotiations between the two nations the French Command had given only qualified support for the Soviet pact. While willing to accept an alliance, it never had consented to a military convention. Such reticence, however, did not stem from any particular knavery or naiveté, but rather was the logical consequence of the faulty military doctrinal theories held by the General Staff during the interwar years. The theory of war during the period was based on the "lessons" learned during World War I: that defense was superior to offense and that the use of mass armies would result in a stalemate. In the long war of attrition that would follow, France, behind the relative security of the Maginot Line and the Franco-Belgian defenses, would be able to mobilize its industrial resources and its colonial and overseas allies for the final victorious assault against Germany. Obsessed with the upcoming "lean years" of 1935–1939, when the pool of available conscripts for the French Army would be drastically reduced because of the wartime losses of 1914–1918, the majority of soldiers and politicians stubbornly clung to an outmoded doctrine even when confronted with new ideas from Charles de Gaulle and the adherents of the *armée de métier*.[30]

This, then, was the doctrinal context in which the French military viewed the Soviet pact. They considered it as a mere "adjunct to a basically secure French defensive position."[31] Skeptical about the Red Army's ability to take the offensive, and doubting the French need of such an offensive in any case, the main advantages of the alliance would be those of diverting German forces to the east with the opening of a second front, supporting France's smaller eastern allies, and precluding the possibility of the Reich gaining access to the immense resources that could be supplied by the Soviets. Therefore, it is clear that the French General Staff eagerly sought to keep Russia out of the German camp and that recognition of these negative possibilities appealed to them and stimulated their original interest in the pact when negotiations opened in 1932. Yet it is equally certain that they regarded such a rapprochement as only a temporary expedient until the French military situation improved, and they were firmly convinced that it should not involve a military convention.[32]

By 1936 the Popular Front government found itself confronted with a continuation of the reserved attitude among the soldiers that had predominated from the beginning of the negotiations. Proponents of Loizeau's views were in the minority; while others, including General Maxime Weygand, had become increasingly outspoken in their opposition to the pact. Since it was highly doubtful that Poland and Rumania would permit Soviet troops to cross their territory, the French military remained convinced that direct Soviet action could not be brought to bear upon Germany. Besides, the General Staff considered Polish military forces superior, except perhaps in aviation, to those of the Soviet Union.[33] Moreover, neither the basic military doctrinal concepts nor the High Command's conception of the role that would be played by the Soviets had altered. The truncated pact still retained the advantages of confronting the Germans with a second front, protecting Poland from an eastern threat as long as both Russia and Poland remained allied with France, and providing a potential source of supply for the Little Entente in the event of a war with Germany.[34]

Edouard Daladier, the Minister of Defense, shared the General Staff's increased skepticism about the value of a military convention with the Soviets. He told Delbos that "in the present circumstances, these General Staff conversations are capable of alarming certain friendly powers and of furnishing Germany the easy pretext of attempted encirclement. To my mind this presents grave disadvantages which you are in a better position to appreciate than I am."[35] Evidently Delbos and the Quai d'Orsay did appreciate the importance of such drawbacks, and they made "no secret of their strong dislike for entering into further engagements with the Soviet Union."[36] Consequently, Blum, who had never shared Delbos' early enthusiasm for the pact and had remained hostile for a long time before accepting it, found himself confronted not only with opposition from the military, but from his Foreign Minister and his Minister of Defense as well.[37]

Despite the reticence of the French, the Soviets still hoped to persuade them to accept precise military commitments to supplement the Pact of 1935. On February 17, 1937, Vladimir Potemkin, the Soviet Ambassador in Paris, went to see Blum. Potemkin proposed that Russian military aid to France and Czechoslovakia in the event of German aggression might be rendered in two ways:

1. If Poland and Rumania, both allied to France, agreed to the passage of Soviet troops, then the Soviet Union would be "in a position to lend its assistance with all arms."
2. If Poland and Rumania refused passage for "some incomprehensible reason," Russian aid would be necessarily limited. But Russia would "be able to send ground troops to France by sea . . . and its air forces to Czechoslovakia and France."[38]

In return, Potemkin inquired about the nature of French aid to Russia in the event of a German attack. General Gamelin, Chief of the General Staff, was given the task of formulating the French response. After the usual delay, Daladier handed the French reply to Potemkin on April 10. If France was not to bear the brunt of the German attack, it could respond offensively against the Germans. But initially France could not supply Russia with arms because it would need all of its resources for itself. Moreover, Gamelin doubted that Poland and Rumania could be persuaded to change their minds. Even if they did, they would need all of their own railroads for their own troop movements. Gamelin noted in his memoirs that Delbos approved of the French reply entirely.[39] Paul Reynaud later wrote, "Once more, the Russians took the initiative in giving life to their alliance with us! Once more, they found among us only hesitation, apathy, and antipathy."[40] Indeed, it was a strong rebuff, and Delbos appeared quite satisfied with it. In fact, as Pierre Renouvin has correctly noted, the government did not seem to doubt the conclusions of Gamelin's report.[41]

Blum partially explained the government's failure to override the General Staff's reticence to the postwar Parliamentary Commission. At the end of 1936, Blum's son transmitted to his father words of caution from Czechoslovakia's President, Eduard Benes. Benes warned Blum to exercise "great precautions" in French relations with the Soviet General Staff. The Czech intelligence service, which "enjoyed in Europe a merited reputation," believed that the leaders of the Soviet General Staff were having "suspicious relations" with the Germans.[42] Faced with the possible leakage of French military and diplomatic secrets, Blum and Delbos could hardly endorse a military agreement with the Soviets in February, 1937. It appears doubtful that they were inclined to do so in any case. An indication of Blum's newly found reluctance came in December, 1936, when he told Sir George Clerk, the British Ambassador in Paris, that the Franco-Soviet Pact had become a valuable part of the European structure. He admitted, however, that "he wished to see it preserved, but not to grow teeth."[43]

During the spring of 1937, Minister of Aviation Pierre Cot, probably the most ardent supporter of a military accord with Russia in the cabinet, continued to press for closer military collaboration. All he obtained was Blum's permission to make an indirect attempt for a commitment of Soviet air support. The existing relations between France and Czechoslovakia and between Russia and Czechoslovakia provided the basis for Cot's endeavor. France would maintain its existing aerial commitment to Czechoslovakia; and if a similar agreement between the Czechs and Soviets could be devised, France would derive the same benefits as it would from a direct agreement with the Soviets. Ultimately, a three-way Franco-Czech-Soviet link would be produced. The negotiations began, but had not been completed by the time Munich effectively removed Czechoslovakia from the French security system.[44]

There is some evidence that Delbos may have given qualified support to Cot's scheme. Articles in *Pravda* and *Izvestia*, on the occasion of the second anniversary of the signing of the Franco-Soviet Pact, reflected Soviet uneasiness and disappointment over French failure to supplement the pact with a military agreement. The Soviet press argued that the French attitude encouraged Hitler's hopes of wrecking the Franco-Soviet Pact. It warned the French that the Soviet Union could dispense with the help of other countries, but that other countries, if they really desired to consolidate the peace, could not dispense with Soviet aid. France had far more to gain from the pact than the Soviet Union, which was perfectly able to defend its own frontiers without foreign help.[45] The Soviet charges may have prompted Delbos' speech of May 9, in which he declared that no one was more determined than he to respect the Franco-Soviet Pact and to preserve its significance.[46]

A few days later, however, he confided to Eden that the French had no intention of entering into any military agreement with Russia. What they now envisioned was something which would be entirely harmless and reasonable—the mere exchange of information between the Military Attachés on both sides. He felt that France's continued refusal to engage even in such limited collaboration would be interpreted as an affront by Russia. Such an arrangement existed between France and other allied governments. Therefore, nothing would be lost by according the same status to the Soviets. Delbos recognized that, for a variety of reasons, there was no immediate danger of Russia throwing herself into the arms of Germany. But he believed that France must give the Soviets some measure of satisfaction on this point. Otherwise they might begin to prepare the ground in such a way that it would be easy to open the road between Moscow and Berlin if and when such an opportunity did arise. It was these preparations for a possible reorientation of Soviet foreign policy that Delbos wished to anticipate and prevent. Eden protested that this "extension of Franco-Russian collaboration would be interpreted as restricting in a new and dangerous way the liberty of action of the French government in European politics." Delbos, however, was convinced that any postponement would merely intensify Soviet suspicions. Moreover, he noted that technical contacts in aeronautics were urgently needed. Soviet air assistance would be indispensable if Czechoslovakia, whose defense he considered vital to French interests, were to be attacked by Germany. He declared, "We will not drop Czechoslovakia. We could not do it without disappearing from the map of Europe as a power of the first order."[47] Delbos was willing to move closer to the Soviets, but not significantly so. In fact, any new conversations with them would be more to assuage their anxieties than to move toward meaningful cooperation. Delbos was resolved to make haste very slowly with the Soviet Union.

This attitude became very clear three days later. On May 18, in the course of a tour through Europe, Maxim Litvinov stopped off in Paris and visited with Delbos. The French Foreign Minister indicated that the Ministers of Aviation and Marine had agreed on the necessity of military conversations, but that the Minister of Defense, Daladier, had not yet made known his response.[48] This further delay probably did not disappoint Delbos. The communiqué issued at the conclusion of Litvinov's meetings with Delbos and Blum gave no indication that any military conversations would be forthcoming in the near future. The statesmen merely "congratulated themselves on the friendly state of the relations between their two countries as well as on the identity of view of French and Soviet policy."[49] They reaffirmed their fidelity to the Franco-Soviet Pact, but generally it was one of Maurras' "communiqués habituels," which said nothing of importance.

The May meetings proved to be the last effort to initiate meaningful military conversations aimed at reinforcing the general Franco-Soviet Pact of 1935. In June, 1937, the great purge of the Soviet High Command began. Marshal Tukhachevsky, Chief of the Soviet

General Staff, and eight of the highest-ranking military officers were arrested, tried, and executed. The charges of treason against the accused appear in retrospect to be bogus accusations by Stalin to achieve the removal of his political rivals. But in view of the Czech warnings to Blum, the situation was hardly of a nature to inspire French confidence in the Soviet military. Any thoughts of military talks quickly dissipated from French minds. One finds it difficult to believe, however, that there was great disappointment at the Quai d'Orsay. In December, 1937, when Delbos made his tour of Eastern European capitals, the absence of Moscow in his itinerary was conspicuous. Coulondre correctly noted that "in spite of all the excuses that will be forthcoming, this will not ameliorate Franco-Soviet relations and restore confidence."[50] Indeed, French policy had been orientated in a new direction.

There can be little doubt that Delbos shares, along with the General Staff and other cabinet members, the responsibility for the failure of the French to negotiate and implement a significant military agreement with the Soviet Union. But from the standpoint of this study, the important question involves the radical change in Delbos' attitude. In other words, why did Delbos, after his unqualified support of the pact before his advent to the Quai d'Orsay, undergo such a sudden volte-face upon becoming Foreign Minister? Why did he refuse, for the better part of a year, to seize upon the Soviet feelers to initiate serious military conversations? The French documents reveal disappointingly little about the answers to these questions. Therefore, any conclusions must necessarily be in the nature of conjecture. What has been learned of Delbos' attitude in other areas, however, makes it clear that several factors helped to determine his policy.

It must be remembered that it was the British Alliance, not the Russian, that constituted the keystone of Delbos' and Blum's foreign policy. Therefore, they were reluctant to do anything that would compromise the Franco-British entente. There is evidence that the conservative British government clearly distrusted the Soviets for obvious reasons and did not desire an effective Franco-Soviet alliance.[51] Orme Sargent, Assistant Undersecretary of State for Foreign Affairs, noted, "It is reassuring to be told that neither the General

Staff nor the Quai d'Orsay wish to enter into further engagements with Soviet Russia."[52] On several occasions London made it quite clear that it did not favor closer Franco-Soviet relations. In May, 1937, just prior to the last real Soviet effort to prod France into participating in military conversations, Sir Robert Vansittart, Permanent Undersecretary of State for Foreign Affairs, told Charles Corbin, the French Ambassador in London, that in his personal opinion "the French Government would do well to stave off still further if they could such military conversations. If they transpired, . . . the Germans would probably seize on this as a pretext for wrecking the negotiations with regard to a Western pact and would throw all the blame on France."[53] A few days later, when Delbos informed Eden of the French plan to exchange military information, the British Foreign Secretary told him that "he much regretted this decision . . . because he foresaw that such collaboration between the French and Russian Governments would be bound to become public and might easily . . . have most serious psychological effects, both in this country [England] and in the lesser countries of Central Europe."[54] Given Delbos' inclination above all to maintain the Franco-British alliance, the words of caution from responsible British officials did not encourage him to pursue vigorously negotiations that would lead to an effective Franco-Soviet alliance.

One historian has written that "it was a rare Western statesman who could, as Winston Churchill did, overlook ideological quarrels and concentrate on the German menace."[55] In this respect, Delbos differed little from most other statesmen of his time. Indeed, his instructions to Coulondre upon the latter's departure for Moscow in the fall of 1936 are quite revealing. The persistent attacks by the French Communist party against his policy of nonintervention in Spain made him suspect that the Russians might be planning to push France into a conflict with Germany.[56] Moreover, he resented what he considered to be Soviet interference in the domestic affairs of France. Although a leader in the left wing of the Radical party, Delbos was undoubtedly upset at the wave of strikes that swept over France after the advent of the Popular Front. One scholar, Peter Larmour, has said, "The Radicals suddenly became frightened when they discovered that their Communist playfellows had turned into a mass of striking men. They were never to feel easy with them again."[57] Alexander Werth wrote, "The Radical rank-and-file were beginning to distrust the Communists almost as much as they had distrusted the Fascists in the past. . . . They felt that, under the pressure of the June strikes, legislation had been enacted which would be ruinous to the small manufacturer and trader."[58] French Communist tactics antagonized many who might have supported a reinforced Soviet Pact, and the repeated criticism of Soviet interference at the Radical Party Congress at Biarritz in the fall of 1936 reflected this increased alienation.[59] It is probable that Delbos could be included in the mainstream of Radical thought on this matter. Moreover, Delbos, like most other officials, probably believed that the activities of the French Communists were due to instructions from the Comintern, which, in turn, merely reflected the international designs of the Soviet Union. Therefore, it was up to Stalin to bring a halt to those activities before confidence could be restored in Soviet intentions and meaningful negotiations could be initiated.[60] Max Beloff noted the paradox that ideological considerations remained subordinate to Soviet international intentions, but that the local needs of the French Communists demanded left-wing action. In the long run the two requirements were incompatible and contributed to the deterioration of Franco-Soviet relations.[61]

In addition, as passions over the Spanish war heightened and no progress was made toward strengthening the Franco-Soviet Pact, Communist press attacks upon Delbos became increasingly vigorous. When Delbos failed to include Moscow in his trip through Eastern Europe in December, 1937, Gabriel Péri openly attacked him in L'Humanité for following the dictates of Britain at the expense of other French allies, namely, Russia and Czechoslovakia.[62] Prior to the governmental crisis in January, 1938, Péri wrote, "We want a Foreign Minister at the Quai d'Orsay, who is not the mute of the Little Entente."[63] Péri even went so far as to call for the removal of Delbos. He said that it was obvious that a "Minister who has a record as deplorable as that of M. Yvon Delbos must not resume his place at the Quai d'Orsay."[64] The attacks obviously upset Delbos. Sir Eric Phipps, the British Ambassador in Paris, reported, "M. Delbos spoke to me last night bitterly about recent Communist attacks upon him. They were, he said, clearly inspired by Moscow, where the slightest sign of a détente between Germany and France . . . aroused absurd and unjustified suspicions."[65] It is clear that a good deal of latent hostility existed between Delbos and the French Communist party, which he considered an instrument of Moscow.

Another factor that must have influenced Delbos was the conviction of the majority of the French military that the Red Army was not strong enough to support France in a general European war. In fact, it has been suggested that General Gamelin considered Rumania a greater military asset than the Red Army.[66] More fundamental, however, for doctrinal reasons already cited, the French High Command had displayed considerable reluctance about the Soviet pact from the beginning; the great purges, which seemed to confirm Czech warnings that there were pro-German sympathizers in the Soviet High Command, shattered whatever confidence existed. As D. W. Brogan put it, "the execution of Marshal Tukachevsky especially startled a country with a conscript army which, it was realized, might have found itself taking the field in alliance with a power whose high command was conspiring with the common enemy."[67] Precisely how much Delbos shared in this lack of confidence in the Soviet military is unknown, but apparently neither he nor Blum made any effort to counteract the military's reservations. Phipps observed that "there is no doubt that the latest Moscow trials and the execution of so many leading Soviet generals created the most unfortunate impression in [France], and that Franco-Soviet relations at the present time . . . are far from being marked by any cordiality or intimacy."[68] Etienne de Croy, Léger's private secretary, who was generally considered well informed about questions of French policy, confirmed that the faith of many of those who had formerly been among the pact's most fervent supporters had been badly shaken by the events in the Soviet Union.[69]

One of the most important factors in the General Staff's reluctance to initiate military conversations was the fact that Russia did not share a common boundary with Germany. Any Soviet military aid in the event of war would have to cross Polish and Rumanian territory in order to strike a blow against the Reich. These two countries, however, refused to permit any Soviet troops on their soil. Both countries had bad memories of past relations with Russia, and they feared that once Soviet troops entered, they would never leave (a fear that was justified by the postwar Soviet occupation of Eastern Europe).[70] As

Léon Noël, the French Ambassador in Warsaw, put it, "the conclusion of the Franco-Soviet Agreement created a scandal in Warsaw. Poland . . . feared that . . . the assistance promised to France . . . would mean for herself a Russian invasion . . . if Russian troops, even as Allies, entered Polish territory, they would never leave it."[71] Lord Chilston and Sir Howard Kennard, the British Ambassadors in Moscow and Warsaw, agreed that "in the event of a Franco-Polish war against Germany, the Poles would probably prefer to have a neutral rather than an allied Russia on their eastern frontier."[72] Moreover, the Poles feared the influence that the Russians might acquire in Central Europe through their pacts with France and Czechoslovakia. Their *Grande Puissance* complex led them to guard zealously their newly found postwar status, and they resented anything that seemed to show that France attached more importance to Russian than to Polish friendship.[73] The French encountered similar difficulties with the Rumanians, who also feared any Soviet troops on their soil, although they apparently might have been convinced to accept them in an emergency.[74] In any event, a basic contradiction existed in France's Eastern European policy. The smaller countries, with the possible exception of Czechoslovakia, distrusted and feared the Soviet Union. They regarded with great apprehension any attempts by the French to strengthen their ties with the Soviets. An effective Franco-Soviet Pact might have led these small states to turn to Germany for an accommodation, thereby eventually resulting in a Germanized *Mitteleuropa*.[75] On the other hand, if France neglected the Soviets in an effort to please its smaller Eastern allies, it then ran the risk of having Russia isolating itself entirely from European affairs. Even worse, it was conceivable that the Soviets might seek a rapprochement with Germany, a threat that they frequently repeated to the French.[76] This was the dilemma that confronted Delbos when he assumed his post at the Quai d'Orsay, and it seems to have shaped his policy until the summer of 1937.

As previously suggested, an opinion that was widely held in France, and particularly in French military circles, was that the value of the Franco-Soviet Pact was to prevent a German-Soviet rapprochement, which many feared despite Hitler's repeated anti-Bolshevik tirades.[77] Phipps, then the British Ambassador in Berlin, noted that "if Russia, after copiously watering her red wine, were ready to abandon France and *wished* to fall into the German arms, those arms would probably be very willing to receive her."[78] The French considered German opposition to the pact as an indication of its worth. They believed the Germans felt that the pact was an obstacle to their pursuing either of two policies: (1) an attempted German-Soviet rapprochement, or (2) the conclusion of a Western pact which would allow them a free hand to attack Russia. In other words, the Germans realized that the pact helped to strengthen the status quo in Europe and made it more difficult for them to proceed with their expansion toward the east. Therefore, while the Soviets undoubtedly regarded the pact as a first step towards a military alliance with France, the latter utilized it to serve a somewhat negative purpose. It was a bit of preclusive diplomacy which prevented Russia from joining the German camp and thereby barred Germany from gaining access to Russia's immense resources and manpower.[79] Consequently, the French hesitated to discard the pact completely, but continually procrastinated in the face of Soviet attempts to initiate military conversations.

Even though the Soviets were disappointed by the French delay, it appeared doubtful that they would go so far as to terminate the pact at this early stage. After all, even if the pact did not live up to expectations, it still retained some value for them. It might become very useful in the event of a combined attack by Germany and Japan. It is not clear what they would have gained by terminating it at this early date without substituting something in its place.[80] But the fact remained that some effort had to be made to resolve the contradiction in French policy. Paul-Boncour told the postwar Parliamentary Commission, "The great difficulty [was] the tense relations of Russia with its Polish and Rumanian neighbors. Of course, we did not want to sacrifice our alliance with these countries. Consequently, it was necessary to blend a new Russian Alliance with our former alliances with Poland and Rumania."[81]

In the light of the fitful actions taken by Delbos, it is apparent that he sought to resolve the contradiction in France's eastern policy and to create the blend referred to by Paul-Boncour. The Franco-Soviet Pact of 1935 would be maintained, but no military agreement would be concluded. On the other hand, the Soviets would not be put off to such an extent that they would seek a rapprochement with

Germany and thereby tear up their pact with France. De Croy put it thus: "Were a rapprochement between Germany and the Soviet Union to become an imminent possibility, it would be possible to 'infuse' into the Pact sufficient substance to transform it into an instrument the benefits of which the Soviet government would not lightly relinquish. Meanwhile, the Pact, while always at hand in case of need, was sufficiently indefinite in form not to be embarrassing to the French."[82] In May, 1937, Delbos had considered Soviet pressure sufficient to warrant them a sop in the form of an exchange of military views and information. But apparently with the execution of the Soviet generals in June, even this plan was abandoned.[83]

The reluctance of France to conclude an effective military pact with the Soviet Union is partially explained by British influence, the behavior of the French Communist party, and the attitude of the General Staff. The antagonism between France's Eastern European allies and the Soviet Union compounded the dilemma confronting Delbos and the Quai d'Orsay. Their solution was an attempt to keep Russia dangling on a string without creating any additional strain upon French relations with Poland and Rumania.

It is interesting to speculate about what could have developed if the Soviet purges had not enabled Delbos and the French to climb down from the fence post upon which they sat for the first year of the Popular Front. Perhaps as a short-term policy Delbos' maneuver held some merit. But it would have been very difficult to keep the Soviets in suspense forever. As subsequent events showed, Stalin was not one to be bothered by ideological probity; and Coulondre admitted that although official contacts between Moscow and Berlin did not take place, he was "not sure that during this whole period certain secret talks had ever ceased."[84] It is clear, however, that as Soviet internal disruption continued, that country became a less desirable ally for both France and Germany alike. Consequently, during the second half of 1937, with the reduced possibility of Germany and Russia joining forces, Delbos could view the situation from a new position. He decided to shelve any closer relations with the Soviet Union. Instead, he sought to revitalize the French alliances with the smaller Eastern European states. Perhaps Delbos was among those Frenchmen who were in Coulondre's mind when he wrote, "For the Polish trees, people did not see the Russian woods. And they committed a two-fold miscalculation: the first concerning the value of Poland as an ally, disproved in 1938; and second concerning the strength of her army, disproved in 1939."[85]

7

Frustration: Efforts to Revive French Influence in Eastern Europe

"Franco-Polish friendship will receive a new consecration by means of a cordial search for the most useful forms of cooperation between the two friendly nations." This was the promise Delbos made to the Chamber of Deputies on June 23, 1936.[1] Instead, diplomatic relations with Poland proved to be another exercise in futility for Delbos and the Popular Front. A Franco-Polish alliance after World War I was a natural development. France had traditionally sought to counterbalance a potential Central European threat through Eastern European connections. French security still required a "barrier to the east" of Germany. But in postwar Europe Russia was in chaos and the French feared the revolutionary ambitions of the new Soviet regime. In fact, France became the principal supporter of the *cordon sanitaire* designed to contain Russia. Moreover, France had worked for the reestablishment of a large Poland at the Versailles Peace Conference. In 1920 French assistance helped sustain the new state by helping the Poles repel the Soviets from the gates of Warsaw.[2] The interests of France and Poland coincided to such an extent that the two countries signed a secret military agreement, whereby the two allies agreed to support each other in the face of unprovoked German or Soviet aggression. The French promised to arm and train the Polish army, and collaboration between the two General Staffs was established.[3] As the largest of the newly created Eastern European states, Poland became the bastion of the French security system designed to contain Germany in the east.[4] The pact of 1921 was supplemented with another treaty of guarantee in October, 1925.[5]

But Poland distrusted the Franco-German cooperation of the Locarno era, and it did not appreciate France's support of the Little Entente. The strains that became evident after 1926, when Colonel Joseph Beck became Polish Foreign Minister, increased sharply after Hitler's rise. Both powers made independent efforts to come to terms with Germany.[6] In January, 1934, a Polish delegation led by Beck signed a ten-year Nonaggression Pact with Germany. The two governments agreed to settle their problems by "direct negotiations."[7] After 1934 Franco-Polish relations steadily deteriorated. The French efforts to bring Russia back into the mainstream of European affairs were regarded as a mistake by the Poles. Beck felt that the French were pushing the Eastern European states into Russia's arms.[8] Naturally, the conclusion of the Franco-Soviet Pact increased the Poles' distrust of France. Their obstinate refusal to allow Soviet troops on Polish soil helped to deter any desire some Frenchmen may have had for a military alliance with Russia.[9] Moreover, French inaction during the Rhineland coup increased Poland's inclination to straddle the fence between its formal commitments with France and its pact with Germany.[10] It has been said that "the simple intention of riding two horses at once can lead to some exceptionally strenuous acrobatics."[11] Indeed, many in French governing circles regarded Beck's acrobatic maneuvering with great repugnance.[12] Franco-Polish relations were not very cordial, to say the least, when the Popular Front assumed office.

Although the Rhineland episode temporarily relieved the pressure on the east, the Poles were not optimistic about their pact with Germany, particularly inasmuch as Nazi activity concerning Danzig increased. Threatened by the military revival of its two neighbors Germany and Russia, Poland sought to stave off the day when a war of rival ideologies might be fought out upon her soil. Such a war would inevitably lead to another partition of Poland. Consequently, the Poles began to reconsider the advantages of strengthening their ties with France.[13] The new Popular Front government promised to seek closer cooperation between the two countries, but in the light of Beck's pact with Germany, the French first sought to determine the Polish position.[14] Consequently, when the Polish government requested funds for a rearmament program, as well as French military and technical advice, Daladier, as Minister of Defense, expressed an unwillingness to supply the Poles with this type of aid and information as long as their relations with Germany remained undefined. Blum then stated, "We cannot live this way. We are bound by an alliance with a state and a people, yet we have so little confidence in them that we hesitate to deliver them arms, designs, plans—for fear that they will betray us and deliver them to the enemy. We must settle the question one way or another. We must know whether the Poles are our allies or not."[15]

In June, 1936, Delbos summoned Léon Noël, the French Ambassador in Warsaw, to Paris for meetings and instructions. Noël met with Blum, Daladier, and Delbos. It was decided that he should renew a previous French invitation to General Edward Smigly-Rydz, Pilsudski's heir and head of the Polish government, to visit Paris for meetings with the French General Staff in an attempt to reach an understanding between the two armies. Noël, however, had an alternative suggestion. Before France extended any financial aid to the Poles, two conditions should be imposed. First, the funds should be used for the development of Poland's own armaments plants. The second and more important point concerned Colonel Beck. It was no secret that Smigly-Rydz did not care for Beck's diplomatic maneuvering. Therefore, Noël believed that the French should bluntly say to the General, "The French government is wholly disposed to aid you, but you know that wrongly or rightly, the French have no confidence in M. Beck. The Chamber will refuse, and French opinion will make it impossible, we fear, to permit the grant of an important loan to Poland so long as he retains the Foreign Affairs portfolio."[16]

Noël later wrote, "M. Yvon Delbos . . . fully shared my point of view and adopted my proposition. He was convinced, in particular, . . . that he should himself undertake to make it understood to General Smigly-Rydz that the French government could not consent to what was asked of it if Colonel Beck was not removed."[17] So Delbos gave his full sanction to Noël's plan, and he took it upon himself to demand Beck's removal as the prerequisite for the desired French aid.

In the meantime, Blum and Delbos proceeded to lay the groundwork for Smigly-Rydz' visit by sending General Gamelin to Warsaw for a "man to man, soldier to soldier" talk with him.[18] Gamelin, during his visit to the Polish capital, August 12 to August 16, broached the subject with Smigly-Rydz in order to prepare the way for Delbos. But he immediately noticed a retreat by Smigly-Rydz, who began to extol the diplomatic talents of Beck. "It is necessary for us to be on good terms with Germany," the Polish General remarked. He defended Beck by noting that during the Rhineland crisis the latter had clearly aligned himself with France. Gamelin departed feeling that "Noël was under some delusion as to what could be obtained from the General in this matter. . . . I found out later, from M. Léger, that M. Yvon Delbos had met the same reserve as I did."[19]

Smigly-Rydz in turn visited Paris for nearly two weeks at the beginning of September. During the usual round of receptions, he was greeted with considerable cordiality and given a sumptuous luncheon by the President of the Republic at the Château de Rambouillet. Since the French had dragged their feet concerning the loan that the Poles sought, and had produced a proposal that was unsatisfactory to the latter only a few hours before Smigly-Rydz' departure from Paris, this occasion at Rambouillet turned into a lively working session.[20] The main French participants were Delbos, Blum, Noël, Vincent Auriol, Minister of Finance, and some military officers led by Gamelin. Smigly-Rydz was accompanied by the Polish General Chief of Staff, Waclaw Stachiewicz, and the Polish Ambassador in Paris, Juliusz Lukasiewicz, and some lesser officials. Delbos had intended to raise the issue about Beck at the luncheon. But Smigly-Rydz broached the question first. Noël recorded the conversation:

> "And what about M. Beck?" he [Smigly-Rydz] spontaneously asked our Foreign Minister. Forewarned as he was by myself of the feelings that Colonel Beck aroused in France, if Smigly-Rydz expressed himself in this manner, he did it because he wished to take an expression of French feelings back to Warsaw. He wished to utilize it for dismissing a minister in whom he had not the slightest confidence. Contrary to the prearranged "set-up," M. Delbos evaded the issue. To the General's question . . . he contented himself by responding: "I know him. I met him at Geneva; he is an intelligent man." Then he changed the subject. I tried in vain to get back to the issue. The Rambouillet Agreement was negotiated and signed without any other mention of Beck or his policy being made.[21]

Seeking to understand why Delbos rejected the opportunity to attempt to force a change in Polish policy, Noël speculated that Beck wielded enough influence in important French business circles to deter Delbos. This argument seems rather dubious. Delbos never appeared to be unduly concerned about business influence in foreign affairs. Perhaps a more logical explanation is that it was not in Delbos' character to meddle willingly in the internal affairs of a foreign government, whether or not he agreed with the policy of that regime. It must be recognized that Noël's plan could have been highly embarrassing if antigovernment sources had gotten wind of it. Moreover, Gamelin argued, "It is always difficult and often dangerous to intervene in the internal policy of allies and to plot the removal of persons. If the interested parties learn of it, one risks incurring their hostility." Certainly Gamelin's report of Smigly-Rydz' reluctance to dismiss his Foreign Minister could not have encouraged Delbos to believe that the plan would work. In fact, Gamelin indicated that Delbos "met the same reserve as myself, and had not considered it wise to insist."[22] In addition, Blum, who had been in on the initial plan, also failed to take up the question at Rambouillet. It has been suggested that such a clear anti-German maneuver would undermine Blum's simultaneous efforts to achieve a détente with Germany. Assuming this to be true, perhaps the Premier ordered Delbos to relinquish the plan.[23] Evidently, whatever the reasons, the two men decided that the game was not worth the candle. But, of course, the lack of evidence on this point must necessarily place any explanation solely in the realm of conjecture.

In any event, the main concern for the Poles, and the main topic of discussion at Rambouillet, was military credits. A lengthy exchange ensued concerning the nature and amount of the credits, the interest rate, and a control clause, through which the French sought to control the use of the loan, before France agreed to extend 2.6 billion francs in credits, arms, and cash for Poland's rearmament program.[24] But France got little in return for its loan. No plan of military cooperation was developed.[25] On the important political question of cooperation between Poland and Czechoslovakia, Smigly-Rydz told Blum: "You can assure President Benes for me that fortifying the Czech-Polish frontier is a waste of time and money." In addition, he held out some vague hope that the Czech and Polish General

Staffs would be able to get together.[26] Of course, these assurances held little consolation for the Czechs two years later in the aftermath of Munich. Noël believed that Colonel Beck benefited most from the Rambouillet Accords. "When he learned that the French government had agreed to the advances and the supplies requested, without laying down any political counterdemands, without even expressing the desire for a real change in the attitude of Poland's diplomacy toward us, Beck was greatly relieved."[27] The meetings with Smigly-Rydz had been cordial enough, but little was accomplished that would indicate that the alliance was anything more than a formality.[28] The Poles' position atop the fence held too many advantages for them to want to climb down.

Nevertheless, the Rambouillet Accords raised expectations at home and abroad of better and closer relations between France and Poland. For example, for the better part of the next year the British wondered what the French had received in return for the financial aid they had given to the Poles. In a speech on February 4, 1937, Delbos fed these hopes by declaring that the Franco-Polish Alliance had been reinforced by the visit of Smigly-Rydz.[29] Delbos did derive some satisfaction from his conversations. Upon inquiring about the nature of Poland's reaction in the event of a German attack on France or Czechoslovakia, Smigly-Rydz gave assurances that Poland would carry out its obligations of assistance to France and that Czechoslovakia could count on Poland to honor its responsibilities to the League of Nations. In case France and Czechoslovakia became jointly involved in a war, Poland would fulfill its obligation as France's ally.[30] Although Smigly-Rydz had reaffirmed Poland's obligations to France, he had carefully avoided making any definite commitment to Czechoslovakia alone. In fact, Blum had been rebuffed when he sought assurances that Poland would not use French arms against Czechoslovakia. Moreover, Smigly-Rydz, in response to a suggestion by *Le Temps* that Poland had undertaken an obligation to Czechoslovakia, ordered the Polish Ambassador in Paris to issue a formal denial that he had discussed Poland's relations with any other nation. Beck also sought to nip in the bud any rumors that Poland had made any commitments to the Czechs.[31] The French, who were hoping to create a solid bloc of smaller Eastern European states against German aggression, were naturally exasperated by the Polish evasion.

Other less meaningful benefits accrued from the conference. Noël felt that the granting of French funds considerably ameliorated relations between the two nations. He noted that lower echelons of the Polish army and Polish intellectuals increasingly favored the French connection. Moreover, the Polish-German amity cooled somewhat, and the Polish press increasingly criticized Germany.[32] These were nice fringe benefits, but they counted for relatively little in an authoritarian state such as Poland. As Noël noted, "Beck and his school continued to act in the same way as before, although with more prudence."[33]

One of the most disconcerting aspects of Franco-Polish relations for the rest of Delbos' tenure at the Quai d'Orsay centered around Poland's refusal to support French efforts at creating an Eastern European bloc to oppose German expansion. The *sine qua non* of an effective Eastern bloc was active cooperation between Poland and Czechoslovakia. But the Poles showed no inclination to develop close relations with the Czechs. It is true that Smigly-Rydz assured Delbos at Rambouillet that Poland would observe its commitment under the League in the event of an attack upon Czechoslovakia. Benes, the Czech President, suspected, however, that Poland would remain neutral in case of aggression against Czechoslovakia. He speculated that Poland's reluctance to establish close relations with Prague, in spite of several Czech offers of a friendship pact, was due to its fear of Germany.[34] Be that as it may, an important cause of Polish antagonism towards Czechoslovakia involved rival claims to the district of Teschen. The Poles were convinced that the Czechs had taken an unfairly large part of this area while Poland had been fighting the Bolsheviks in 1920. Moreover, Beck distrusted the Soviet-Czech Alliance of 1935, and he claimed that the Comintern used Prague as a center for anti-Polish activities. These were just a few of the antagonisms the Poles harbored against the Czechs.[35] All of this led Litvinov to believe that Beck sought to isolate Czechoslovakia from the rest of the Little Entente.[36]

Delbos continued to do all he could to bring about an improvement in relations between the two countries. Realizing that Britain might help, he instructed Corbin to ask Eden to encourage Poland to improve its relations with Czechoslovakia.[37] But nothing came of this new approach. In June, 1937, the Poles requested that a tri-

partite agreement between France, Germany, and Poland be negotiated concerning Germany's eastern boundary. Delbos angrily declined to entertain such an idea. He deemed that the Polish plan
was outrageous, and it convinced him that Colonel Beck had been
completely won over to the German camp.[38] As the summer wore
on, Beck sought to determine exactly what the French obligations
to Poland would be under the Treaty of 1925 in the event of aggression against Poland. But the French preferred not to commit themselves and gave a vague reply.[39]

A deterioration of Polish-German relations, due to increasing
Nazi pressure about the minorities question, and the general disintegration of the European situation during the summer of 1937
evidently convinced Beck of the need to play up the Franco-Polish
connection. In September, while returning from Geneva, Beck stopped
in Paris to talk with Delbos. He told Delbos that in view of the
gravity of the general situation in Europe, he wished to renew his
assurances that Poland would fully honor its obligations as an ally.
He undoubtedly did this in the hope of inducing France to clarify
its obligations to Poland.[40] Beck's assurances merely repeated those
he had given in March, 1936, in the aftermath of the Rhineland crisis.
But his *démarche* had the effect of putting relations between
the two countries on a more favorable footing. Although Delbos
had made little headway in obtaining closer Polish-Czech relations
or in getting the Poles to allow Soviet troops on Polish soil, he may
have felt that Beck would now be more inclined to move in that
direction.

Meanwhile, Delbos made an effort to strengthen the Little Entente. The alliance between Czechoslovakia, Rumania, and Yugoslavia, based on three bilateral treaties concluded in 1920 and 1921,
was initially intended to prevent Hungarian revisionism. France concluded a treaty of alliance with Czechoslovakia in 1924, which was
followed by treaties of understanding and friendship with Rumania
and Yugoslavia in 1926 and 1927. Although a political raison d'être
existed for the Little Entente, the collaboration between the states
was never based on a stable economic foundation.[41] Ultimately, the
reoccupation of the Rhineland severely undermined the confidence

that the Little Entente powers had in French support. They began to wonder "if France abstained from acting when its own vital interests were at stake, would it not have good reasons for remaining passive when ours are in peril."[42] They asked France, "Now that Germany has occupied the Rhine again, would you come to our aid in the event of a threat to our security?"[43]

The consequences of French inaction soon became apparent. On August 29, 1936, the pro-French Rumanian Foreign Minister, Nicolas Titulescu, was replaced by the more cautious Victor Antonescu in a new government headed by Georges Tatarescu.[44] Increasing numbers of Rumanians such as Antonescu began to see advantages in neutrality. In Antonescu's words, "Our policy . . . is more discreet than formerly, but it is also more circumspect. The principles remain fundamentally the same, but the methods have changed, notably vis-à-vis Poland and Italy. The Rumanian government . . . keenly desires a rapprochement with those two powers." He warned that public opinion was becoming increasingly hostile to an alliance with the Soviets.[45] Additional support for a neutral Little Entente standing between the democratic and totalitarian powers became evident.[46] In Yugoslavia, the President of Council, Milan Stoyadinovitch, told Blum, "We cannot solidify our relations with France. . . . We are now obliged to reckon with the German danger which you have allowed to emerge and spread."[47] He began moving closer to the Italians by concluding a commercial pact in September.[48] Even Czechoslovakia, the closest of France's eastern allies, began to hint about the need to find common ground for a rapprochement with Germany.[49]

This sudden desire on the part of the Little Entente states to pursue a policy of *sauve qui peut*, forced Delbos to develop a plan for revitalizing France's alliances in Eastern Europe. In October, 1936, after some prodding by the Czechs,[50] Delbos indicated his willingness to examine, "with all the necessary discretion," proposals to strengthen France's ties to the Little Entente.[51] On November 10, 1936, he informed the Little Entente states that France was ready to pursue parallel negotiations with each of them, while they conducted meetings with each other for strengthening this alliance. The French negotiations would become operative only after the other three powers had arrived at a consensus.[52]

The Czechs responded quickly. On November 11 and 12 they submitted their proposal for a Mutual Assistance Pact between France and the Little Entente. The plan was divided into two parts. It included a protocol which stated the obligations of the Little Entente states. In the event that one of the three states became the object of unprovoked aggression, the other two states would immediately come to its aid under Articles 15, 16, and 17 of the Covenant of the League of Nations. Article 3 of the Czech proposal added that "in principle, all engagements towards a third state that relate to the general policy of the Little Entente will be henceforth contracted by the three member states collectively."[53] This article was meant for France, because the other part of the Czech proposal consisted of a "Treaty of Mutual Assistance between the French Republic and the States of the Little Entente." Article 2 stated that "in the event that . . . France or whichever of the states of the Little Entente would be . . . the object of unprovoked aggression, the states of the Little Entente, and reciprocally France, will lend immediate assistance."[54] Here was a pact designed to replace the individual French treaties with Czechoslovakia, Rumania, and Yugoslavia.

On January 11, 1937, Delbos made the French counterproposals, along with his observations about the Czech plan. Although he approved of the general format of the proposed Mutual Assistance Pact, he felt that his objections were significant enough to warrant a completely new scheme. Basically he had three criticisms of the Czech plan, for which he proposed remedies.

First, he noted that while France would be contracting significant new obligations towards two members of the Little Entente, the Czech plan did not assure any significantly closer cohesion among the Little Entente states themselves. Then he stated, "In drawing up our scheme, our dominant preoccupation has been that . . . an effective solidarity between Prague, Belgrade, and Bucharest shall in practice be the condition of the execution of our own undertaking." Therefore, he proposed, "France only undertakes to help one of the three states if that state is already assured of the effective support of its two associates." In addition, French assistance would be conditional upon a request from the Little Entente. It would be impractical and imprudent, for example, for France to go automatically to the aid of the Little Entente in the event of an attack by Hungary.

Secondly, Delbos noted that the Czech proposal closely paralleled that of the Franco-Soviet Pact. Due to the hostile state of world opinion towards the Soviet Union, stemming from its actions in Spain, he felt that it would be a mistake politically and psychologically to reproduce merely the text of the pact. Such a move would be interpreted as "an indirect method of building up a bloc extending from Moscow to Paris by way of Bucharest, Belgrade, and Prague." He feared that this would provide Germany with fresh ammunition for denouncing its alleged encirclement. It would also be likely to disturb British opinion.

Accordingly, and this constituted his third criticism, he declared, "It is in our interest . . . that we should appear to be desiring understandings of a wider sort." In other words, the nature of the Czech proposal seemed to be too limited. Delbos believed that no "point" should be made against Germany or any other state. He felt that the agreement should appear to have a provisional character in order that it might be renounced as soon as a wider agreement embracing other powers could be negotiated. This, of course, was aimed at the reservations the pact might evoke in the countries that were involved.[55]

Delbos believed that his proposal went far enough to ascertain whether the project had any chance of success. Both he and the Czechs were well aware of the possibility of opposition among the Little Entente states. Their anticipations quickly proved to be well founded. When Czech Foreign Minister Kamil Krofta offered the Czech plan to the French, he suggested that it be presented to Belgrade and Bucharest as a French plan in order to assuage their sensitivities.[56] Delbos had also observed increasing opposition to such a pact in Belgrade. Consequently, when he made his proposals to the Czechs in January, Delbos advised that to ensure the success of the scheme, they should be presented to Belgrade and Rumania as a French plan.[57] Nevertheless, resistance from Rumania and Yugoslavia soon became apparent.

In Rumania, Antonescu did not conceal his antipathy toward the proposals for the Mutual Assistance Pact. Despite the French camouflage, he felt certain that the plan had originated in Prague. He believed that Germany would regard the proposals as provocation. It would be far better for Czechoslovakia to come to terms with

Germany.[58] Antonescu again conjured up the specter of Soviet troops utilizing Rumania as a corridor for rendering aid to Czechoslovakia. Once the Russian troops came in, would they ever leave? He noted that many were convinced that France's position had greatly declined and would not improve. On the other hand, German and Italian influence was stronger. He told the British that the countries of the Little Entente did not wish to become associated with the Axis powers, but in view of France's weakened condition, the inclination was strong.[59] Antonescu recommended that France sign separate agreements similar to the Franco-Polish Pact with each of the three Little Entente states. He felt that this would not be as provocative as the plan being proposed, and that it would have a steadying effect on Central and Eastern Europe.[60] But the French wanted more effective cooperation among the Little Entente states themselves. Antonescu's plan would eliminate that desirable aspect of the French proposal.[61]

Delbos' plan encountered similar opposition in Yugoslavia. Stoyadinovich argued that Yugoslav aid to Czechoslovakia in the event of an attack by Germany would have to be sent across two hostile countries—Austria and Hungary. Meanwhile, Yugoslavia would be leaving its own frontiers open to attack by Italy.[62] For the same reason, he was not impressed with the argument that Czech troops would come to Yugoslavia's aid in the event of Italian aggression. They, too, would have to pass through Austria and Hungary. In addition, aid from French troops might well be held up by the new German fortifications. Stoyadinovitch saw advantages for France in the proposed pact because of the fact that it would be partially relieved of its responsibilities to Czechoslovakia. The Czechs would also be the beneficiaries of more support. But he failed to see how Yugoslavia would benefit from the plan. Even though the French hinted that they had won Antonescu over, he believed that the wish was father to the thought.[63] He argued that the rapprochement between Germany and Italy had only been "temporary and occasional," but implementation of the French plan would bring the two powers together in a closer and more durable relationship. As a great power, France need not worry. But Yugoslavia would be immediately exposed to economic reprisals. Besides, he assured France, "Germany does not any more dream of attacking Czechoslovakia than France."[64] In retrospect, this was quite a statement. At any rate, Stoyadinovitch clearly intended to remain free from any commitment to the proposed Mutual Assistance Pact.

Opposition also existed in another important quarter. On November 8, 1936, Delbos had the French Ambassador in London, Charles Corbin, relay to Eden the intentions of France to engage in negotiations for a Mutual Assistance Pact with the Little Entente. Anticipating Yugoslav reluctance, he asked the British to use their influence to encourage the Belgrade government to approve the plan.[65] Eden replied that he understood that the Yugoslav objections stemmed from their fear of Russia. But he added that he was pleased at the resumption of French efforts to regroup the Little Entente, "which too often appeared balanced between contrary influences."[66] Yet Eden's reply belied the real dissatisfaction at the Foreign Office over the French proposal. Orme Sargent, Assistant Undersecretary of State at the Foreign Office stated:

> I think we are entitled, in view of the guarantee we have given [France] to exercise a definite control over her policy in the East of Europe, and in this particular case we would be justified in pointing out that we disapprove of her undertaking the fresh commitments implicit in the present draft pact. We have always accepted that she is pledged to assist Czechoslovakia: we have, though unwillingly, acquiesced in her giving a similar pledge to Soviet Russia; but we cannot agree that she should now give further pledges which might easily bring about a fresh quarrel with Italy and further strengthen the Italo-German Entente while at the same time involving France in the irrelevant intricacies of Danubian and Balkan politics. If she wishes to strengthen Czechoslovakia in her present precarious position, surely the simplest and most obvious manner is to make it abundantly clear to Germany that she intends to carry out her present obligations towards Czechoslovakia.[67]

Sargent thought that if the French persisted, Britain should indicate to them that Czechoslovakia should first show that it had not been able to reach an "honourable and durable settlement with Germany." Such a pact, if concluded, should be constructed in a manner that would assure Polish and Italian interests in Central Europe. Alexander Cadogan added, "I hope indeed that we may do whatever may be possible to dissuade the French from this crowning folly." Another Foreign Office official added, "I hope that we shall tell the French Government quite frankly that we will have nothing to do with it and deprecate it sharply—[sic] It would be infinitely better that we should shoulder the blame for preventing it than, . . . [that we,] by being over-diplomatic, should allow the negotiations to go a yard further; for, if they leak out, much irretrievable harm will be done in Europe."[68]

Despite this opposition at the Foreign Office, supplemented by pressure from Rumania on Britain to give advice and "directive" to Paris, cooler heads prevailed. Eden did not attempt to exert any conspicuous pressure on Delbos to drop the plan. Perhaps he realized there was no need to do so. When he presented the British position, he merely recounted the main points of Rumanian and Yugoslav opposition, as well as the possible repercussions in Rome and Berlin. He refused to believe that the situation was as somber as the French claimed. He concluded by indicating that "perhaps . . . there existed other means for shielding [Czechoslovakia] than by concluding a pact the efficacy of which is so uncertain."[69] Eden had made British reluctance clear without putting himself in the position of having to assume responsibility for the plan's defeat. He did not have to. He probably realized that Rumanian and Yugoslav opposition would be enough to force Delbos to abandon or at least shelve the project. Indeed, in March, 1937, Yugoslavia applied the *coup de grâce*.

In early February, 1937, Stoyadinovitch told the French that a representative would be sent to Rome to examine the possibilities of an entente with Italy. He had in mind a "Gentleman's Agreement" similar to that between Britain and Italy. Despite French counsels of prudence, Stoyadinovitch insisted that this proposal did not mean a reorientation of Yugoslav policy.[70] On the following day he declared to the Yugoslav Chamber, "My policy is neither germanophile, francophile, anglophile, nor italophile. I have a yugoslavophile policy and neither recognize nor want any other foreign policy."[71] Stoyadinovitch was beating a hasty retreat from closer ties with France and the West. On March 27, 1937, Yugoslavia signed a Nonaggression Pact with Italy. The two states agreed to remain neutral in a war with a third power. They would consult in the event their "common interests" were endangered.[72]

Conclusion of the Italo-Yugoslav Pact can only be regarded as the final setback for Delbos' project. He believed that a German attack on Czechoslovakia was imminent. Therefore, it was essential to show Germany that the Czechs would be solidly supported by France and its Little Entente allies. The best way to impress this fact upon the Germans, Delbos concluded, was by an effective Mutual Assistance Pact. If this common front failed, the Little Entente would dissolve and Rumania and Yugoslavia would fall under Axis influence.[73] The Italo-Yugoslav Pact was a clear indication of the reorientation of Yugoslav policy and the resulting internal loosening of ties within the Little Entente.

When Stoyadinovitch visited Paris in the fall of 1937, Delbos took him to task for his actions. The Frenchman was irritated because Stoyadinovitch had not kept France informed of the negotiations with Italy. He stated that Hitler and Mussolini appeared intent upon intimidating Europe, and the only means of preventing this was to confront them with a solid block of countries, united in resistance. He implied that Yugoslavia had allowed itself to be written off as a country that gave them a carte blanche for aggression.[74]

There can be little doubt that Delbos' plan amounted to a bold new French initiative to strengthen its position in Eastern Europe. In effect, the scheme involved a sizable increase in France's Eastern European commitments. Under the pact France would have undertaken, at the request of the Little Entente, to go to war with Italy, Hungary, Bulgaria, or Greece in defense of Czechoslovakia, Rumania, and Yugoslavia. In return, however, France merely gained the possibility of receiving Rumanian and Yugoslav aid in the event of a German attack. Therefore, it appears that Delbos' main objective, in the wake of the Rhineland crisis, was the restoration, among the Eastern European states, of confidence in France as a great power. To be sure, some advantage would have accrued to Czechoslovakia in the form of two closer allies. But the pact would not have added much to France's existing security arrangements. It was certainly no substitute for an effective Franco-Soviet military pact.

But the point is academic. The important fact remains that Delbos' first attempt to strengthen France's prestige and position in Eastern Europe had foundered upon the rocks of Rumanian and, especially, Yugoslav opposition. Throughout the spring of 1937 Delbos continued to try to establish some arrangement in Eastern

Europe. But he admitted his "despair" at being unable to develop a policy that would keep Eastern Europe from falling into German hands. Whenever he suggested to the Little Entente states that they should cooperate in opposing German expansion, they replied that France was not strong enough to protect them without British support.[75] But Britain showed no willingness to become involved in the defense of Eastern Europe.

As we have seen, French relations with Poland had deteriorated. Beck visited Rumania in the hope of developing an anti-Soviet front. He believed that Poland's best opportunity for safety in the immediate future lay in allowing Germany to preoccupy itself by driving southward through Austria and Czechoslovakia.[76] In addition, Czechoslovakia was pressuring France with a mild form of blackmail. Benes had made overtures for a rapprochement with Germany, even to the point of allowing the Germans to inspect Czech military preparations. Germany had refused the offer.[77] But the Czech initiative again reflected a lack of confidence in French strength. Moreover, Mussolini had informed Kurt von Schuschnigg, the Austrian Chancellor, that he would do nothing to prevent Austria from falling into German hands. Furthermore, he told the Austrian that he opposed any Danubian combination.[78] Perhaps it was due to the roadblock in Eastern Europe that Delbos considered warming up to the Soviets in the late spring of 1937. When the purges made him reluctant to follow that path, however, he was thrown back upon making a renewed effort at revitalizing the French position in Eastern Europe.

By fall, Delbos may have believed that the momentum of renewed Franco-British cooperation and success at Nyon, however limited it may have been, would encourage the Eastern European states to cooperate in a security arrangement with France. Besides, he had other reasons for thinking that a new initiative might be successful. As we have seen, increased German pressure concerning Danzig and the Polish Corridor had led Beck to act more favorably towards France. In addition, in November, when Delbos admonished Stoyadinovitch for his maneuverings with Italy, the latter had held out some hope of cooperation. He told Delbos that Yugoslavia's interests remained with the Little Entente, the Balkan Entente, the League of Nations, and, even more, with France. He was still convinced that the Rome-Berlin Axis was not durable. Ultimately, France,

Italy, Yugoslavia, and the Little Entente would find themselves united against the German peril. Although British feebleness in the Abyssinian affair and French inaction during the Rhineland crisis gave some reason for anxiety, Yugoslavia would side firmly with Czechoslovakia and France in the event of aggression against the Czechs. He noted, however, that it was quite flattering to him personally and to his small country to receive visits from Neurath and Count Ciano, the German and Italian Foreign Ministers.[79]

It is difficult to determine when Delbos thought of making his own trip to the Eastern European capitals. By early November he had decided that his new attempt to breathe new life into the decaying French security system in Eastern Europe should take the form of such a trip. Conceivably he wished to offset the effects of Lord Halifax's visit to Germany in November.[80] Or perhaps he hoped to emulate Louis Barthou's highly successful whirlwind tour of Eastern European capitals in May, 1934. Barthou had given the statesmen of those countries the impression that France had a strong policy and would not abandon Eastern Europe to German penetration. What is more, Barthou had showed himself strong enough to implement that policy.[81] As we have seen, before leaving on his trip Delbos went to London with Premier Chautemps to confer with Chamberlain and Eden. This new manifestation of Franco-British cooperation, as well as the British expression of interest in Central Europe in the final communiqué, must have been reassuring to Eastern European statesmen. But Delbos undoubtedly lost some of his freedom of action, if not determination, as a result of the meeting. Britain, after all, did not give a firm commitment to aid in the defense of Austria and Czechoslovakia. As he left on his trip, Delbos must have been well aware of Britain's great reluctance to become involved in a war for the defense of Eastern Europe. Yet the meeting did give Delbos the added prestige of being able to speak for Britain.

On December 2, one day after returning from London, Delbos departed for a three weeks' "tour of friendship" in Central and Eastern Europe. He undoubtedly wished to test the extent to which France could count on its eastern allies, and hoped to revitalize French ties in the area by reassuring them of France's commitment to their security.[82] As his train passed through Berlin on its way to Warsaw, Delbos received a surprise visit from Neurath. It was a clever gesture, coming as it did barely two months before the Anschluss. The visit, which lasted ten minutes in his train compartment, had been unsolicited by the Frenchman, but he took the opportunity to pose questions to the German Foreign Minister. When Delbos asked why Germany rejected proposals for a "general settlement," Neurath replied that it was a mistake to try to settle everything at once. The best method was to settle matters bit by bit. Neurath did not respond unfavorably to Delbos' suggestion of an air pact. He said that to show how friendly German feeling towards France was, a group of Hitler Youth had wanted to come to the station with bouquets![83]

In Warsaw on December 3, Delbos was met by Colonel Beck and was the object of an enthusiastic public reception. Delbos saw the President of Poland, from whom he received the highest Polish decoration. He discussed with Smigly-Rydz the application and effects of the French loan for military rearmament resulting from the Rambouillet Agreement. He then held conversations with Beck. But apparently both men deliberately refrained from bringing up controversial questions.[84] This dismayed Léon Noël. On the train the French Ambassador in Warsaw had insisted that Delbos speak very seriously to Beck about the continuing Polish-Czech differences. Noël considered that this problem "was an intolerable obstacle to the fulfillment of French diplomatic aims." But according to Noël, Delbos avoided raising the question with Beck.[85] Later, however, Delbos said that he had indeed discussed Czechoslovakia. Beck had replied that Czechoslovakia was the center of Comintern propaganda against Poland. Delbos merely pointed out that the Czech government need not be held responsible for this.[86] Evidently he did not wish to pursue such a sensitive question any further, let alone to demand that Poland improve its relations with Czechoslovakia.

During the remainder of his stay in Poland, which included a visit to Cracow, little of significance was discussed. Beck expressed his interest in colonies for Poland in the event that a redistribution of colonies occurred. He hoped that Poland's need for raw materials and its surplus population would not be forgotten.[87] Delbos did warn Beck of possible repercussions from his meddling in Danzig.

If the Danzig constitution continued to be violated indiscriminately, the League might be forced to consider withdrawing its High Commissioner. Beck was shocked enough to speak enthusiastically about the League, the only time he showed any regard for the international organization.[88]

For the most part, however, the Delbos-Beck conversations were rather vague and inconsequential.[89] Perhaps most significant was the apparent effort by Delbos to improve the psychological relations between the two governments. "Every effort was for once made by the French to respect Polish susceptibilities."[90] Delbos felt that his London visit prior to this trip had helped to create a more favorable atmosphere.[91] The fact that Neurath had visited Delbos also impressed Beck. Sir Howard Kennard, the British Ambassador in Warsaw, reported that Delbos changed his itinerary in order not to go from Warsaw to Prague because of the mistrust between the two countries. Moreover, throughout the entire visit France's bonds with Russia and Czechoslovakia were played down. When the Czech Minister in Warsaw appeared at the station to welcome Delbos, he was urged to leave, and he hurriedly disappeared before the train arrived.[92] Delbos' reluctance to broach the sensitive Czech question is another example of his desire to soothe the Poles. Conceivably, in the light of past relations between the Popular Front and Poland and the deep distrust of Beck at the Quai d'Orsay, Delbos felt it would be difficult to create substantially better relations between the two governments during a visit of only four days.[93] It would be better to restore confidence between them gradually. Sound as his plan may have appeared, however, time was running out on France.

Delbos continued on to Rumania, which was on the verge of a general election and in a state of turbulence. Upon his arrival in Bucharest on December 8, however, Delbos again received an enthusiastic welcome from the populace. In spite of their recent efforts to become more neutral, King Carol, Premier Tatarescu, and Antonescu—still the Foreign Minister—were also friendly. Discussion centered upon trade relations, mechanization of the Rumanian army, and collective security. Antonescu wondered if the French commitment to Czechoslovakia, which had been pledged repeatedly, would be carried out in the event of aggression against the Czechs. He noted that France had tied itself to Britain's apron strings by pursuing nonintervention in Spain and by rebuffing Soviet attempts to conclude a military pact. Antonescu inquired if Britain would deter France from acting in defense of Czechoslovakia as it had during the Rhineland crisis.[94] With the benefit of hindsight, his doubts appear quite justified. When Delbos raised the question of a Franco-Rumanian Alliance to replace the treaty of friendship between the two countries, the Tatarescu government said that it would consider such a pact if Yugoslavia agreed to a similar treaty.[95] The Rumanians were still hiding behind a Yugoslav shield while they waited to see in which direction France would move in the next crisis.

Delbos' visit to Yugoslavia was generally considered to be the most delicate and difficult part of his trip. It will be remembered that under Stoyadinovitch's direction, Yugoslav foreign policy had been developing along neutralist lines. He had been the most intransigent opponent of Delbos' Mutual Assistance proposal, and it had been the Italo-Yugoslav Pact which had applied the *coup de grâce* to the idea. In addition, Stoyadinovitch had just returned from a visit to Rome prior to Delbos' arrival, and it had been announced that he would soon pay a visit to Berlin. His maneuvering had created considerable hostility in Paris.[96] When Delbos arrived in Belgrade from Bucharest on December 12, he was greeted by a frenzied crowd that had gathered outside the station. As Delbos and Stoyadinovitch left the station, there were pro-French and antigovernment demonstrations. Cries of "long live France" and "long live Delbos" were mixed with shouts of "down with Stoyadinovitch," "down with the government." Special precautions had been taken to maintain order, and the demonstrations were promptly and ruthlessly suppressed. At one point the police fired upon a group of demonstrators, who, in the best French tradition, had thrown up a barricade.[97] The results were one dead and several wounded. As Alexander Werth noted, it was as much an anti-Stoyadinovitch as it was a pro-French outburst.[98]

On his first day in Belgrade, Delbos conferred with Stoyadinovitch. The latter declared, "I hope you do not for one moment doubt that in the hour of need, the Yugoslav army would be at your disposition." Delbos probably recognized that these words were not to be taken at their face value.[99] In return, Delbos let the Yugoslavs know that the French considered the Yugoslav army to be deficient.[100] Little else resulted from the visit. Delbos was entertained at a luncheon by King Paul and at a banquet by Stoyadinovitch. The latter gave a speech, in which he mentioned Yugoslavia's desire for friendly and constructive collaboration with France. He considered it necessary for Yugoslavia, on the one hand, to cultivate and maintain existing friendships and, on the other, to remove all causes of conflict and misunderstanding within the scope of Yugoslavia's interests and frontiers. Sir Ronald Campbell, the British Ambassador in Belgrade, considered the remarks to be an apologia for Stoyadinovitch's visit to Rome.[101] Perhaps his statement should have been viewed as an indication of his intention to remain as neutral as possible.

The remainder of Delbos' time was taken up with assorted ceremonial visits, receptions, and addresses. On the third and final day he signed three commercial agreements designed to supplement the Franco-Yugoslav Treaty of Commerce of 1929. On December 14 Delbos departed for Prague. He told Campbell that he was markedly more satisfied than he had expected to be. But Stoyadinovitch had not committed himself to anything. He probably felt unable to agree to any definite declaration on Franco-Yugoslav relations for fear of offending German and Italian sensibilities.[102] Werth later noted that Stoyadinovitch "was only too glad to see the last of Delbos."[103]

As his train made its way across Hungary on its way to Prague, Delbos remarked to one of the journalists in his car: "At last we are going to see some real friends."[104] President Benes, Foreign Minister Krofta, and Premier Hodza were all considered friends, and, indeed, Delbos received an euthusiastic welcome in Prague. The speeches were all affectionate in their tribute to Masaryk, the man with whom the French had cooperated to such a great extent to form the Czech state in 1919 and who had made Czechoslovakia an "eastern bastion" in the French security system.[105]

It will be recalled that the British were quite concerned about what Delbos would say in Prague. During his conversations with the British Ministers in London, it had been agreed that Delbos should press the Czechs to consider concessions on the matter of German minorities. When Delbos raised the question with Benes, the Czech President assured him that the Sudetens, who comprised 21 percent of the total population of Czechoslovakia, would get that percentage of posts in the public services. He added, however, that this could not be done suddenly. In certain districts this percentage could not be allotted. But in other districts as much as 50 percent would be allotted to maintain a balance. Benes pointed out, map in hand, that autonomy for the Sudetens could not be considered. They were scattered about in a long, wormlike pattern which was not even continuous. Besides, he felt that friendly collaboration between the Czechs and Germans was not only possible but probable.[106] Evidently Delbos was satisfied that the Czech government would do everything possible to meet the legitimate claims of the Sudetens, and he did not pursue the matter further. In the course of an official reception, Delbos met the two Parliamentary representatives of the Sudetens. He was impressed by the fact that they attached "great importance to the desirability of a friendly understanding between Germany and France." They emphasized their loyalty to Czechoslovakia, but they stressed their opposition to being treated as a minority.[107]

The Germans, who had displayed little interest during most of Delbos' trip, naturally were quite concerned about his conversations with the Czechs. Ernst Eisenlohr, the German Minister in Prague, reported that Delbos desired a détente between Germany and Czechoslovakia. It did not matter what method was used, multilateral or bilateral negotiations, as long as a peaceful settlement could be reached.[108] Eisenlohr noted that the conversations were held without being accompanied by any anti-German reproaches, either public or private.[109] The theme that dominated the conversations was whether and how Czechoslovakia's relations with Germany could be improved, and what repercussions this might have on Franco-Czech relations. Benes had informed Eisenlohr earlier that

> whether developments in Europe would lead once more to the strengthening of the League of Nations, or whether the struggle between the Great Powers would remain the decisive factor in the development of Europe, would determine whether he could seek the security of his country, as hitherto, on a collective basis or would have to follow the example of, say Yugoslavia, and settle relations with his mighty neighbor by direct negotiations with her.[110]

This was a rather ominous threat to the French, in view of the Yugoslav action, that Czechoslovakia might try to make the best deal possible for itself, unless better collective security arrangements were worked out. For the moment, Benes emphasized that "the visit was a complete success and a great and harmonious manifestation of Franco-Czechoslovak friendship."[111]

Czechoslovakia gave the Frenchman an affectionate farewell. At Cheb, on the Czech-German frontier, Delbos was greeted by the playing of the "Marseillaise" and the Czech national anthem. Delbos emphasized once again the "indissoluble bonds uniting the two countries." But Werth noted the irony when he wrote: "It was through Eger (or Cheb as the Czechs called it) that Hitler made his triumphant entry into the Sudetenland in October 1938."[112]

On December 19, 1937, Delbos' train steamed back into the Gare de l'Est. Werth summed up the trip in the following manner:

M. Delbos, smiling his gentle smile, came out of the train and said: *"J'ai fait un excellent voyage."* That was for the afternoon papers. A few days later, before the Foreign Affairs Committee of the Chamber, M. Delbos, as an honest man, admitted that the *voyage* had not been as *excellent* as all that. No doubt, the ordinary people in Poland and Jugoslavia and Rumania still felt deeply attached to France and all that France stood for; but the Governments—no. The Czechoslovak Government alone was as wholeheartedly pro-French as were the Czech people.[113]

Indeed, what can be said for the results of what proved to be Delbos' and France's last attempt to revitalize its security system in Eastern Europe? Perhaps Chautemps' description of the Polish attitude as being "allied but not really friendly" would be best applied to all of the countries visited, with the exception of Czechoslovakia. The tête-à-tête conversations with the heads of government in the four states neither produced nor anticipated any treaty agreements. Perhaps, as Delbos emphasized to press correspondents in Prague, "the purpose of his tour had been a moral one, and this had been achieved."[114] Given the failure of his attempts to conclude a Mutual Assistance Pact earlier in the year, it is probable that anything of that nature remained out of the question in the fall of 1937. Certainly then, the outcome of his visit can only be judged against the background of the previous year. In addition, if, as has been suggested, he made the trip to offset the effects of Lord Halifax's visit to Germany and to emulate Barthou, maybe it is true that all he sought at this time was a consolidation of France's moral position among the states of Eastern Europe. Perhaps the psychological reassurance gained from his trip could be used as an opening wedge into a more comprehensive mutual-security scheme at a later date.

But events during the next few weeks showed that if indeed this was his hope, it proved to be ill-founded. Delbos had scarcely left Rumania when the elections in that country toppled the Tatarescu government. Although Tatarescu and his Foreign Minister, Antonescu, had not beaten a path to the French door and had opposed Delbos' Mutual Assistance Pact, it was nevertheless considered friendlier than the Beck government in Poland, and certainly more friendly than the rightist Goga government which replaced it.[115] It was even rumored that Delbos' visit might have influenced the elections in favor of those who opposed drawing closer to France and thereby closer to Russia.[116] This, of course, is difficult to gauge.

In Warsaw, Noël had warned Delbos that "after your visit, Beck will not delay in going to Germany." Delbos exclaimed, "He will not dare." A few weeks later Beck made his trip to Berlin, where Hitler renewed his assurances that differences over minorities and Danzig could be resolved without difficulty. "On his return to Poland, Colonel Beck did not conceal the satisfaction that he derived from this meeting. Hitler had implied to him that he was determined 'to settle,' in a short time, the Austrian question."[117] Beck obviously was still determined to remain astraddle his fence for fear of getting his feet wet on the wrong side. Delbos' trip to Warsaw had little effect on Polish policy, psychologically or otherwise.

The Yugoslav leader, Stoyadinovitch, also made his trip to Berlin. Important economic interests required good relations with Germany. Yugoslavia's improved economic relations and *bon voisinage* with Italy were additional reasons for not incurring the ill will of Rome and Berlin.[118]

Consequently, whatever good will and psychological solidarity Delbos succeeded in attaining quickly dissipated. But one other ramification of Delbos' trip must be examined. There can be little doubt that Delbos' failure to include Moscow on his itinerary further damaged Franco-Soviet relations. Count Schulenburg, the German

Ambassador in Moscow, reported that Litvinov had attended the Brussels Conference in November, 1937, solely for the purpose of personally inviting Delbos to visit Moscow. When Delbos refused, Litvinov prematurely left the conference in a "huff."[119] Robert Coulondre, the French Ambassador in Moscow, noted that "despite all the excuses which could be presented," the French snub would hardly "ameliorate Franco-Soviet relations and restore confidence."[120] Schulenburg reported, "Delbos' journey . . . which took him to Warsaw, Bucharest, and Belgrade without touching Moscow, had caused great resentment in authoritative quarters here." Schulenburg added that the Soviet leaders were so "miffed" that the rebuff "was partly responsible for the Soviet attempt to interfere in the French cabinet crisis in January, 1938, and to bring about the removal of Delbos."[121] Whether this is true or not is beside the point. The fact is that by November, 1937, Delbos had definitely decided to strengthen France's relations with the small states of Eastern Europe rather than those with the Soviet Union. As we have seen in the last chapter, Delbos had been prompted by several reasons to make a decision that would have great implications. As Daniel Brower noted, Delbos' snub and the ensuing campaign by the Communists to dump Delbos may have been directly related to the worsening of Franco-Soviet relations in late 1937 and early 1938.[122]

On the other hand, Delbos' trip obtained little in the way of lasting results. With the benefit of hindsight, we can judge that he most certainly bet upon the wrong horse by choosing the small Eastern European states over the Soviet Union to contain Germany in the east. Delbos undoubtedly placed too much hope in his efforts to recreate a bloc of French allies in Eastern Europe. It is doubtful, given their basic antagonisms toward each other, that such a grouping could have been formed and, much less, been effective in the face of a real German threat. This point should have been made clear by the failure of Delbos' proposed Mutual Assistance Pact. By the fall of 1937, Delbos was operating from an increasingly weakened position, and his trip offered too little too late to the small Eastern European states. As Charles Corbin, André François-Poncet, and Georges Bonnet have pointed out to this writer, German and Italian ambitions had become all too clear to the Eastern European statesmen.[123] Seen in this light, France's failure to act during the Rhineland crisis had a profound effect upon them. This must be seen as the decisive factor in the decline of French influence in Eastern Europe. Even if it was not too late when he assumed his post, as Corbin has suggested, Delbos was not Barthou. He was not the man to reassure those statesmen.[124] But in all fairness to Delbos, the German and Italian threats were not nearly as great in 1934 as they were in 1937.

8

Contrasting Policies
towards Italy and Germany

"Every effort should be made to reach reconciliation with Germany but . . . Italy should be treated with contempt and disdain as a relatively unimportant jackal."[1] This statement, which Delbos made to Ambassador Bullitt in August, 1937, goes a long way towards explaining the Popular Front's policy towards Italy. Indeed, the French policy makers scarcely concealed the disdain that they held for their "Latin sister." As early as 1933 Delbos considered Mussolini to be an "imperialist and megalomaniac dictator."[2] There is little evidence that he changed his opinion as Foreign Minister. In fact, as he also admitted to Bullitt, both he and Blum "loathed Mussolini intensely."[3] Consequently, diplomatic relations between Italy and the Popular Front government started at a low ebb and progressively worsened.

Count Ciano, the Italian Foreign Minister, once observed that relations between the two countries had always been rather stormy and that, "though violent love was apt to alternate with equally violent quarrels," there were no fundamental causes of friction between the two countries.[4] The two Latin sisters "were accustomed to scratch and kiss each other alternately without either the scratch going very deep or the kiss being very significant."[5] Indeed, the resentment and bitterness that had been built up between them by June, 1936, stood in stark contrast to the close Franco-Italian friendship of the Stresa Front days of early 1935. When Mussolini invaded Abyssinia in October, 1935, he probably hoped that his agreements with France would dissuade it from applying economic sanctions. When France reluctantly destroyed these hopes by adhering to the League's sanctions, relations between the two countries deteriorated sharply. The League's action did not effectively halt the Italian aggression, but it was sufficient to incense Mussolini.[6]

As long as French rightists like Laval and Pierre-Etienne Flandin formulated French foreign policy, there always remained the chance that the Stresa Front could be recreated once the Abyssinian crisis diminished. But when the Popular Front government of Léon Blum took office in June, 1936, its association with the Communist party and the Franco-Soviet Pact "were like red rags to a bull." The Italian fascist press lost all restraint in its attacks upon the new government.[7]

The problem of economic sanctions against Italy was the first great international issue with which the Blum government had to deal. For all practical purposes, Italy had won the war, but the sanctions still remained in effect. It was a delicate problem. The end of sanctions meant de facto recognition of Italy's conquest and acknowledgment of the League's defeat.[8] Once again, however, the new government was anxious, if possible, to conform to the British position. In May, 1936, before assuming office, Blum went to London to confer with Eden. He declared that he "definitely did not want to raise sanctions as his first act as Prime Minister." He would prefer to keep them on for a time. He then made a most revealing statement, according to Eden: "In reference to the relations of Signor Mussolini and Herr Hitler, M. Blum expressed his conviction that it would not be possible to keep the two dictators apart. Sooner or later their policies would converge."[9] It is quite clear that neither Delbos nor Blum was inclined to take any initiative at Geneva to abolish the sanctions, but they were willing to support any British steps in that direction.[10] In his first foreign-policy statement on June 23, Delbos indicated to the Chamber the government's sentiments on the problem. He acknowledged that France had bound itself with sanctions, despite its affinities with the Italian nation. After all, it was a French tradition to honor its obligations and fulfill its duties towards justice and humanity. France could not fail to respect its obligations to the League Council, which had unanimously decided that Italy had committed an act of aggression. But in the light of the existing circumstances, "the maintenance of sanctions would amount to no more than a symbolic gesture without real efficacy."[11]

On July 15 sanctions were raised. This source of irritation having been removed, the time might have been right for a new Mediterranean pact and a reconstituted Stresa Front.[12] Indeed, there is evidence that perhaps Italy may have made several efforts in that direction. Through Jean-Louis Malvy, a member of the French Senate, Mussolini hinted that if France took the initiative at Geneva in dismissing the League's moral condemnation of Italy, he would be "disposed to collaborate closely with France on all problems."[13] A few days later Mussolini told Hubert de Lagardelle, a French journalist, that he was ready to examine the eventuality of a Mediterranean pact, once the British naval agreements directed against Italy had been removed.[14] Ciano also suggested to Count Charles de Chambrun, the French Ambassador in Rome, that his government desired to collaborate with France and the League if the sanctions were raised. He even said that Italy would refrain from demanding recognition of its position in Abyssinia.[15] Even though these Italian *démarches* preceded the removal of sanctions, and must therefore be open to suspicion, there is no evidence that Delbos or Blum would have taken them seriously in any case. No effort was made to reply, even after the sanctions were raised. Blum had indicated to Eden, during their meeting in May, that it might be embarrassing to call off the sanctions and then immediately plunge into negotiations with Italy for a Mediterranean pact.[16] Perhaps the real reason, however, was his distrust of Mussolini. As he admitted to the postwar Parliamentary Commission, "I was entirely convinced, since the German-Austrian agreement of July, 1936, that a real rapprochement between Italy and France was no longer possible." After agreeing to German influence over Austria and Central Europe, Mussolini would be forced to turn to the Mediterranean for his adventures. Here he would conflict with French and British interests.[17]

Mussolini's blatant disregard for the French nonintervention scheme in Spain made Delbos and Blum even less disposed to negotiate a rapprochement with Italy. The Italians presented their moral and material support to Franco as an ideological crusade against Bolshevism. An ideological war that Delbos consistently repudiated loomed just over the horizon. The Italian press repeatedly charged that France was aiding the "Reds" in Spain and that it was therefore the enemy of law and order in Europe. It jubilantly noted the succession of strikes in France and the continued decline of French influence in Europe as examples of the inability of the decadent democratic system to cope with modern conditions.[18] Furthermore, the French could only view with grave concern the growth of Italian influence in the Balearic Islands.[19] The establishment of bases there by an unfriendly power could cut France off from its North African colonies.

At the same time, de facto cooperation between Germany and Italy over Austria and Spain led those two countries into a de jure partnership with the announcement of the "Rome-Berlin Axis" in November, 1936. There is evidence that Mussolini first warned France that he had received overtures from Hitler and that he said: "If the attitude of the French government is not soon modified towards myself and towards Italy . . . then I will accept Hitler's propositions."[20] Perhaps Delbos and Blum did not relish being held up by an open case of blackmail, or they may have felt, as Blum noted, that it was already too late to detach Italy from Germany. In any event, once again Delbos and the Quai d'Orsay did not respond; and on November 1, following Count Ciano's visits to Berlin and Berchtesgaden in October, Mussolini announced the birth of the Axis.[21]

Relations between the two countries continued to worsen during the fall. In October, Delbos and Blum decided to retire de Chambrun as Ambassador to Rome, probably because of his Italophile sympathies.[22] It was agreed that René Doynel de Saint-Quentin would be his successor, but Mussolini decided that his credentials must be addressed to Victor Emmanuel III, "King of Italy" *and* "Emperor of Ethiopia."[23] The French believed that this gesture was clearly aimed at them because the American Ambassador, William Phillips, had just been accepted in the usual fashion. De Chambrun protested, but Ciano told him that the decision was irrevocable.[24] At the end of October, Delbos talked about the matter with Vittorio Cerruti, the Italian Ambassador in Paris. Cerruti insisted that France show its good will towards Italy by recognizing the King of Italy as the Emperor of Ethiopia. Delbos replied that France's attachment to the League and its responsibilities in Europe prevented it from granting what would be tantamount to recognition of Italy's annexation of Ethiopia. Cerruti warned of the bad effect the absence of a French Ambassador would have in Rome. Delbos laconically replied that "this absence is compensated for by [your] presence in Paris."[25] For the remainder of Delbos' tenure at the Quai d'Orsay, French representation at the Quirinal was handled by Counsellor Jules Blondel, acting as Chargé d'Affaires. Only after Blum reassumed the premiership in March, 1938, did France make plans to send an Ambassador.[26] This suggests that Delbos himself may have been the chief roadblock to normalizing relations with Italy, particularly since Chautemps was decidedly more pro-Italian than Blum. Perhaps, as some suggest, this vacancy at the French Embassy, the Farnese Palace, for two critical years was an important lost opportunity.[27] Delbos' posture gives little indication, however, that he would have favored a rapprochement with Italy, in any case.

To be sure, he did occasionally profess his desire to develop closer relations. Before the Chamber on December 4, 1936, he noted that there were more factors uniting than dividing Italy and France. The only real difference between them arose out of France's obligations to the League. But then, obviously referring to the ambassadorial impasse, he asked, Why should Italy ask of France initiatives that it did not ask of others? He expressed his hope that a general solution could be found for the questions dividing them. But, just as he had failed to put forth any proposals in his meeting with Cerruti, he made no new suggestions upon which a solution might be based.[28] Again, on January 2, 1937, after the conclusion of the Anglo-Italian "Gentleman's Agreement," Delbos stated that he was "delighted at the joint decision of the British and Italian governments to make known the friendly character of their relations."[29] He gave no indication, however, that France wished to join the agreement, although his desire to remain close to Britain indirectly made France a party to it.

The fact that relations with Italy were not about to be improved can be seen in the speeches of Blum and Delbos during the next few weeks. Blum, speaking at Lyon, and Delbos, at Châteauroux, both made virtual *tours d'horizon* of the international situation. But they did not even mention Italy.[30] Moreover, Blum later admitted that at the end of January, 1937, Cerruti brought him a special message from Mussolini. The Italian Ambassador said that Mussolini "detests Hitler" and that he felt an "insurmountable repulsion" for him. Furthermore, Mussolini was convinced that "if France and Italy were closely united, nothing in the world could resist this bloc of 80 million Latins." The only question separating the two "Latin sisters" was Spain. If, however, France would allow Franco to establish himself in Spain, Mussolini would obtain Franco's good will and friendship for France. Blum replied that although he also wished to improve Franco-Italian relations, the best way would be for Italy to honor the Nonintervention Agreement in Spain. Both Delbos and Léger agreed to Blum's rebuff of the Italian *démarche*.[31]

Although proponents of the Gentleman's Agreement anticipated that it would modify Mussolini's attitude toward the Spanish war, quite the contrary happened. During the spring and summer of 1937 Italy continued to increase its shipments of arms and troops to Franco. By October there were sixty thousand Italians fighting in Spain.[32]

In the meantime, Delbos' smoldering antagonism toward Italy increased apace. Fuel was added to the fire when he attempted to conclude the Mutual Assistance Pact in Eastern Europe. The Italians, who regarded it as being anti-Italian as much as anti-German, applied the *coup de grâce* to the pact's slim chances of success by concluding an entente with Yugoslavia.[33] By detaching the Yugoslavs from the Little Entente, Mussolini effectively ruined the proposed Eastern pact that Delbos so eagerly sought. When Neville Chamberlain and Camille Chautemps, the new French Premier, indicated their desire to appease Mussolini, Delbos was further irritated.[34] Ambassador Bullitt reported that Delbos "was in disagreement with Chautemps' policy of rapprochement with Italy. . . . Both he (Delbos) and Blum loathed Mussolini intensely and believed that Chautemps' efforts to reach reconciliation with Italy would be interpreted by Mussolini as a sign of weakness. They (Delbos and Blum) believed that Mussolini would merely be encouraged to further violence." He feared that Chautemps' efforts would only lead to "further outrages" by Italy. Moreover, he said that he was furious with Chamberlain and Eden for having initiated a rapprochement with Italy. It was in this connection that he referred to Italy as being a "relatively unimportant jackal."[35]

As we have seen, Italian aggression at the end of the summer of 1937 demolished the hopes that Chamberlain and Chautemps had for an understanding with Italy. Spurred on by the Italian submarine attacks against neutral shipping in the Mediterranean and the flagrant

Italian celebrations over Italy's contribution to the Nationalist victories at Bilbao and Santander, Delbos responded by engineering the Western success at the Nyon Conference in September, 1937. His attitude during the entire negotiations indicated his smoldering hostility towards Italy. His goal was the termination of Italian aggression in the Mediterranean. That goal was achieved as the naval attacks quickly subsided, but Delbos' action was hardly calculated to win friends in Italy.

As Delbos promoted a hardening of the French attitude during the late summer and fall of 1937, anti-French feeling grew in Italy. The bitterness among Italians toward France led Sir Eric Drummond, the British Ambassador in Rome, to observe that "mutual distrust and dislike are an almost constant factor in Franco-Italian relations." He reported that "most Italians are aroused to a high pitch of exasperation." Even Italian moderates wondered if it would be possible to establish *bon voisinage* on mutually satisfactory terms. France's position during the Abyssinian War and the Spanish Civil War was proof of its desire to continue its old policy of discouraging the growth of a potentially powerful neighbor.[36]

On October 30, 1937, Cerruti left a communiqué at the Quai d'Orsay recalling that the French Ambassador had not been replaced since de Chambrun had been called home on October 31, 1936. The Italian government could not tolerate the resulting *"disparité"* in diplomatic representation any longer. Therefore, Cerruti had been instructed to return to Italy for an "indefinite leave" on the following day, October 31.[37] It was a blunt quid pro quo scarcely designed to improve relations between the two countries.

Toward the end of November the Italian press found a new occasion to unleash violent attacks against France. According to the Italian press, César Campinchi, the French Minister of Marine, had declared in a speech at Toulon that Corsica must be defended by every means against inevitable Italian aggression. The island would be needed as a base for an offensive to "bring fascism to its knees."[38] Campinchi denied the statements attributed to him. A semiofficial statement published on November 28 supported Campinchi's denial and asked that an end be put to the press attacks against France. They could only be harmful to relations between the two countries.[39] The whole affair led Delbos to observe that the Italians were "behaving like lunatics."⁴⁰ Eden later reported to the British cabinet that in discussing Italy during their visit to London prior to Delbos' trip through Eastern Europe, the French Ministers had "shown more signs of irritation than on any other subject." Delbos and Chautemps had agreed that it was desirable to improve relations with Italy. But they had insisted that before any negotiations could be undertaken, a halt must be made in Italian press polemics and propaganda such as those leveled against Campinchi. Eden later relayed this message to Count Grandi, the Italian Ambassador in London.⁴¹ Keith Feiling, Chamberlain's biographer, wrote that during the meeting "French contempt for Italy was much in evidence."⁴²

Relations between the two countries remained bad for the rest of the year. The continued press campaign against France led Blondel to wonder if it might be leading up to a rupture of diplomatic relations. The Chargé d'Affaires' pessimism was echoed by François Charles-Roux, the French Ambassador at the Vatican, although he did not discount the possibility that the disquieting outbursts against France might be intended for internal consumption.⁴³ During the early weeks of 1938, however, aside from isolated incidents which were played down by both sides, the press attacks abated.⁴⁴

It will be recalled that in February, Chamberlain decided to make an approach to Italy aiming at another "Gentleman's Agreement." Delbos did not wish to take the initiative for a rapprochement with Italy, but he did not oppose Chamberlain's efforts. On February 25, during a debate in the Chamber of Deputies, Delbos indicated that he agreed with Chamberlain's approach concerning a Mediterranean agreement. But he declared that a final liquidation of the Abyssinian question would be possible only if an end was put to the dispatch of men and munitions to Spain and if a stop was put to propaganda directed against France.⁴⁵ This proved to be Delbos' last statement on the problem, but it showed that he had not greatly altered his attitude. Relations between the two countries did not improve during the remainder of his tenure at the Quai d'Orsay.

"France is and remains by far the [i.e., Germany's] most terrible enemy," wrote Adolf Hitler in *Mein Kampf*.⁴⁶ Delbos early recognized the Nazi and fascist threats. In 1933, not long after Hitler's seizure of power, he noted the danger that existed for France "while Germany is prey to the spirit of revenge, inflamed by misery and despair."[47] He argued that the "disturbing states of mind of the Germany of the steel-helmeted barons, magnates, and Nazis and of fascist Italy, who did not even take the trouble to conceal their belligerent designs against our allies and ourselves," were the most important reasons for concluding an alliance with the Soviet Union.[48] For him "the surest means of calming pan-Germanism and fascism [is] to remove the assistance that they anticipate."[49]

As we have seen, for the next three years Delbos ardently promoted the Franco-Soviet Pact as the German threat continued to increase. In the years prior to the Popular Front, of course, the most manifest indication of Germany's resurgence was its Rhineland coup only three months before the Blum government took office. Due to the timidity displayed by the Sarraut government, the French military, and its British ally, France did nothing. Frenchmen were shocked and alarmed at Hitler's brazen repudiation of the Locarno Treaty, but they were more interested in considering Hitler's proposals than in condemning his action.

France, Britain, and Belgium conferred in March; the Council of the League denounced Germany's violation of the Versailles Treaty; and peace plans were formulated. On May 6, after consulting with the French, the British addressed a questionnaire to the Germans to attempt to establish a basis for negotiating a settlement. Confronted with only verbal protest, Germany saw little need to negotiate. Hitler reacted to the British effort with feigned annoyance, and the questionnaire went unanswered.[50] It was the misfortune of the Popular Front government that it assumed power in the aftermath of the Rhineland coup. In the intervening three months Hitler's gamble had become a *fait accompli*.

Nevertheless, the new French government was determined to reach a reasonable understanding with Germany. Despite warnings by the French Ambassador in Berlin, André François-Poncet, that Hitler was a "pirate chief," ready to attack any weak ships that passed by, Blum indicated that he would be ready to send Delbos to Berlin if there was a possibility of an arrangement.[51] In their foreign-policy statement on June 23, 1936, Delbos told the Chamber and Blum told the Senate that "the *Rassemblement populaire* have always fought for a Franco-German entente." After all, Jean Jaurès had lost his life because of his fervent desire for peace between the two peoples. They were determined to pursue the Locarno policy for the honor and security of the two countries. Chancellor Hitler had on several occasions proclaimed his wish for an agreement with France. The government had no desire to doubt his word; but even though they sincerely desired an agreement, it was not possible to forget facts and the lessons of past experience. The declaration then recalled the repudiation of the military clauses of the Treaty of Versailles; the repudiation of the Locarno Pact; the presentation by the Locarno Powers of concrete proposals to arrive at a basis for a new security agreement; the presentation by Germany of counterproposals rejecting any system founded upon mutual assistance except with the Locarno Powers; and, finally, the entrusting of the British government with the task of elucidating certain points by means of a questionnaire to which the German government had not yet made a reply. Would the government reply tomorrow? "In any event, France will examine the German suggestions in the sincere desire to find the basis of an agreement, but such an agreement can not be realized unless it adheres to the principle of indivisible peace without a threat to anyone."[52] During the debate that followed the government's declaration, Delbos expressed the hope that the Germans would soon reply to various questions that had been put to them. Otherwise it would be necessary to reexamine the question of the Rhineland Pact.[53] "It was a strong hint that France wanted something done about Germany's failure to respond to the Locarno Powers."[54]

Blum later recalled that during July, he and Delbos had made two efforts, once in Geneva and once in London, to resolve the questions raised by the remilitarization of the Rhineland.[55] At Geneva on July 3, Delbos, Blum, Eden, and Van Zeeland, the Belgian Prime Minister, agreed that it would be necessary to call a meeting of the three Locarno signatories to reexamine the Rhineland situation in the light of Germany's refusal to answer the British questionnaire of May 6.[56] As we have seen, Delbos adamantly refused to agree to the British suggestion to have Germany included in the conference. Moreover, he felt that "the first order of business had to be to settle the situation created by the German initiative of March 7 and to negotiate afterwards . . . a new accord destined to replace the

Rhineland clauses of the Locarno Pact."[57] The three powers met in two sessions on July 23, with Delbos leading the French delegation at the morning session. They agreed to a vague statement in which they envisaged that European problems would be solved by another meeting, which would be expanded to include other interested powers. In the afternoon session Blum indicated the willingness of the French to talk with the Germans on an equal footing about all subjects, although he warned the delegates that "the perils that exist today are not peculiar to France and Germany." The three powers ultimately proposed a new five-power conference at which they would negotiate a new agreement designed to replace the Rhineland Pact of Locarno. Invitations to participate would be sent to Germany and Italy.

Delbos, however, remained skeptical that the five-power meeting would produce results.[58] His doubts proved to be well founded. The British did not deliver the invitations until September 17,[59] and the Germans procrastinated until October 12 before replying. In their response to the British note, the Germans merely reiterated the plan that they had proposed on March 31. Essentially, they proposed a nonaggression pact between Germany, France, and Belgium which would be guaranteed by Britain and Italy. In other words, the German reply rejected the inclusion of other interested powers, a prerequisite that Delbos had sought. By implication it rejected any eastern pact, particularly one involving the Soviet Union. Moreover, whereas the former Locarno Pact adhered to Article 16 of the Covenant of the League of Nations, the German reply denied the necessity of including the League in any deliberations over violations of the new pact.[60] Since Delbos and other French policy makers sought an eastern pact to accompany a western pact as well as a continuance of the League's role, the German reply was unacceptable. In addition, Delbos contended that the German idea of having Britain and Italy "intervene only as guarantor powers manifestly does not respond to the necessities of the present time." Although he admitted that the German note did not allow for optimism about the future of negotiations, Delbos believed that it would be a mistake to abandon the attempt.[61]

In the meantime, French contacts with Germany were proceeding along another route. On August 26, 1936, Hjalmar Schacht, the German Minister of National Economy and President of the Reichsbank, went to Paris to return a courtesy visit paid to him by Emile Labeyrie, Governor of the Bank of France. André François-Poncet later described Schacht as being "a cynic, a frantic blusterer, a person possessed of unbridled ambitions. Schacht threw his lot in with National Socialism; he foresaw its rise to power, contributed to it, and was rewarded accordingly. Yet he did not consider that the advantages he gained were proportionate to his merits."[62]

But the French Ambassador also noted that he was an intelligent man whose financial wizardry enabled the Nazi regime to commit enormous resources to rearmament without incurring inflation. He was well respected in world financial circles.[63]

In August, 1936, Schacht decided that the time was right to put forward Germany's colonial claims. His motives for doing so are debatable. Perhaps because he had "always been a zealous upholder of the colonial idea," he believed that Germany's need for raw materials and agricultural products could be fulfilled by regaining economic rights in the former German colonies.[64] Or perhaps he envisaged the acquisition of colonies as a method of diverting Hitler away from embarking upon a war over Czechoslovakia.[65]

Although his position as Reichsbank President did not carry diplomatic status, it often required him to meet with foreign leaders on official business; and Schacht used these opportunities to combine political and economic discussions. This is what he envisaged in August, 1936, when he obtained Hitler's permission to discuss with France the question of colonies for Germany. The Führer had been more interested in what Schacht termed "those fantasies of *Mein Kampf*," or expansion into Eastern Europe. But the Reichsbank President felt his superior might be bending. If concessions could be gained from the British and French, perhaps Hitler might become converted to colonial expansion.[66] Before setting off to Paris, Schacht talked with François-Poncet. The latter reported to Delbos that Schacht was very concerned about the European armaments race and the possibility that war might break out. He noted that Schacht wished to talk with various French officials, including Blum, Delbos, Auriol, Chautemps, and Daladier. François-Poncet advised them not to hestitate to speak openly with Schacht.[67]

Upon his arrival in Paris on August 26, Schacht met with several French officials. The first meeting was at a state dinner attended by

Delbos, Labeyrie, Auriol, and several other Ministers. At this gathering Schacht expounded upon Germany's economic difficulties, its lack of raw materials, and its consequent need for colonies. He made an appeal for cooperation between France, Germany, and Britain in colonial and economic matters. After this general meeting Schacht expressed his desire to talk with Blum alone before leaving Paris. Blum doubted that a special meeting would produce any significant results, but he consented.[68]

The news of Schacht's visit produced considerable excitement in Paris among the Socialists and Communists. Therefore, on August 28, while the press corps thought Blum was merely walking in the Hôtel Matignon gardens and waited for him at the front gate, Schacht was whisked in through a back gate on the Rue de Babylone for a secret meeting with the Premier.[69] In spite of Blum's doubts as to its value, the meeting went well, and he was surprised when Schacht proceeded to develop his ideas more fully "though without noticeably greater precision."[70] Schacht maintained that the question of colonies and raw materials was now of vital importance to Germany. He wished to see confidential negotiations between France, Germany, and Britain started as soon as possible. The outcome could be a German guarantee of a general European settlement and its agreement to the reduction and limitation of armaments, if in return Germany could obtain some satisfaction in the colonial sphere. Schacht explained, however, that it was impossible for Germany to give any direct guarantee to Russia. But Blum understood him to mean that Germany would guarantee that it would not attack Russia. Blum reiterated that France could not conceive of a general disarmament agreement that excluded the Soviet Union. Schacht hedged. He did not foresee the complete exclusion of Russia, but he noted that an agreement with the Soviets need not be concluded immediately. It would be necessary to go slowly. Besides, Schacht argued, Blum must remember that Germany's ideology presented an insuperable obstacle to a direct agreement with the Soviets. Blum retorted that he doubted whether ideological differences were as important in diplomacy as it was sometimes thought. After all, Tsarist Russia had consummated an alliance with prewar Radical France, and it was the Right in France that had authored the Franco-Soviet Pact of 1935. The relieving of French apprehensions about Germany, which had brought on such a policy, would be the simplest way to solve the situation. Schacht appeared impressed and said that he would repeat the argument to Hitler.[71]

Blum stated that his greatest fear was that should negotiations fail, the diplomatic situation might be seriously aggravated. He maintained that "we will renounce neither our engagements nor our friendships, and that we will do nothing which may justify the suspicions of powers upon whom we count in case of a grave crisis." He made it clear that France wanted a general European settlement, not merely an agreement with Germany. Once a general settlement and a reduction of arms had been achieved, it would not be impossible to have conversations on Germany's colonial requests. Blum told Schacht that the British, as France's ally, must be consulted on such conversations. But he said, "I am ready to engage in conversations immediately." Schacht replied that it would be necessary for him to report the results of his meetings to Hitler and get his approval. But he urged that conversations between the three powers start as soon as possible. He insisted upon secrecy to ensure the success of the negotiations. Schacht even urged Blum to go to London immediately and tell the British of the outcome of the Paris meeting; Blum replied that such a trip was not consistent with maintaining secrecy. It would attract less attention if he were to inform Eden when the latter passed through Paris on his way to Geneva.[72] Before Schacht departed, Blum made it clear that he should remember to report two points to Hitler. First, "I do not want our desire for peace to be turned against France." Second, "success is only possible in a certain atmosphere." He warned that French public opinion "will not indefinitely tolerate new surprises. It will be impossible to convince it if . . . there is not a détente, if we do not organize now a kind of truce."[73]

After his meeting with Blum, Schacht returned to Berlin to report to Hitler and to lay before him the French position. He suggested that the French Ambassador in Berlin be invited to Berchtesgaden for an unofficial conversation. This Hitler did. On September 2 François-Poncet paid his visit. Hitler declared his support of Schacht's initiative before he launched into a tirade about the Bolshevik menace confronting Europe. "The Franco-Soviet Pact was, in this regard, an error, an appalling mistake." He conjured up the specter of a

Communist takeover in France, an eventuality which he would consider as having international implications. Between France and Germany there was no longer a serious dispute. The Saar and Alsace had been settled, "so an entente with France was still possible; like Dr. Schacht . . . he was ready to investigate it thoroughly." But he was skeptical about obtaining a colonial domain for Germany. "The French, he said, will subordinate their consent to that of the English; the English will take refuge behind the French. Both, finally, will only give up the colonies which do not belong to them! It is necessary, however, to understand that in order to live, Germany cannot do without raw materials. My task is as simple as it is pressing. I have to assure a people of 67 million the possibility of work and support. Germany wants to gain the means, amicably. If not, it will procure them another way."[74]

On September 20 Blum gave a full account of Schacht's proposal to Eden as the latter passed through Paris on his way to Geneva. The British Foreign Secretary was astonished at the method used by the Germans to put forth their "feeler," although Schacht had conveyed German inquiries before. He warned Blum that since "the French Government had been more forthcoming in the matter of colonies than His Majesty's Government," he thought it important that they "should both guard against the dangerous possibilities that such reports foreshadowed." He added that there was a danger in negotiations started on the basis that France and Britain were willing to discuss Germany's desire for colonial compensation, even though that basis was combined with a German intimation of a desire for a European settlement and for an agreement for the reduction and limitation of armaments. "It was true," Eden reported, "that the German attitude . . . appeared to constitute a considerable advance, but when accurately defined the German proposals . . . might be found to mean a great deal or very little. Even if they only meant very little, we should have been committed to a discussion with Germany of her desire for satisfaction in the colonial sphere. That was something that I at any rate could not agree to at present." Blum agreed that he disliked the German method of procedure. On the other hand, he was very reluctant to allow such an opportunity for a European settlement, if it was one, to slip by. He asked, "Were we to shut the door? Were we to offer a flat refusal?" After some discussion it was decided that Eden should formulate the British position.[75]

On October 2 Eden warned Blum, "In my opinion Schacht was clever, if not cunning." He expressed the fear that Germany wished to commit Britain and France to colonial conversations while retaining freedom of action, and "Blum acquiesced good-naturedly, and did not pursue his exchanges with Schacht."[76] As Blum later admitted, "negotiations, therefore, were stillborn."[77] He did not desire to override British opposition.

One student of Schacht's visit to Paris, Earl Beck, correctly noted that the real question is " 'Out of whose hat had he pulled the rabbit?'—where did he find this plan for the future of world peace?"[78] In other words, did Schacht's initiative really constitute a sincere effort at establishing a viable peace, or was it merely a pipe dream conjured up by a cunning maneuverer who was hopeful of increasing his stature in German political circles? In view of Hitler's past proposals and conduct, Beck came to this conclusion: "That Hitler authorized Schacht to make these additions to Hitler's proposals of March seems dubious."[79] Further evidence that Schacht acted on his own initiative is provided by Blum. He told Eden that Schacht had stated that "he had no mission from the German Chancellor to discuss these matters," although Hitler was aware of his visit.[80]

Nevertheless, Hitler's disclosure to François-Poncet that he had "authorized M. Schacht to pursue the path in which he was engaged," indicated some high-level support for Schacht's proposal.[81] It is doubtful, however, that this interest in colonial acquisitions would have been more than a temporary diversion for Hitler, although he might have considered it to be useful. After all, he seriously doubted that Britain and France would concede any of their colonial holdings. But having made the offer of a general European settlement and arms limitation in exchange for colonial concessions, the onus for the failure of the proposals would fall upon Britain and France. Moreover, the negotiations would distract world attention away from Eastern Europe. It is here, after all, that Hitler's main thrust for Lebensraum was directed, and there is little evidence that he ever seriously considered giving up his designs in that area in exchange for a colonial empire overseas. In any event, the negotiations did not ever begin.

For the purpose of this study, one must wonder what opinion

Delbos held on the Schacht initiative. It is difficult to discover. He did meet with Schacht while the latter was in Paris. But the editors of the *Documents diplomatiques français* tell us that no record of this meeting can be found in the French archives.[82] Moreover, the other published French documents are unrevealing on the matter. Therefore, any estimate of his role and viewpoint must be largely based upon conjecture. At this early stage of the Blum government's tenure in office, Delbos was in close agreement with Blum on matters of foreign policy. In their foreign-policy statement of June 23, they had committed themselves to finding the basis for an agreement with Germany. Therefore, it is unlikely that he would have opposed at this point any effort to that end. Indeed, in a foreign-policy debate in the Chamber on July 31, he had reiterated the French desire for an agreement with Germany. He expressed the belief that no territorial difference existed between the two countries, and that it was "false to say that Franco-German antagonism is the origin of all the ills of Europe." Franco-German relations were only a part of much wider and more general problems.[83] Delbos later confided to Ambassador Bullitt that both he and Blum were most anxious to initiate direct conversations with Germany. They had both believed since 1919 that peace in Europe could not exist except on the basis of a complete reconciliation between Germany and France. He added: "It is a horrible absurdity that at a [*sic;* time?] like the present when I believe that Germany desires peace with France and France ardently desires peace with Germany, Europe should be plunging toward war because the two countries stand scowling at each other like dogs."[84] At about the same time Delbos told Count von Welczeck, the German Ambassador in Paris, that he believed that the entire French nation desired a settlement with Germany, "now or never." Neither France nor England wanted to bar the door to Germany's desires. Delbos proposed that Germany "should have raw materials, colonies, and loans, in return for which the only compensation required [of Germany] was *peace.*" But peace "could be attained only by deeds, not declarations. The most important prerequisite was the creation of an atmosphere of peace, without which the tender little plant of understanding could not thrive. One of the prime requirements was a disarmament of minds, not of armies." He believed that as long as the state-controlled German press continued to depict

France as a decadent country, disintegrating and standing on the verge of Bolshevism, an understanding would remain impossible. "If Germany wished to rejoin the concert of Europe . . . and was willing to observe [its] standards, . . . the door was open for successful negotiations."[85]

It is clear that Delbos wanted to begin negotiations with Germany in an effort to insure the peace of Europe. Why then did he not seize upon Schacht's visit and proposals to lead France into initiating such conversations? There appear to have been two reasons. One explanation can be found in Germany's actions in the Spanish Civil War. On at least two occasions, Delbos told German representatives in Paris that a solution in Spain was the precondition for initiating conversations concerning the German claims and a possible general European settlement. On December 11 he told the German Chargé d'Affaires that he believed that "the continuance of the [Schacht] negotiations depended upon the improvement of the general atmosphere. After the settlement of the Spanish crisis we could, as [Delbos] repeated several times, discuss all questions affecting Germany." He was of the opinion that joint action by the great powers in mediating the Spanish war would improve the general atmosphere and also form a point of departure for further Franco-German collaboration.[86] On December 24 Delbos repeated to Welczeck, "in a calm and decisive tone," that the Spanish question appeared to him to be most acute. The continuation of ideological warfare in Spain must inevitably lead to a world war. Therefore, he suggested the following steps in pursuing meaningful Franco-German negotiations:

1. Collaboration in isolating and extinguishing the Spanish conflagration.
2. Creation of an atmosphere conducive to peace.
3. Discussion and satisfaction of Germany's wishes and, at the same time, settlement of the Locarno question.
4. Limitation of armaments.[87]

There is little doubt that Delbos, as the principal organizer of the nonintervention scheme, could hardly initiate negotiations with a power that was one of the blatant violators of that plan. This would certainly create an embarrassing situation for the Blum government. Moreover, as he told Welczeck, the possibility of a massing of German troops in a country with which France had a vulnerable frontier made many French patriots uneasy. Delbos warned, "France could not permit the fate of this neighbor country to be decisively influenced . . . by another power, no matter whether the latter sympathized with the Right or with the Left."[88]

The second explanation for Delbos' reluctance to pursue Schacht's proposal vigorously—although not necessarily second in his own mind —was the British reluctance to consider Schacht's proposal seriously. Once again, at the risk of seeming redundant, it must be made clear that Delbos valued the British alliance above all else and was unwilling to take any initiative that might arouse their displeasure. Delbos admitted to Bullitt that Welczeck was essentially correct in his assertion that Schacht's visit had not been followed up by the French due to British resistance. "The British frowned because Schacht had mentioned colonies." Delbos said that the French willingness to discuss the colonial problem disturbed the British. He added, however, that "although France must be extremely careful to maintain her present good relations with England, the French Foreign Office would remain independent enough to indulge in direct conversations with Germany."[89] Yet one point remains clear: Once again the British viewpoint had prevailed. Their apprehension about Schacht and their reluctance to consider colonial concessions helped to deter Delbos and Blum from pursuing the conversations. Moreover, there is little reason to believe, in spite of Delbos' assurances to the contrary, that France would embark upon any serious negotiations without first consulting with the British. Blum had made this quite clear to Schacht during their meeting. After all, why throw away whatever good will had been gained with Britain by entering into any direct negotiations with Germany to which the former might object.

Nevertheless, one scholar, Nathanael Greene, has written, "Both Delbos and Blum were committed to an accommodation with Hitler: Delbos on the condition that Germany assist in bringing hostilities in Spain to a speedy conclusion, Blum on the condition that Germany signify her will to disarm."[90] They continued to leave the way open for possible negotiations and used every opportunity to indicate their willingness to talk. On December 4, during a Chamber debate on foreign affairs, Delbos clearly stated his German policy. While recognizing the differences in ideology, he declared that "nothing is more

necessary for the tranquility of Europe than a Franco-German rapprochement." But, in an obvious reference to the Rhineland, he asserted, "In order to understand each other it is necessary on both
sides to avoid threats and slights. This is not the impression that we
get when treaties on which our security depends are torn up uni-
laterally." He expressed his desire that all obstacles to a rapprochement be removed. To assure Germany of France's peaceful intentions,
he reiterated that France had no desire for hegemony in Europe or
for an encirclement of Germany; it sought only "a general effort
towards economic recovery and towards disarmament." France would
not dispute any of Germany's legitimate claims, but he warned that
it would not permit any nonaggression treaty in Western Europe,
along the lines of another Locarno, to "constitute for any one of its
signatories a blank check [blanc-seing] authorizing them to pursue
elsewhere a policy of aggression." Therefore, France sought a general
European settlement to prevent the possibility of aggression any-
where.[91]

Blum, who concluded the debate with a statement of his own,
supported Delbos' declaration by saying, "We remain ready in any
manner, on any grounds, for political, economic, and technical conversations that will permit a general settlement of European problems."[92] As we have seen, Delbos followed up his statement with
conversations with the German representatives on December 11 and
23. The theme was the same. France was willing to make concessions
as long as the Spanish war could be ended and a general European
settlement sought. He was convinced that these need not be insurmountable obstacles in the path of negotiations.

The efforts of Delbos and Blum in the fall and early winter of
1936 appear to have been the high point of their attempts to negotiate a settlement with Germany. As 1937 wore on, the continuing
German intervention in Spain, the apparent solidification of the
Berlin-Rome Axis, the increased possibility of German aggression
against Austria and Czechoslovakia, the inclination towards neutrality
in Belgium and Eastern Europe, and continuing German rearmament,
all appear to have promoted a hardening of attitude towards Germany. To be sure, the Frenchmen never tired of calling for a Franco-
German and general European settlement. At Lyon on January 24,
1937, Blum emphasized that the French government did not doubt

for a moment Hitler's expressed desire for peace. Perhaps an economic deal could be worked out between the two powers, but it was impossible to deny the interrelation of political and economic questions. What country would give help to another unless it could be certain that the resources contributed would not someday be turned against it? In other words, "How can economic agreement be conceived independently of a political settlement?" A convention for the limitation of armaments would necessarily form an essential part of any general European settlement. He concluded that there was a close connection between the Franco-German problem and the European problem as a whole. If the Germans would give proof of their will to cooperate, France was ready to collaborate with them without reservations.[93]

At Châteauroux, a week later, Delbos replied to a speech that Hitler had made to the Reichstag on the previous day. He gladly noted that the Führer had affirmed his desire for peace and that he had refrained from attacking France. In fact, Hitler had affirmed that "peace is our supreme good: Germany will do what it can to contribute in detail to this work." Although Hitler had done nothing to strengthen European confidence by his earlier repudiations and denunciations, no doubt he was turning over a new page in declaring himself ready to collaborate loyally in the future. Delbos echoed Blum's words when he reiterated that the economic reconstruction of Europe would depend upon an atmosphere of peace and upon the supervision and limitation of armaments. In this regard, he said, "We will ask nothing from Germany that would not be asked of everyone, including France itself." Convinced that war was not inevitable, France would leave untried no procedure of conciliation, no initiatives, and no efforts at understanding. "The sole limit to this desire for peace is our inflexible resolution to defend ourselves if we are attacked and to remain faithful to the obligations that we have undertaken."[94]

Despite these overtures by Delbos and Blum, the Germans did not reply with concrete proposals of their own. Delbos did reveal to Bullitt some of his ideas for reintegrating Germany into the economy of the rest of the world. A first step envisaged bilateral negotiations for the reduction of tariff barriers. Second, he and Blum had envisioned the creation of consortia to develop parts of Africa.

They would be based upon French, British, and American money and German machines. To complete the entire plan, Germany would be given a colony, probably the Cameroons. All of the European colonial holdings would be exploited by the international consortia which could utilize German products. In this way German manufacturing genius could hopefully be turned away from war production. At the same time, efforts would be made to reach an arms-limitation agreement with Germany. He declared, "You cannot expect France or any other nation to help supply Germany with iron and steel in order to receive it back in the form of shells and bombs."[95]

Delbos indicated that he had no other plans for a settlement with Germany. There is little indication, moreover, that even this proposal got off the ground. A deterrent may have been the German reply on March 16 to two British notes of November, 1936. The British had reiterated the need for a new Western pact to replace the Locarno Agreements. The notes had put forth the British view on the problems facing the powers and had invited the powers to indicate their opinions on the most advantageous method of resolving the differences between the powers.[96] The German reply rejected a guarantee to Britain in any new Western pact. The agreement should be limited to a nonaggression pact between France and Germany which would be guaranteed by England and Italy. But the British and Italian guarantee would not become effective until both powers had decided that there had been aggression. Delbos bluntly noted that "in view of the close working agreement between Germany and Italy—if not alliance—and the knowledge which has been gained . . . as a result of the Spanish experience as to the degree of reliance that may be placed in the good faith of Italy, the value for France of any such supposed guarantee is only too evident." The German reply allowed no role for the League of Nations to decide whether aggression had occurred. "Germany was proposing . . . to wipe out the League of Nations and the whole system of security in Europe as it exists today."[97] Moreover, Delbos believed that the German proposal also would have dropped the French mutual-assistance treaties with Poland, Czechoslovakia, and Russia by preventing France from going to the assistance of those countries. A new Franco-German nonaggression pact would have bound France not to come to the aid of those countries should a conflict with Germany break out.[98] "The German

reply was in effect negative, and does not advance matters at all."
He believed that the proposals had been made "more for the purpose
of gaining time than with any hope that they might be accepted."[99]
The German rebuff apparently was a real setback for whatever
hopes Delbos may have retained for a general European settlement
based upon a Franco-German rapprochement. During the next few
months he began to reorientate his thinking, and he made no effort
to approach the Germans. At the end of May, however, Schacht
turned up in Paris once again, this time to open the German pavilion
at the World's Exposition. After the usual ceremonies, Schacht again
met alone with Blum. The latter sharply scored the Reichsbank
President for the impression he had spread that Blum was responsible
for the failure of their earlier initiative. Convincing the British had
been "difficult and ticklish." Blum argued that Schacht "had been
somewhat mistaken when he assured me that I should find the British
Government much better disposed . . . than I might imagine as far
as the colonial question was concerned." Besides, in his Lyon speech,
Blum noted that he had kept the door open for further discussions.
But no German reply had been given. Blum reiterated once again
the French position. A preliminary meeting should determine whether
a political settlement was possible. After all, he asked, "How can
a country be expected to contemplate economic conventions capable
of increasing the strength of another country which it fears may be
an aggressor?" Blum clearly showed his impatience with Schacht and
the German tactics. He emphasized, "There are two illusions that
Berlin must give up: the first is that they will succeed in separating
Great Britain and France; the second is that through a latent revolutionary crisis, France is being destroyed as a factor in European
affairs. . . . Not at all! I do not know what the future of our government will be; I do not know how the political situation will evolve;
but France will not disintegrate." He declared that the time was past
when the peace of Europe depended solely upon a Franco-German
rapprochement, although it was still a necessary condition. But he
said, "It is impossible for us to conceive of bilateral Franco-German
agreements that disregard the rest of Europe and that will paralyze
us in any European conflicts in which our vital interests or our signature might be at stake." Moreover, neither Britain nor France would
accept a League of Nations "not only reduced to its lowest terms in

the present but deprived of all capacity for development in the future."
Blum laid down his proposals around which conversations could
begin:

1. General settlement of European problems
2. General limitation of armaments
3. The drawing up of conditions for Germany's reentry into
   the League of Nations.[100]

Joel Colton has correctly noted that Blum's comments reflected
a hardening of his attitude towards Germany.[101] The German Foreign
Office observed that the Blum statements could not offer a suitable
basis for initiating more extensive negotiations and that Blum "was
not really ready to offer us anything tangible at all but did . . . re-
iterate the familiar demands for a general settlement." It noted that
"the compensation that he was still ready to offer us in August,
1936, concessions to our colonial demands, he expressly termed in-
appropriate." The Germans wondered how Blum "could believe that
we would be prepared to regard this repetition of time-worn French
demands, accompanied only by quite vague promises to make concessions to us, as a serious offer to negotiate."[102]

Quite probably Blum did not expect anything serious to develop,
and neither did Delbos. As we have seen, the Axis refusal to observe
strict nonintervention in the Spanish war had increasingly antagonized
the French Foreign Minister.[103] In addition, only a day after the
Blum-Schacht conversations, the *Deutschland* incident and the German retaliatory bombardment of Almeria had incensed Delbos. Confronted with the German decision to withdraw from the control
scheme and the nonintervention discussions, Delbos and Blum could
hardly be expected to embrace Schacht and his vague proposals.
There is probably some truth to Schacht's later contention that "Hitler
spoiled everything by his intervention in the Spanish civil war."[104]
It is difficult, however, to disagree with the Wilhelmstrasse's view
that the Schacht initiatives had not been a "missed opportunity" for
improving Franco-German relations.[105] Despite French willingness
to make concessions, little of substance had come from the German
side. Moreover, the frequent French and British proposals for initiating meaningful negotiations for a Western pact had repeatedly met
with German intransigence. In fact, Delbos believed that the German

reply of March was designed to destroy the very basis of France's security system. In any event, by November Schacht had fallen out of favor with Hitler and had been removed as Minister of National Economy, although he remained as President of the Reichsbank.[106] Any further chance of utilizing Schacht's efforts to create a Franco-German entente, if indeed the opportunity ever really existed, disappeared.

During the summer of 1937 there was a marked stiffening of Delbos' attitude towards Germany. The Spanish question was undoubtedly the most significant factor in Delbos' change of posture. After he had sharply deprecated the German retaliatory bombardment of Almeria following the *Deutschland* incident, he became further dissatisfied when the Germans withdrew from the naval patrol scheme following the *Leipzig* incident. Meanwhile, the Germans continued to violate the Nonintervention Agreement and to press for the recognition of belligerent status for General Franco. In Delbos' opinion, Franco should be recognized as a belligerent only after all foreign volunteers had been withdrawn from Spain and effective controls had been initiated to prevent their return. But Germany and Italy remained cool towards any such plan, and the usual stalemate occurred in the Nonintervention Committee. Delbos became increasingly frustrated and bellicose as the summer wore on. He may even have considered opening the Franco-Spanish frontier to material bound for the Republicans. When the Italian naval attacks began in August, Delbos reacted strongly by calling for a united Western response. He only acquiesced to inviting Germany to the Nyon Conference in order to persuade Britain to permit Russian attendance. When the latter openly blamed Italy for the attacks, Germany chose to find the "unproved accusations" a convenient excuse for refusing to attend. It is unlikely that Delbos shed any tears over the German announcement.

By fall, Delbos warned that France and Germany would "commit the most tragic error if they did not continue to try to come to an understanding."[107] But Phipps was probably correct in reporting that Franco-German relations were "scarcely cordial." Furthermore, he believed that most Frenchmen considered that a satisfactory settlement with Germany was "fundamentally impossible."[108] Delbos increasingly feared that Germany was about to make a move against

Austria or Czechoslovakia.[109] Therefore, in November he began to formulate plans for his tour through Eastern Europe in order to revitalize France's prestige and alliances in that area. As we have seen, however, before departing, Delbos and Chautemps traveled to London to obtain a clarification of the British position and to learn the results of Lord Halifax's recent visit to Germany. Delbos had been very concerned lest Halifax had given encouragement to a German adventure in Czechoslovakia.[110] Consequently, major attention was focused upon the German problem during the Franco-British meeting on November 29–30. After Halifax's report on his trip, Delbos voiced his skepticism about German intentions in Austria and Czechoslovakia. He warned that Germany really sought to absorb those countries. He thought that there was little likelihood of an immediate German intervention in Czechoslovakia, but that "the Germans expected to get what they wanted in due course." As has been previously indicated, Chamberlain feared that the French Ministers might pressure the British into taking a more resolute stand in Central Europe.[111] But they did not.

On the subject of colonial concessions to Germany, a topic that had been discussed for over a year since Schacht had first proposed it, the British showed little more inclination to attempt to satisfy the German demands. An indication of Delbos' revised attitude was that he made no effort to pressure the British into reconsidering their position. He appeared quite satisfied that the "French and British Governments would make no proposals and that proposals would have to come . . . in the immediate future from the German side." Since he anticipated that the Germans would not put forth any such proposals, perhaps the question was in his own mind a dead issue.[112] In any case, the familiar Franco-British position was reiterated. No negotiations on colonies would take place before a discussion of other matters that would form the basis of a general settlement. The questions of disarmament, Germany's return to the League, and the conclusion of a Western pact were still regarded as essential elements in a general settlement which had to be reached before the colonial question could be broached.[113] In the light of the Hossbach Memorandum,[114] about which Delbos could not have known, there was little likelihood that Hitler would accept a plan that he had rejected earlier. In other words, the Franco-British position was justifiably tantamount to abandoning the question.

Delbos appeared relieved when he informed Bullitt of the outcome of the London Conference. It is quite apparent that he had given up any hopes of a rapprochement with Germany. Instead, he had again opted for strengthening the bonds with Eastern Europe, which had been designed to contain Germany. When he was met by Neurath at the railway station on his way through Berlin a few days later, he bluntly told the German Foreign Minister that the Western powers could only offer concessions if Germany was prepared to contribute its share towards a general settlement. He asked why Germany always seemed to resent any suggestion of such a settlement. Neurath replied that he believed it was a mistake to try to settle everything at once, that "the right method was to settle matters bit by bit."[115] This must have helped to confirm Delbos' belief that Germany had no intention of agreeing to a general settlement. After a year and a half of seeking a détente with Germany, he had been vindicated in his original belief that Germany constituted a most dangerous threat and that France must revitalize its security system in Eastern Europe before it was too late.

One wonders why, despite Hitler's obvious disinclination, Delbos made repeated overtures to negotiate a rapprochement with Germany, but did not make a similar effort with Italy. The explanation probably resides in a number of factors of varying importance.[116]

Many Frenchmen on the Left had a particular distaste for Mussolini, the first of the fascist dictators, which frequently did not extend with the same vigor to Hitler's brand of fascism.[117] Although a man of the moderate Left, Delbos undoubtedly found Mussolini's fascist regime particularly reprehensible. The parties of the Left and Center in France instinctively rejected the principles of the totalitarian state. Furthermore, as certain forms of fascist doctrine became increasingly popular among groups of the extreme Right—such as the Action Française, the Croix de Feu, and the Jeunesses Patriotes, among others—there was an increased polarization in French domestic politics. The Left regularly spoke of the riots of February 6, 1934, in terms of fascism and antifascism. It increasingly regarded the fascist Ligues as symbols of opposition to social reform and of oppression of the working classes.[118] There can be little doubt that the increased polarization of French domestic politics influenced diplomatic decisions to a certain extent. Mussolini was obviously a symbol of the rejection of the fundamental beliefs of individual freedom that Delbos undoubtedly shared with the rank-and-file of his party.[119] Yet having said all of this, there is little evidence to suggest that Delbos allowed ideology to play a very significant role in the determination of his policy towards Italy. Moreover, the same ideological considerations, if they were significant to Delbos, would have prevented him from seeking a rapprochement with Germany as well. What little difference there was between the totalitarian regimes of Italy and Germany was not sufficient to determine policy in the eyes of the French Left.

Another explanation for Delbos' attitude toward Italy might be found in strategic considerations and the repeated acts of aggression committed by Mussolini. As René Massigli, a former Director of the Political Section at the Quai d'Orsay noted, Mussolini had consistently broken agreements and promises during the twenties and thirties. Italian aggression in Abyssinia and Spain merely added to a long list.[120] As a believer in collective security, the League of Nations, and the need for general disarmament, Delbos must have been increasingly irritated as Italian aggression systematically violated the Covenant of the League, compromised the principle of collective security, and made nations threatened by aggression unwilling to consider disarmament. Moreover, the blatant Italian assistance sent to Franco compromised the nonintervention plan that Delbos had been so instrumental in initiating. Furthermore, should Italy establish itself in the Balearic Islands as a result of its participation in the Spanish war, it could directly threaten French communications with North Africa.[121] Strategically this would create an intolerable situation in case of a general European war. Finally, if Franco won the civil war, it would place another hostile state on France's vulnerable southern flank.

Mussolini's policy in Central and Eastern Europe must have also been disconcerting to Delbos. As we have seen, the Italo-Yugoslav Pact effectively destroyed Delbos' hopes of concluding a mutual-assistance pact among the Little Entente states. In addition, the announcement of the Rome-Berlin Axis could scarcely encourage the Eastern European states to believe that France could effectively come to their aid in the event of combined Axis aggression. It appeared as if Italy was intent upon destroying the French security system in Eastern Europe. Surely, then, Mussolini's actions were bound to alienate Delbos. Yet Germany also had intervened in the Spanish war and had continued its massive rearmament program; and its reoccupation of the Rhineland created a more direct threat to France's security than Italian presence in the Western Mediterranean. Italian acts of aggression and considerations of security, although important, cannot fully explain Delbos' refusal to normalize relations with Italy.

Jules Moch, Blum's Secretary-General of Staff Services, told this writer that both Italy and Germany were intensely disliked by the leaders of the Popular Front government. But in order to insure the peace, it was necessary to have negotiations with those who had the ability to make war and thus destroy the peace. He said that the feeling existed that the Italians posed no threat to France in a war. They had never been successful in warfare and never would be.[122] Here is the crux of the matter. The policy makers of the Popular Front, including Delbos, consistently refused to take Italy seriously.[123] In other words, as Léon Archimbaud, a Radical Socialist Deputy and long-time political associate of Delbos', explained it, the rank-and-file of the Radical party were convinced that Germany presented the real danger to France. Although the Italian danger might become acute within a few years, it "was a small matter indeed compared to the larger issue."[124] Delbos himself once told Eden that Mussolini was a question mark, but that Germany was the real problem, and no efforts should be spared to improve relations with that country.[125] This implied that no immediate effort needed to be made to reach a settlement with Mussolini. It was true that there were natural affinities between the two Latin countries. Yet one observer noted that the French liking for the Italians was not "untinged with contempt." The French never felt for Italy the "Schwärmerei" of the Germans or the admiration of the Victorian Englishman.[126] Another observer believed that "the French had a sort of ingrained contempt for the Italians and the Italians knew it."[127] The French disdain for the Italian military was quite obvious. After all, was there not a direct line from Adowa to Caparetto to Guadalajara?[128] Henri de Jouvenel, when asked what he thought of the Italian army, is said to have replied, "Eh bien, le départ serait magnifique!"[129] It was a point that continually rankled the Italians and helped to aggravate the tension between the two countries. The Italians began to feel that they had to show France their military worth.[130]

In any event, to a large extent, the repeated failures by Delbos to seize upon the Italian feelers to start negotiations appear to have been due to his own refusal to take Mussolini and his overtures seriously. Perhaps he was correct in believing that the Italian dictator was merely maneuvering to obtain time to consolidate Franco's victory in Spain. Whether, like Léon Blum, he considered Italy irrevocably tied to Germany, as the Rome-Berlin Axis and the Anti-Comintern Pact appeared to suggest, is not clear.

As Lloyd Thomas, the well-informed British Chargé d'Affaires suggested, his policy may also have been influenced by another line of reasoning. In the long run, Italian and German interests in Central Europe and Austria were incompatible. Italy had always been an opportunistic and "vacillating friend" of France. As soon as Mussolini became disenchanted with his new-found bedfellow, he would see that it was in Italy's best interest to rejoin the Western camp. In the meantime, the best policy would be to make the Franco-British camp as strong as possible. No effort should be made to pursue Mussolini, because he would merely interpret it as a sign of weakness. Besides, if left alone, he would see more quickly the disadvantages of his alliance with Hitler. The ultimate result would be the detachment of Rome from Berlin.[131]

This explanation must certainly remain in the realm of conjecture. But several points are clear. Neither ideological nor strategic considerations, while they cannot be rejected out of hand, were dominant factors in Delbos' policy. It is quite evident, however, that from the time of Mussolini's offers of good will and cooperation until his refusal to accredit Saint Quentin as French Ambassador in Rome, Delbos consistently refused to regard the Italian dictator seriously. Instead he chose to pursue Hitler with repeated overtures. Whether Mussolini could have been detached from Berlin is unclear. But Delbos made no effort to find out. On the other hand, the futility of his efforts to achieve a rapprochement with Germany became manifestly clear during the last few weeks of his tenure as Foreign Minister.

9

Resignation

As early as February, 1937, Delbos began to consider the possibility of a German invasion of Austria and what France's response to such an action would be. He observed that while France had promised to protect Czechoslovakia in the event of an invasion, it had no obligations to protect Austria.[1] During the last year of his tenure at the Quai d'Orsay, Delbos became increasingly concerned about the Austrian question. On April 22, Ambassador Bullitt observed that both Delbos and Alexis Léger, the Secretary General at the Quai d'Orsay, were apprehensive that Hitler might decide within twelve months "to provoke a Nazi revolt in Austria and support it by so-called 'volunteers' from Germany."[2] By the end of the month Delbos was of the opinion that "Hitler could now take Austria at any time he might choose without creating serious international complications."[3] Delbos believed that France was no longer strong enough to maintain the status quo in Central Europe against the combined strength of Germany and Italy. He remained emphatic: If Germany attacked Czechoslovakia, "France would immediately declare war on Germany"; but "France alone could not possibly march to the support of Austria." Mussolini had made it clear to Kurt von Schuschnigg, the Austrian Chancellor, that he would do nothing to prevent Austria from falling into Germany's hands. Delbos was "at his wits end to devise a method of meeting the problems which had now arisen."[4] By this time it was quite apparent that his proposed mutual-assistance pact for Eastern Europe never would be adopted. Moreover, his project for a rapprochement between Austria, Czechoslovakia, and Hungary really never got off the ground.[5] As we have seen, Delbos

181

tried to salvage the French position by making his tour through the Eastern European capitals in the fall of 1937.

Early in November, Franz von Papen, the German Ambassador in Austria, visited Paris. He was informed that France "would fulfill to the limit" its treaty obligations to Czechoslovakia. With regard to Austria, however, the French merely told von Papen that France would "view with disfavor any change in the status of Austria." Von Papen's visit strengthened Delbos' belief that Hitler's next move would be directed against Austria rather than Czechoslovakia. He speculated that von Papen's trip had been made to "ascertain whether France would react more violently to a German move against Czechoslovakia or to a move against Austria."[6] Von Papen later informed Neurath that Chautemps considered a reorientation of French policy in Central Europe as "entirely open to discussion." The French Premier "had no objection to a marked extension of German influence in Austria that was obtained through evolutionary means."[7] By the end of November, 1937, Ambassador Bullitt found Delbos "extremely apprehensive that Germany would in the near future make some sort of drive against Austria." The Germans clearly "were determined one way or another to incorporate Austria in the German Reich." He remained convinced that Germany would not move immediately against Czechoslovakia.[8]

It will be recalled that during the London Conference of November 29-30, 1937, Delbos and Chautemps had reiterated their opinion that although Germany might not immediately invade Czechoslovakia or Austria, "the Germans expected to get what they wanted in due course." The Frenchmen believed that France and Britain could either disinterest themselves or adopt a conciliatory attitude about the state of affairs in Central Europe (evidently resistance was not an alternative). It was noted that the Stresa Declaration had been the last statement of support for the territorial integrity of Austria as a necessary element in European peace. Delbos and Chautemps observed that although Italy's concern with Austrian affairs had waned, they could not believe that Italy had entirely disinterested itself in the fate of that country. They believed that the Austrian situation had to be taken into consideration in any negotiations with Germany.[9] Yet, as we have also seen, Delbos had nearly given up hope that a general settlement with Germany could be negotiated. Therefore, that path to securing Austria's position was probably closed from the start. It was decided that neither France nor Britain would announce in advance that it would go to war in defense of Austria against German aggression. On the other hand, neither would they renounce their support for Austria. In other words, "only the event could prove what would happen." Delbos added, however, that Czechoslovakia was a different matter. After all, France had treaty obligations to support the Czechs immediately in case of a German attack.[10] The point to be noted, as Delbos admitted after he returned from his trip through Eastern Europe, is that he increasingly feared a German move against Austria. But he had no constructive plans to prevent it. Instead, he characterized his policy as being one of "wait and see."[11]

In retrospect, the watershed of Delbos' tenure at the Quai d'Orsay came with the obvious failure of his trip through Eastern Europe. As can be seen by his policy of "wait and see," he was now virtually at a loss as to what was to be done. As the German pressure concerning Central Europe increased during the first two months of 1938, his sense of bewilderment, frustration, and exhaustion increased correspondingly.

Meanwhile, significant events came with disconcerting rapidity. On February 4, 1938, Hitler carried out a wholesale shake-up in the German military and the Foreign Ministry. Field Marshal Werner von Blomberg, General Werner von Fritsch, and Foreign Minister Baron Konstantin von Neurath, along with sixteen other high-ranking generals, all remnants of the old, conservative ruling class, were replaced. Hitler took personal command of the armed forces, with General Wilhelm Keitel heading his military staff. Joachim von Ribbentrop became the Foreign Minister. Hitler now was ready to begin carrying out the plans he had laid down on November 5, 1937. No further interference would be forthcoming from the military or the Foreign Office.[12]

On February 12, 1938, Hitler invited Chancellor von Schuschnigg to Berchtesgaden. Subjected to tremendous pressure by Hitler and his generals, Schuschnigg was given an ultimatum demanding that he appoint the Austrian Nazi Artur von Seyss-Inquart as Minister of Interior, grant a general amnesty to all Austrian Nazis, and incorporate the Austrian Nazi party in the government-sponsored Fatherland

Front.[13] Faced with the threat of German invasion, Schuschnigg replied, "We are not alone in the world. That probably means war." After discounting Italian and British aid to Austria, Hitler retorted: "And France? Well, two years ago when we marched into the Rhineland with a handful of battalions—at that moment I risked a great deal. If France had marched then, we should have been forced to withdraw. . . . But for France it is now too late!"[14]

Later that afternoon Schuschnigg submitted. This nazification threatened to turn Austria into a German satellite. During the weeks that followed the Berchtesgaden meeting, the Austrian Nazis became increasingly belligerent as Seyss-Inquart's police became more ineffective. On March 9 Schuschnigg finally decided to call for a national plebiscite to be held on March 13. He hoped that a favorable vote would unite the nation in opposition to an Anschluss. Schuschnigg's move precipitated the final crisis. Hitler was enraged at the Austrian Chancellor's display of independence, and he ordered the German army to march into Austria not later than March 12, the day before the proposed plebiscite.[15]

What were Delbos and the French doing during this period? As so frequently occurred during the interwar period, at a time of international crisis France was going through a bewildering change of government, combined with acrimonious debate over foreign policy. During the fall and winter of 1937, the Chautemps government had been confronted with renewed labor unrest, which extended even to the public services. Intransigence on both sides hindered Chautemps' efforts to arbitrate the situation. The domestic crisis was aggravated further by a new financial crisis and a weakening of the already unstable franc. On January 14 Chautemps called for a vote of confidence. After a sharp exchange with Ferdinand Ramette, the Communists decided to abstain from supporting the government. The resulting breach in the Popular Front coalition led Chautemps and his cabinet to resign on the following day. For the next three days the crisis continued as Georges Bonnet and Léon Blum made abortive efforts to form a government. Finally, on January 18, President Lebrun asked Chautemps to form another government. He agreed, but the Socialists refused to participate in the new cabinet and were replaced by Radicals.[16] Consequently, just as an international crisis was looming on the horizon, the domestic absurdity *de Chautemps à Chautemps* was rocking France. When Chautemps presented his new government to the Chamber, one deputy, André Albert, remarked before the vote, "The bigger the Government's majority, the less time will it last."[17] Indeed, the government obtained a record vote of confidence of 501 to 1 with 105 abstentions! Yet it was destined to live a precarious existence. Opposed by both the Communists and the Right, it was only reluctantly supported by the Socialists. Nobody expected it to be any more than a *ministère de transition* which, after an early defeat, would be replaced by a wider combination under Herriot.[18]

Another dimension of the January cabinet crisis was that of foreign policy. It was widely rumored, particularly on the Right, that the crisis was deliberately provoked by the Communists, who disapproved of the government's foreign policy. They were alarmed that France and Britain, in the aftermath of Halifax's trip to Germany and the ensuing trip to London by Delbos and Chautemps, might contemplate a rapprochement with Germany. This would disrupt the already lukewarm Franco-Soviet relations.[19] The evidence at our disposal makes any conclusive assessment of this interpretation impossible. But several facts are clear. As we have seen, Delbos, Blum, and Chautemps had consistently evaded Moscow's request that negotiations be started for a military convention to strengthen the Franco-Soviet Pact. Moreover, Delbos had rebuffed Litvinov's invitation to visit Moscow during his trip through Eastern Europe. By the end of the year, Gabriel Péri began launching bitter attacks in the Communist organ *L'Humanité* against the government's subservience to London and the wishes of the Little Entente. The attacks continued into the new year, until finally Péri openly called for the ouster of Delbos. On January 15, in the midst of the cabinet crisis, Péri wrote that a "minister who has a record as deplorable as that of M. Yvon Delbos must not resume his place at the Quai d'Orsay."[20] When Delbos retained his post in the new Chautemps Ministry, Cogniot wrote in *L'Humanité* that "the Hitlerian circles are happy . . . at the maintenance of M. Delbos at the Quai d'Orsay."[21] Although the Quai d'Orsay officially denied Soviet pressure for an extension of the Franco-Soviet Pact, it was rumored that Delbos encouraged the *Petit Parisien*, France's most widely read morning newspaper, to publish an article exposing the Communists' motives for the cabinet crisis.[22] Although there is no proof of this, Delbos was unmistakably upset over the attacks against him. He bitterly told Phipps that the charges were "clearly inspired by Moscow."[23] Whether the attacks were inspired by Moscow is uncertain. The important fact is that Delbos obviously believed that he was the victim of unjustified Communist attacks.

On January 21 the new Chautemps government promised to continue the foreign policy of the previous governments. It professed faith in the League of Nations, but assured the Chamber that a great effort would be made in national defense.[24] During the ensuing month, as the new government sought to establish itself domestically, international tensions continued to mount. As we have seen, on February 4 Hitler reshuffled his military and diplomatic corps. Delbos, Léger, and Chautemps apparently misread the implications of the move. They believed that Neurath and other moderates in the German military would continue to influence foreign policy decisions, and that "von Ribbentrop would not be allowed to run wild at the Foreign Office."[25] It apparently took some time for them to see that Neurath had been "kicked upstairs" to a powerless post and that Hitler now could act without fear of opposition from the Wilhelmstrasse or the military. After the implications of Schuschnigg's visit to Berchtesgaden became clear, Delbos despairingly asked a number of French journalists, "How can we interfere in a quarrel between a country of 70,000,000 and a country of 7,000,000, and with all the guns on the side of the former?"[26]

On February 20, 1938, Hitler delivered one of his most violent speeches before the Reichstag. At the same time, Britain was in the throes of a cabinet crisis brought on by the resignation of Anthony Eden as Foreign Secretary. The announcement of Eden's resignation, coming on the same day as Hitler's speech, "caused the deepest commotion in Paris."[27] Phipps observed that "it would be difficult to exaggerate the dismay and consternation amounting almost to panic which reigned in Paris" when the crisis first arose.[28]

Alexander Werth had noted, "It was a fearful blow to M. Delbos. It looked as though his policy to which he had clung in spite of everything, was finally crumbling."[29] That evening Phipps was summoned to the Quai d'Orsay, where he found Delbos, Chautemps, Léger, and Corbin, all of whom were "gravely perturbed" at the news of Eden's resignation. Delbos and Chautemps begged the

British Ambassador to remind Chamberlain that a radical change in British policy could produce disastrous results in France. They added that they were concerned over Hitler's threatening speech.[30] Despite Chamberlain's reassurance, sent to Paris that same night,[31] Bullitt found Delbos in a state of "acute depression" on the following day: "He said that the entire policy he had attempted to carry out for the past two years had been destroyed. There was nothing for him to do but give up his shoes. He could not think of any constructive policy. The British Government had made it clear that Britain would do nothing to prevent the absorption of Austria by Germany. France could not attempt to protect Austria alone. It was clear, therefore, that Austria would fall into the hands of Germany within a very limited time. It would then be the turn of Czechoslovakia." Bullitt added, "Delbos made it entirely evident that he desired to be out of office as soon as possible. I derived the impression that Chautemps will find it difficult to prevent his resignation and in consequence the fall of the government."[32] Phipps also noted that Delbos was so personally affected by Eden's resignation that he offered his resignation to Chautemps several times.[33] Evidently, however, Chautemps rejected Delbos' resignation and persuaded him to stay on at the Foreign Ministry. Perhaps Delbos did not wish to provoke another cabinet crisis—which would inevitably occur with the resignation of a Foreign Minister—so close upon the heels of the January crisis.

Even though Chamberlain, in a speech before the Commons on February 21, promised that Eden's resignation would in no way affect the close Franco-British relations, his speech on the following day could hardly have allayed Delbos' fears that Britain would not oppose an Anschluss. He stated that the League was unable to provide collective security for anybody and added, "I say we must try not to delude small weak nations into thinking that they will be protected by the League against aggression."[34] If after Halifax's indiscretion at Berchtesgaden in November, 1937, Hitler needed more proof of Britain's unwillingness to act, he now had it.

On February 26, after appearing before the Foreign Affairs Commission of the Chamber four days earlier, Delbos participated in a prolonged foreign-policy debate. It proved to be his last statement before the Chamber as Foreign Minister. Werth observed that he was "a tired and disappointed man" as he said to the deputies:[35]

[France] has never ceased to affirm, and it affirms today, that Austrian independence is an essential element of European equilibrium. Several speakers, notably M. de Monzie, have emphasized the gravity of the present situation in Austria. This is indeed a problem of European security as well as of international honor. When I think of Austria I think also of the other countries in the same Danubian region exposed to the same dangers. The setting up of a hegemony over Central Europe is not admissible in the economic sphere any more than in the political sphere. . . . I wish to affirm once again—and I think that in this I am interpreting the views of the Chamber—the affection of France for [Czechoslovakia] and for its courageous government . . . and I wish to declare once more that should the occasion arise, our obligations toward Czechoslovakia will be faithfully kept.[36]

The important implication to be derived from his statement was that France would unequivocally honor its commitments to assist Czechoslovakia, which would mean war. But, although the independence of Austria was an "essential element" of European peace, Delbos made no commitment to come to its aid in the event of German aggression. The distinction did not escape Count Welczeck, the German Ambassador in Paris. He reported, "It is not to be inferred from [Delbos'] statements . . . that an energetic step is to be expected of France in the Austrian question."[37]

Other important speeches during this second day of debate were made by Flandin, Reynaud, and Chautemps. Flandin was greeted by shouts of "Heil Hitler!" "Heil Flandin!" "A Berlin!" He argued for a policy of retrenchment in French foreign policy—France should limit its obligations. "But," he said, "we ought to make sure that we are able to carry them out." Paul Reynaud followed and declared that France was at the crossroads. It was faced with the choice of either maintaining the European equilibrium or of giving up its role in Europe, abandoning its allies, entrenching itself behind the Maginot Line and waiting. He warned against the day when "our colossal neighbor will make things so unbearable to the pride of a noble people that we will be thrown into war, without friends, without honor."[38]

Chautemps concluded the debate for the government. He reiterated Delbos' statement by declaring that France could not go back on its commitments to Czechoslovakia. But he made no such commitment to Austria. He merely said that France could not disinterest itself in Central Europe.[39] Nevertheless, a vote of confidence in the government was passed 438 to 2, with 163 abstentions.[40] The vote created an impression of agreement on foreign policy, but the agreement was only superficial. The frequently acrid debate indicated a much deeper divergence of opinion.

In the meantime, events were racing toward a climax with regard to Austria. On March 1 Delbos' "most intimate collaborator" confessed that Delbos and the Quai d'Orsay were deeply depressed about the progression of events.[41] Hitler had little cause to delay, since he must have been quite sure by then that neither France nor Britain would act to defend Austria. When, on March 9, Schuschnigg announced his decision to hold a national plebiscite to determine Austria's future, Hitler was incensed and flew into action. On March 11 German frontier officials closed the Austro-German border and several ultimatums were delivered to Schuschnigg. He was ordered to call off the plebiscite, resign, and bring in the Austrian Nazi Seyss-Inquart to form a new government. With the German army poised for invasion, the Austrian Chancellor had little time to salvage the situation. He asked for the immediate advice of the British government,[42] but got this reply: "His Majesty's Government cannot take the responsibility of advising the Chancellor to take any course of action which might expose his country to dangers against which His Majesty's Government are unable to guarantee protection."[43]

What would France do? Nothing! The government had fallen when Chautemps had resigned on the previous day, March 10. Delbos, however, remained at the Quai d'Orsay as acting Foreign Minister. During the fateful day of March 11, he summoned Count Welczeck to the Foreign Office. He probably did not yet know the full extent of the German move, but he emphasized to the German Ambassador "the alarm and anxiety of the French government" about reports of the Austro-German situation. Welczeck pleaded ignorance about the situation. But he indicated that Germany and Austria considered themselves to be one big family, and since they "wished to settle big or little family quarrels between ourselves alone, we had to refuse any advice, however well meant." Delbos replied that "Europe, too, had to be considered as one big family in which absolutely every conflict affected the other members of the family."[44] But the German Ambassador, in the light of his observations about the debate of February 25–26, knew that the German move would not lead to active French intervention. Indeed, Delbos had given up hope long before the event occurred. Not once since he first began to fear the possibility of an Anschluss, over a year before, had he promised to defend Austria. Czechoslovakia had been reassured numerous times, but not Austria. As Léger observed during the crisis, France had no legal or moral commitment to act in defense of Austria.[45]

General Gamelin recorded that on the afternoon of March 11, Chautemps—who, like Delbos, remained until a new cabinet could be created—decided that "without the entire concurrence of the British, no military measures were to be taken."[46] On the following morning Delbos, Daladier, Chautemps, and Georges Bonnet, the Minister of Finance, met at the Hôtel Matignon. Daladier informed them that the military had decided to proceed with the military measures already prepared, but "on the condition of obtaining the British collaboration already asked for by the Foreign Office."[47] The British reply came that afternoon. They had already made it known to Vienna that they could not advise the Austrians. Léger now reported that "Britain would refuse any strenuous démarche."[48] Meanwhile, Jules Blondel, the French Chargé d'Affaires in Rome, asked to see Count Ciano, to make an inquiry about the Italian position. He received a curt message back that if the object of the interview was Austria, that was a subject regarding which the Italian Government "had no reason to concert with either France or Great Britain."[49] The British reply, coupled with an Italian rebuff of Blondel's inquiry, confirmed what Delbos had realized earlier—France was isolated. France settled for a strong protest against the "coercion supported by violence" used against Austria.[50] In the early evening of March 11, Schuschnigg resigned; and on the next day the German army moved into Austria unopposed.[51]

Why did Delbos fail to push for strong retaliation against the German aggression? Probably, as Professor Pierre Renouvin has argued, the most decisive element in French minds was the need for British cooperation, just as it had been so important in so many other decisions. But Britain never considered resorting to arms over Austria.[52] For years no British government had denied that a closer union between Germany and Austria was inevitable. They had only expressed a desire for "reasonable solutions reasonably achieved."[53] Delbos had refused to act against Britain's wishes many times before, and he knew well its attitude on this matter. Therefore, it is not surprising that he refused to act this time. In all fairness to Delbos, however, in his position of Acting Foreign Minister it would have been difficult for him to make decisions, the results of which would fall upon the shoulders of his successor at the Quai d'Orsay.

On March 14, 1938, Léon Blum finally formed a new government, and Joseph Paul-Boncour became the new Foreign Minister.[54] Delbos had served his only stint at the Quai d'Orsay. The question that remains to be answered is, of course, why did Blum not choose to keep his friend Yvon Delbos at the Quai d'Orsay? Perhaps another aspect of the question is why Delbos, obviously anticipating the impending Anschluss, did not try to dissuade Chautemps from resigning, thus creating a weakened France in the face of German aggression. Unlike Chautemps, whose motives are at best questionable,[55] Delbos would appear to have had several logical reasons for his departure. One scholar has concluded that he may have believed, along with Chautemps, Bonnet, and the observers at the British Foreign Office, that Blum's effort at reestablishing the Popular Front was an unviable solution for France's problems.[56] Another explanation may reside in the possibility that Blum and Delbos no longer agreed as closely on foreign affairs. This might have been particularly true with regard to the Spanish question. One of the first actions taken by the second Blum government was to further "relax" the restrictions on arms and men going to Spain over the French border. Delbos was still committed to strict nonintervention in Spain.[57] Some observers believe that, given the weakness of his government, Blum may have felt the need to bring in the most prestigious individual possible to the Quai d'Orsay to give some appearance of strength to his cabinet. Paul-Boncour, the long-time French representative at Geneva and a widely respected political figure, had that sort of prestige.[58]

Although these probably were important elements in Blum's decision not to include Delbos in his government, the most important factor was that Delbos no longer wished to remain in the government.[59] It will be recalled that he had only reluctantly accepted the appointment in the first place. For nearly two hectic years he had remained at his post through a bewildering series of wars, diplomatic crises, abortive negotiations, conferences, trips, and domestic difficulties. There is little doubt that Delbos was a tired and disappointed man. After the obvious failure of the effort to revitalize France's position in Eastern Europe, and the unwillingness of Britain to commit itself firmly to the defense of that area, he felt a sense of despair that he could do nothing to salvage the situation. He could think of no policy beyond that of "wait and see." But that was tantamount to no policy at all. As 1938 came and progressed, his weariness and despair led to submission and passiveness. When the invectives of the Communist press became increasingly acrid, he grew bitter. But if the failure of his trip through Eastern Europe was a cruel disappointment, Eden's resignation was the final blow. Given the cooperation and close identity of viewpoint between the two men, the event was a crushing blow to Delbos. As we have seen, he had tried to resign then, but had been urged to stay on. By March, however, he could not have been persuaded any longer, even if Blum had tried—and there is no indication that he made the effort.

10

Conclusion

What conclusions remain to be drawn from two years of decision making that were linked so inextricably with the declining fortunes of France? We have examined Delbos' policies and actions in the areas that were of most concern to the French. Although France had significant interests in the Far East, these were secondary to the considerations of French security in Europe. France could not commit itself to any policy that might compromise its position in Europe to such an extent that Germany and Italy might be encouraged to strike.[1] Delbos was realistic enough to realize that France and Britain could not act alone in the Far East to stop Japanese aggression. They could act only in the event of a general world action to halt Japan.[2] France looked towards the United States to take the lead. If the Americans would assume the major responsibility for restraining Japan, France would collaborate in a general policy for the Far East.[3]

Delbos realized, however, that the United States believed itself far removed from the menace facing the European powers and their interests and did not wish to become involved in any overseas adventures. Therefore, he sought to convince the United States that it was not only French and British interests that were menaced, but also those of the United States. Thus he wrote later, "The thesis of security by isolation will not withstand the test." The freedom and security of the United States would be inextricably tied to that of the other democracies.[4] But the fact remains that the United States and the Far East were peripheral to the main considerations of French foreign policy.

It is necessary to pause and reflect upon the measure of success that Delbos achieved in his quest for ways to reinforce France's security and its position in Europe. To be sure, the balance sheet is a mixed one. If there is a thread that runs throughout Delbos' policy, it is his attachment to the Franco-British entente. In virtually every sphere of policy making Delbos considered the wishes of Britain above all else. There is little doubt that he saw the dangers that confronted Europe more clearly than did the British. But he was unable to induce Britain to adopt a policy of resolute opposition to Axis aggression in Eastern and Western Europe. After he made spasmodic attempts at an independent policy at Nyon and in Eastern Europe, France's reliance upon the Entente Cordiale resulted in its total capitulation to British policy. This was becoming quite clear by the time of the Anschluss, and it became completely manifest at Munich only six months after Delbos left the Quai d'Orsay.

On the positive side of the ledger, however, Delbos was correct in assuming that no guarantee could equal that of the British. As he contended later, close cooperation between the two democracies was "commanded by geography, by history, by a common ideal, and by the gravity of present circumstances."[5] It is undeniable that during his tenure as Foreign Minister, relations between the two countries improved dramatically, if fitfully. From the depths of antagonism and distrust created by the effects of the Abyssinian War and the reoccupation of the Rhineland, their relationship progressed to a state of mutual consideration.[6] Although Delbos modestly gave credit to Blum and Chautemps for being the "great artisans" of the renovation of the Entente,[7] the truth is that he was perhaps more instrumental than any other individual for its revitalization.

He never tired of promoting closer relations between the two countries. Even after leaving the Quai d'Orsay, he repeatedly wrote editorials in La Dépêche de Toulouse, calling for closer cooperation and understanding.[8] He believed that the Nyon Conference was "one of the clearest and most effective manifestations of the Franco-English entente"[9] and maintained that the Entente was "the safeguard of our common security [and] the surest guarantee of world peace."[10] He praised the rearmament effort of the British as an indication of their overcoming the "fog of blind isolationism and extreme pacifism."[11] Yet the fact remains that he never realized that Britain needed France's support as much as France needed Britain's. Instead, in order to avoid irritating the British, he abdicated France's status as an equal partner in the entente. It was a high price to pay for Britain's support. One scholar, David Thomson, has correctly noted: "The main feature of French foreign policy from 1936 onwards was its complete subservience to British policy. . . . The *Quai d'Orsay*, whatever its inclinations, could make no major move that was not correlated with the policy of the British Foreign Office."[12] Even though Delbos made some effort at pursuing an independent policy— a fact too often overlooked by historians of the period—he must ultimately assume a large share of the responsibility for French subservience to British policy.

While Delbos should receive credit for the improvement in Franco-British relations, the fact that he made critical miscalculations while pursuing his policy in other areas is undeniable. He was probably right in making an initial attempt to formulate an effective nonintervention policy in an effort to isolate and curb the explosive Spanish crisis, which threatened to involve all of Europe. Although by their past deeds the totalitarian states had never given any indication that they would cooperate in easing European tensions, Delbos believed that the diplomatic and domestic situation that confronted France made the attempt worthwhile. In view both of the strong warning from the British against becoming embroiled in a war over Spain and of the domestic division in France, his decision to pursue nonintervention is understandable. What is incomprehensible, however, is the fact that despite the proof of repeated Axis violations of the Nonintervention Agreement, he continued to persist in adhering strictly to what quickly became a bankrupt policy. Even after the notable success at the Nyon Conference, Delbos did not sustain the initiative, and once again it passed to the Axis powers. Pierre Renouvin has observed that although the direct results of the Spanish war were modest, it created a "moral tension" in Europe. Moreover, "it enabled Hitler and Mussolini to realize that the British and the French governments were prepared to accept considerable sacrifices in order to avoid general war."[13] Delbos' prolonged pursuit of the farce of nonintervention inevitably places him high among those responsible for demonstrating Western unwillingness to act. In all fairness to him, however, he was not alone in his hope that somehow the policy would help resolve the crisis.

The post-Nyon period was an opportune time for Delbos to take new initiatives to strengthen the French position. Although he did not utilize the occasion to try to stop the intervention in Spain, he did take positive action to revitalize the French position in Eastern Europe. But in the wake of the reoccupation of the Rhineland, Delbos' effort offered too little too late to reassure Eastern European statesmen. Delbos continued to maintain his interest in Eastern Europe after his departure from the Quai d'Orsay. Prior to the Czech crisis he frequently used *La Dépêche* to argue that the defense of Czechoslovakia was essential to "the equilibrium and security of Europe." He warned that the German ambition was "to enslave or annihilate Czechoslovakia and in that way to dominate Central Europe and indirectly all of Europe."[14] Nevertheless, in the aftermath of Munich, Delbos, like most other Frenchmen, breathed a sigh of relief. He wrote: "One fact dominates all others . . . peace, despite all, was maintained. . . . In acclaiming Edouard Daladier and Georges Bonnet, France hailed the retreat from the specter of war, the return to life."[15] There is no evidence to indicate that he ever realized that his policy of strengthening the French alliance system, and therefore French obligations in Eastern Europe, was basically contradictory to the planning of the French General Staff. Paul Reynaud later wrote that the Chamber failed in its duty to point this out. He argued that it should have said: "You think in terms of concrete, continuous front, and firepower. Yet France is committed to come to the defense of Poland and Czechoslovakia in case of a German aggression. How are you going to attack Germany with a defensive army?"[16] Delbos never appeared to consider the problem either.

Meanwhile, as he pursued what proved to be a futile policy in Eastern Europe, he repeatedly shunned Soviet endeavors to strengthen the Franco-Soviet Pact. Although there is no certainty that the Soviets would not have completed their marriage of convenience with Germany in 1939 anyway, it seems certain that Delbos completely miscalculated, for reasons we have examined, the importance of the Soviet Alliance. As Pierre Cot testified after the war: "In 1939, we did not have the support of Soviet Russia. Nothing can obscure this fact. . . . Suppose . . . that the Soviet Union had come to our help. Germany would have been unable to hurl her whole might against us, and the shape of things would have been altered."[17]

Delbos was equally cool towards the Italians. Several times they made what appear to be bona-fide *démarches* to France in the hopes of developing better relations between the two countries. Whether Mussolini really desired a reconstituted Stresa Front to restrain German expansion or merely sought to gain his immediate goals in Abyssinia and Spain is not certain. One cannot be sure that Mussolini truly felt an "insurmountable repulsion" for Hitler, nor is it clear that he was firmly attached to Berlin. It is plainly evident, however, that Delbos made no effort to find out. He refused to consider seriously the approaches made by the Italian "jackal," whom he confessed that he personally "loathed."

On the other hand, he chose to pursue Hitler with repeated overtures for the start of negotiations for a rapprochement between the two countries. But, of course, his labors did not bear fruit. Although it is now obvious that Hitler had no intention of coming to terms with France, Delbos persisted for nearly a year. It seems utterly fantastic that he should repulse the *démarches* by the Soviet Union and Italy, but endeavor to pursue a rapprochement with a state that did not show the slightest inclination to come to an agreement with France. To put it bluntly, he apparently reasoned that France must seek to negotiate with those who posed the greatest threat and had the power to make war. Not only did he evidently feel that neither the Soviet Union nor Italy was a serious threat to European peace, but that they were not worthwhile allies.

When his efforts to induce Germany to negotiate a rapprochement and his efforts to revitalize the French alliance system in Eastern Europe failed, he realized that an Anschluss was inevitable. Disillusioned, tired, and stymied, the only policy that he could formulate was that of "wait and see"; and that was no policy at all. Consequently, during the two months prior to the Anschluss, France drifted aimlessly, a fact that the German Foreign Ministry did not fail to observe. Moreover, unable to devise an effective policy, coming under increasing attacks from the Communist press, and becoming exhausted by the burden of office, Delbos sought to resign his post. Eden's departure from the British Foreign Office was particularly discouraging to him. Finally, less than a month later, on the very eve of the Anschluss, Delbos departed from the Quai d'Orsay after Chautemps' government abruptly fell. He stayed on, however, as acting Foreign Minister during the critical hours of the crisis over Austria. Even if he had been disposed to act, and there is no indication that he or anyone seriously considered an effective reaction, a large segment of public opinion could not believe that the Austrian problem was worth a war.[18]

Some men are born to lead, some achieve leadership through hard work and ambition, and some have positions of leadership thrust upon them. Delbos was hurled, albeit somewhat reluctantly, to high office by the circumstances of the times. However frustrated was his tenure as Foreign Minister, it was not without its achievements, though these tend to be overshadowed by his grievous miscalculations. He early recognized the fascist threat and the danger that it posed for France. But although he was an honest man of courage and conviction, he was miscast for dealing with the crescendo of crises that confronted France. In ordinary times he would probably have gone down in history as a good although unspectacular Foreign Minister. But the times were not normal, and he was not equipped to direct France's foreign policy in such a critical period of its declining fortunes. In all fairness to Delbos, however, we must agree with Joel Colton, who observed that Delbos was "a receiver in bankruptcy."[19] Indeed, the more one studies the diplomacy of the period, the more it becomes evident that the Rhineland crisis was the single most decisive event of the decade before the outbreak of World War II. It was Delbos' misfortune that he was called upon to direct the destinies of France's international interests under the circumstances that prevailed in the aftermath of that event.

The fact remains that Delbos' ordeals were those of a France in peril. His weaknesses as well as his strengths were those which he shared with his own political generation. His achievements, as much as his failures, were those of the society to which he belonged. Indeed, he was truly a man of his times. Unfortunately, France needed more.

Notes

The short references listed below are used for works most frequently cited in the manuscript.

DBrFB   *Documents on British Foreign Policy, 1919–1939* (London: His Majesty's Stationery Office, 1949), Third Series, Vol. I.

Débats, Chambre   *Journal Officiel, Chambre des Députés, Débats Parlementaires* (Paris: Imprimerie des Journaux Officiels, 1936–1938).

DDF   *Documents diplomatiques français, 1932–1939* (Ministère des Affaires Etrangères, Commission de publications des documents relatifs aux origines de la guerre 1939–1945; Paris: Imprimerie Nationale, 1964 *et seq.*), Second Series, Vols. II–IV.

DGFP   *Documents on German Foreign Policy, 1918–1945* (London: His Majesty's Stationery Office, 1949 *et seq.*), Series D, Vols. I–III.

Les Evénements   *Les Evénements survenus en France de 1933 à 1945: Témoignages et documents recueillis par la Commission d'Enquête Parlementaire* (Paris: Presses Universitaires de France, 1947 *et seq.*), Vols. I–IX.

UBCab.   Unpublished British Cabinet Papers, 1936–1938.

UBFO   Unpublished British Foreign Office Documents, 1936–1938.

USFR   *Foreign Relations of the United States: Diplomatic Papers, 1936–1938* (Washington, D.C.: United States Government Printing Office, 1953–1955), Vols. I–II for years 1936–1938.

PREFACE

1. David Thomson, *Democracy in France Since 1870* (New York and London: Oxford University Press, 1964), pp. 199–200.
2. Pierre Cot, "La Politique extérieure de la Troisième République," *in* Jean Benoît-Lévy, Gustave Cohen, Pierre Cot, et al., *L'Oeuvre de la Troisième République* (Montreal: Les Editions de l'Arbre, 1943), p. 39.

CHAPTER 1

1. The author is greatly indebted to the Association "Les Amis d'Yvon Delbos," and especially to one of its members, M. Henri Bonnet, for granting him

access to photocopied unpublished manuscripts written by various members of the Association. These *souvenirs* about various facets of Delbos' character and career have provided the basis for this chapter. The manuscripts cited are those written by MM. Henri Bonnet, Emile Bouvier, René Massigli, Joseph Barsalou, Jules Romains, and Léon Drouart. Subsequent citations will be by manuscript.

2. Bouvier MS. This is the most useful source for Delbos' youth, written by a man who was one of his classmates and comrades during those years and who ultimately became an eminent literary critic. The initial segments of this chapter are largely based on Bouvier's manuscript.

3. Pierre Flottes, "Yvon Delbos," a memorial published in *L'Annuaire de l'Ecole Normale Superieure* (Paris, 1958), p. 49. The importance of his *instituteur* family background cannot be overestimated. This class of French society was well educated, and its members were greatly respected in their communities. Yet for all of this, they did not share in the wealth and privileges to which they believed their training entitled them. Highly ambitious and greatly dissatisfied with their status, they tended to be leftist in their political outlook as they sought recognition.

4. Bouvier MS; Flottes, "Yvon Delbos," p. 50.

5. Lanson had a lasting influence upon many scholars and was noted for his meticulous and scientific study of the sources. His most famous work was *Histoire de la Littérature Française* (1894). For a concise treatment of Herr's influence at the Ecole Normale, and especially on Blum, see Joel Colton, *Léon Blum: Humanist in Politics* (New York: Alfred A. Knopf, 1966), pp. 16–22. For his impact on Jaurès, see Harvey Goldberg, *The Life of Jean Jaurès* (Madison, Wis.: University of Wisconsin Press, 1962), pp. 62–63.

6. Bouvier MS.

7. Bonnet MS; Flottes, "Yvon Delbos," p. 50.

8. Romains MS.

9. Bouvier MS.

10. Massigli MS.

11. Ibid.

12. Interview with Henri Bonnet, Paris, Aug. 30, 1969; Bonnet MS; Bouvier MS; Drouart MS; Georges Suarez, *Nos Seigneurs et maîtres* (Paris: Editions de France, 1937), p. 65.

13. Flottes, "Yvon Delbos," p. 50.

14. Bouvier MS.

15. Ibid.

16. Bonnet MS.

17. Flottes, "Yvon Delbos," p. 50; Drouart MS; carbon copy of the typed *Communiqué de l'Association "Les Amis d'Yvon Delbos"* supplied to the French press on the occasion of the *Inauguration du monument à la memoire du Président Yvon Delbos* at Montignac s/Vézère, Oct. 16, 1966. A copy of the communiqué was supplied to this writer by M. Roger Cler-

gerie, treasurer of the Association and a former secretary to Delbos, at an interview, Boulogne s/Seine, Aug. 29, 1969.

18. H. Bonnet interview; *Communiqué de l'Association "Les Amis d'Yvon Delbos." L'Ere nouvelle* became one of the great Radical dailies to which Edouard Herriot was a frequent contributor.
19. Peter J. Larmour, *The French Radical Party in the 1930's* (Stanford, Calif.: Stanford University Press, 1964), p. 41.
20. Suarez, *Nos Seigneurs et maitres*, p. 62; Friedrich Sieburg, "Persons and Personages: Yvon Delbos," *Living Age*, CCCLII (Mar., 1937), 52. This is an article translated from the *Frankfurter Zeitung*.
21. Larmour, *The French Radical Party*, p. 55.
22. H. Bonnet interview.
23. *Communiqué de l'Association "Les Amis d'Yvon Delbos"*; Drouart MS; Flottes, "Yvon Delbos," pp. 50–51.
24. Larmour, *The French Radical Party*, p. 33.
25. Ibid., p. 41.
26. Interview with Robert Blum, Paris, July 4, 1969; *Gringoire*, May 29, 1936. For further insight into the attitudes of the *radicaux de gestion*, see also Francis de Tarr, *The French Radical Party from Herriot to Mendès-France* (London: Oxford University Press, 1961), pp. 156–59.
27. Larmour, *The French Radical Party*, pp. 41–44.
28. *Dépêche du Midi*, Nov. 16, 1956.
29. *Communiqué de l'Association "Les Amis d'Yvon Delbos"*; *Dictionnaire des parlementaires français: notices biographiques sur les ministres, députés et senateurs français de 1889 à 1940* (Paris: Presses Universitaires de France, 1966), IV, 1310.
30. Bonnet MS; Drouart MS.
31. Yvon Delbos, "Mon récent voyage en Russie" (a speech given by Delbos upon his return, before the Société d'économie industrielle et commerciale, Feb. 17, 1933). The report dealt primarily with social and economic conditions, but he did make a few observations about the need for closer cooperation between the two powers in foreign affairs.
32. Jean-Baptiste Duroselle, "France and the Crisis of March, 1936," *in* Evelyn M. Acomb and Marvin L. Brown, Jr., eds., *French Society and Culture Since the Old Regime* (New York: Holt, Rinehart & Winston, 1966), pp. 252–54.
33. Ibid., pp. 253–54; Larmour, *The French Radical Party*, p. 198. See also John M. Sherwood, *Georges Mandel and the Third Republic* (Stanford, Calif.: Stanford University Press, 1970), pp. 178–83; W. F. Knapp, "The Rhineland Crisis of March 1936," *in* James Joll, ed., *The Decline of the Third Republic* (London: Chatto & Windus, 1959), pp. 67–85; *Times* (London), Nov. 16, 1956.
34. William R. Rock, *Neville Chamberlain* (New York: Twayne Publishers, 1969), p. 101.
35. Larmour, *The French Radical Party*, p. 198.

36. Paul Reynaud, *Envers et contre tous,* vol. II of *Mémoires* (Paris: Flammarion, 1963), p. 366.
37. Bonnet MS; *Dépêche du Midi,* Nov. 16, 1956.
38. *Dictionnaire des parlementaires français,* IV, 1311; *New York Times,* May 2, 1945. The details of Delbos' imprisonment and subsequent transfer are still hazy. It is likely, however, that he was caught, like many others such as Blum and Mandel, in a mad shuffle of political prisoners which occurred near the war's end.
39. *Communiqué de l'Association "Les Amis d'Yvon Delbos"; Dictionnaire biographique française contemporain* (Paris: Pharos, 1950), p. 183; Drouart MS.
40. Bonnet MS.
41. Romains MS. For a running box score of the balloting, which was initially scattered indecisively among fourteen candidates before three or four of the most serious contenders took charge, see *Le Monde,* Dec. 17–24, 1953.
42. Flottes, "Yvon Delbos," p. 52.
43. Interview with Daniel Mayer, Paris, June 30, 1969.
44. Blum interview, July 4, 1969.
45. Interview with Henri Laugier, Antibes, France, July 8, 1969.
46. *La Dépêche de Toulouse,* Jan. 24, 1936.
47. Massigli MS.
48. Barsalou MS. Barsalou's recollections of Delbos' journalistic activities are the best source on the subject.
49. Ibid.
50. H. Bonnet interview; Bonnet MS. Delbos, of course, took great care to attend to the defense of the agricultural interests of his rural constituents too. See the *Dictionnaire des parlementaires français,* IV, 1312, for a summary of his record in agricultural matters.
51. Laugier interview.
52. He took a particular interest in promoting the expansion of educational buildings and facilities, including the creation of *Cité Universitaire* in Paris, the advance of scientific research, and the development of academic scholarships. See the *Dictionnaire des parlementaires français,* IV, 1312, for a summary of his activities on behalf of higher education.
53. Massigli MS.
54. Sieburg, "Yvon Delbos," p. 49.
55. Bouvier MS.
56. Sieburg, "Yvon Delbos," p. 48.
57. Bouvier MS.
58. Blum interview, June 26, 1969.
59. Sieburg, "Yvon Delbos," p. 48.
60. Bouvier MS.
61. Massigli MS.
62. Bouvier MS; Massigli MS; Laugier interview.
63. Bonnet MS.

64. Flottes, "Yvon Delbos," p. 52.
65. Interview with Charles Corbin, Paris, Aug. 25, 1969; interview with Pierre Cot, Paris, July 7, 1969.
66. Laugier interview; Blum interview, July 4, 1969.
67. *Dépêche du Midi*, Nov. 19, 1956.
68. Romains MS.
69. Sieburg, "Yvon Delbos," p. 51.
70. Quoted in Drouart MS.

CHAPTER 2

1. Jean Touchard and Louis Bodin, "L'Etat de l'opinion au début de l'année 1936," in *Léon Blum: Chef de gouvernement, 1936–1937* (Paris: Librairie Armand Colin, 1967), p. 66. This is the published version of the papers and discussion heard at the Colloquium on Léon Blum as Premier, held on Mar. 26 and 27, 1965.
2. Samuel M. Osgood, "The Third French Republic in Historical Perspective," in Gerald N. Grob, ed., *Statesmen and Statecraft of the Modern West* (Barre, Mass.: Barre Publishers, 1967), p. 69. A similar viewpoint was expressed by Alexander Werth, *The Twilight of France, 1933–1940* (New York: Howard Fertig, 1966), p. 15.
3. Colton, *Léon Blum*, p. 109; Werth, *Twilight of France*, pp. 46–49.
4. H. Stuart Hughes, *Contemporary Europe: A History*, 2d ed. (Englewood Cliffs, N.J.: Prentice-Hall, 1966), p. 252.
5. Gordon Wright, *France in Modern Times: 1760 to the Present* (Chicago: Rand McNally & Co., 1960), p. 484; Alfred Cobban, *France of the Republics, 1871–1962*, vol. III of *A History of Modern France* (Baltimore, Md.: Penguin Books, 1965), p. 149; Colton, *Léon Blum*, pp. 125–26.
6. These questions were first posed to this writer by Professor René Rémond at an interview in Paris, July 1, 1969.
7. Edouard Bonnefous, *Vers la guerre, 1936–1938*, vol. VI of *Histoire politique de la Troisième République* (Paris: Presses Universitaires de France, 1965), p. 2.
8. Cot interview.
9. Interview with Jules Moch, Chataigneraie, France, Aug. 28, 1969.
10. *Times* (London), May 21, 1936. The foreign press showed a greater interest in the question of the appointment of a Foreign Minister than did their French counterparts, with the possible exception of *L'Oeuvre*. The sit-down strikes beginning on May 14, and spreading on the twenty-sixth, virtually crowded all else from the pages of the French press.
11. *Le Temps*, May 21, 1936.
12. *New York Times*, May 21, 1936. *L'Oeuvre* on May 20 speculated that Herriot just was not impressed with Blum's offer. On the next day it said that Herriot had promised to "reflect" on the offer, but it was confident that he had not changed his mind.

204

NOTES TO PAGES 24-28

13. *L'Oeuvre*, May 23, 1936.
14. *Le Temps*, May 24, 1936.
15. *Times* (London), May 25, 1936.
16. Laugier interview.
17. Blum interview, July 4, 1969.
18. Bonnefous, *Vers la guerre*, p. 2.
19. Michel Soulié, *La Vie politique d'Edouard Herriot* (Paris: Librairie Armand Colin, 1962), pp. 470–72.
20. *New York Times*, May 19 and 21, 1936.
21. Ibid., May 17, 1936.
22. Colton, *Léon Blum*, p. 142.
23. *Times* (London), May 25, 1936.
24. *Le Temps*, May 27, 1936.
25. *Le Populaire*, May 26, 1936; *L'Oeuvre*, May 26, 1936.
26. *New York Times*, May 28, 1936.
27. Laugier interview. Georges Bonnet supported the point of Delbos' hesitance in an interview, Paris, July 11, 1969.
28. Skeptics of the appointment quickly seized upon Delbos' inexperience. In London, the *Times*, May 27, 1936, observed that Delbos had not been regarded as a "statesman equal to the responsibilities of such a post." The more caustic *Gringoire*, June 19, 1936, reported that upon taking over the direction of the Quai d'Orsay, Delbos told his cabinet, "I am going to need your advice. Foreign affairs are for me a blank page." Of course, the extreme rightist newspaper was virulent in its criticism of the leftist coalition. It retained vivid memories of Delbos' attack against Laval and the Hoare-Laval Plan at the end of 1935. See *Gringoire*, May 29, 1936.
29. Mayer interview.
30. Moch interview.
31. *Je suis partout*, May 30, 1936. The Right's truculent hatred of Blum makes this a highly questionable statement. Besides, Blum's intellectual inclinations undoubtedly evoked in him an appreciation for others with ideas.
32. H. Bonnet interview.
33. Ibid. Bonnet's point was supported by testimony from Robert Blum, Pierre Cot, and Henri Laugier.
34. Moch interview.
35. Interview with André François-Poncet, Paris, July 9, 1969.
36. Blum's testimony in *Les Evénements*, I, 126.
37. Ibid.; Blum interview, June 26, 1969.
38. Blum's testimony in *Les Evénements*, I, 126.
39. Blum interview, July 4, 1969.
40. William E. Scott, *Alliance Against Hitler: The Origins of the Franco-Soviet Pact* (Durham, N.C.: Duke University Press, 1962), p. 251.
41. For the evolution of Blum's attitude toward the Soviet pact, see Scott, *Alliance Against Hitler*; Colton, *Léon Blum*, pp. 119–20 and 210–13; Na-

thanael Greene, *Crisis and Decline* (Ithaca, N.Y.: Cornell University Press, 1969), pp. 96–97.
42. Laugier and Cot interviews.
43. *Débats, Chambre,* Dec. 27, 1935, p. 2810.
44. John T. Marcus, *French Socialism in the Crisis Years, 1933–1936: Fascism and the French Left* (New York: Frederick A. Praeger, 1958), p. 161.
45. Interview with Paul Bastid, Paris, July 3, 1969.
46. *Times* (London), May 25, 1936.
47. Laugier interview and Blum interview, July 4, 1969.
48. Interview with René Massigli, Paris, July 7, 1969.

CHAPTER 3

1. Pierre Cot's testimony in *Les Evénements,* I, 273.
2. A. J. P. Taylor, *The Origins of the Second World War* (Greenwich, Conn.: Fawcett Publications, 1961), p. 119.
3. René Albrecht-Carrié, *A Diplomatic History of Europe Since the Congress of Vienna* (New York: Harper & Row, 1958), p. 302; Jacques Chastenet, *Vingt ans d'histoire diplomatique, 1919–1939* (Genève: Editions du Milieu du Monde, 1945), p. 130.
4. Pierre Renouvin, *Les Crises du XXe siècle, 1929 à 1945,* Vol. VIII of *Histoire des relations internationales* (Paris: Librairie Hachette, 1958), p. 106.
5. Renouvin, *Les Crises du XXe siècle,* p. 105.
6. Alexander Werth, *Which Way France?* (New York: Harper & Brothers, 1937), p. 375.
7. The publication of the French documents for the period was helpful for filling in details and gaining new perspectives on this question. The reduction of the fifty-year rule to thirty years in Britain has made possible the release of many documents that had been previously unavailable. They are particularly valuable for tracing the exchanges between the French and British governments as well as opinions of the British representatives and Foreign Office officials on French policies and actions.
8. Jules Moch, André Blumel, and other close advisors have written only sketchy accounts of the period. Charles Corbin, who was the French Ambassador in England, feels that there are too many published memoirs already. Moreover, the details of the period are too unpleasant to write about. Consequently, he has chosen not to write his own description. Interview, Paris, Aug. 25, 1969.
9. For example, Delbos did not even testify before the postwar Parliamentary Commission of Inquiry. Only Léon Blum's testimony is at all revealing. Given the positions of responsibility held by Daladier and Chautemps, their testimony reveals disappointingly little. Chautemps' memoirs, *Cahiers secrets de l'armistice, 1939–1940* (Paris: Librairie Plon, 1963), are also very thin on the problem.

10. Disagreement over the most prominent factors can be seen from the observations of some of the closest observers and participants in the decision. In interviews with this writer, Jules Moch, Pierre Cot, and Henri Laugier pointed directly to foreign influences, particularly that of Britain. Others, including Charles Corbin, André François-Poncet, and Henri Bonnet, emphasized the domestic considerations as being paramount. Corbin, for example, categorically stated that "Britain did not intervene diplomatically or in any other way" in the French decision to pursue a policy of nonintervention. On the other hand, he conceded that their "inner feelings" on the subject were well known.

11. Wright, *France in Modern Times*, p. 499.

12. Bowers (San Sabastián) to Sec. of State, July 14, 1936, *USFR, 1936*, II, 439.

13. Léon Blum's testimony in *Les Evénements*, I, 215.

14. Herbette (Madrid) to Delbos, July 18, 1936, *DDF*, 2e, II, no. 483, pp. 736–37. See also Herbette to Delbos, July 18, 1936, *DDF*, 2e, II, no. 484, p. 738.

15. Herbette (San Sabastián) to Delbos, July 19, 1936, *DDF*, 2e, III, no. 1, p. 1.

16. Joel Colton, *Léon Blum*, p. 236.

17. Blum's testimony in *Les Evénements*, I, 215–16; Pierre Renouvin, "La Politique extérieure du premier gouvernement Léon Blum," in *Léon Blum: Chef de gouvernement, 1936–1937* (Paris: Librairie Armand Colin, 1967), p. 330. The Spanish request for aid was clarified further a few days later. See Coulondre (Paris) to Delbos (London) and "L'Ambassade d'Espagne à Paris" to Delbos, July 23 and 24, 1936, *DDF*, 2e, III, nos. 17 and 25, pp. 37 and 52.

18. Colton, *Léon Blum*, p. 236; Renouvin, "La Politique extérieure," pp. 330–31. Jules Moch (*Naissance et croissance du Front Populaire* [Paris: Editions du Parti Socialiste S.F.I.O., 1966], p. 45) and Pierre Cot (*Triumph of Treason*, trans. by Sybille and Milton Crane [Chicago and New York: Ziff-Davis Publishing Co., 1944], p. 338) agree that there was little hesitation in the decision to send arms.

19. Cot, *Triumph of Treason*, p. 338.

20. Ibid.

21. Ibid. There is evidence that a leak occurred in the French cabinet as well. The German Ambassador in Paris reported that a member of the cabinet had confirmed the anticipated arms shipment to him. See the Ambassador in France (Welczeck) to the Foreign Ministry, July 23, 1936, *DGFP*, D, III, no. 3, p. 4. No evidence has come forth on the identity of the informant.

22. Blum's testimony in *Les Evénements*, I, 217; Cot, *Triumph of Treason*, p. 338.

23. Cited in Cot, *Triumph of Treason*, p. 338; André Blumel, "La Non intervention en Espagne," *in* Georges Lefranc, *Histoire du Front Populaire* (Paris: Payot, 1965), p. 462.

24. *L'Action Française*, July 23, 1936.

25. Renouvin, "La Politique extérieure," pp. 331–32.

26. Blum interview, July 4, 1969.
27. See Cordell Hull, *The Memoirs of Cordell Hull* (New York: The Macmillan Co., 1948), I, 476; Straus (Paris) to Sec. of State, July 27, 1936, *USFR, 1936*, II, 448. These sources have provided the basis for the arguments put forth by Dante A. Puzzo, *Spain and the Great Powers, 1936–1941* (New York: Columbia University Press, 1962), p. 87; Hugh Thomas, *The Spanish Civil War* (New York: Harper & Row, 1961), p. 219; Arthur H. Furnia, *The Diplomacy of Appeasement* (Washington, D.C.: The University Press, 1962), pp. 209–10.
28. Colton, *Léon Blum*, pp. 237–38.
29. Blum's testimony in *Les Evénements*, I, 216.
30. Cot, *Triumph of Treason*, p. 338.
31. Massigli (Geneva) to Delbos, July 3, 1936, *DDF*, 2e, II, no. 386, p. 590.
32. Laroche (Brussels) to Delbos, July 8, 1936, *DDF*, 2e, II, no. 407, p. 613. At this point Britain desired that the Germans be invited to the conference, which would have as its goal "a general amelioration of the international situation." Delbos, however, strongly objected to the proposed German attendance on the grounds that since the Rhineland coup they had not given satisfaction to the legitimate demands of the other powers. To invite them would be "publicly to consecrate the final success of the method of the *fait accompli*." Delbos to French Ambassadors in Brussels, London, Rome, Berlin, July 9, 1936, *DDF*, 2e, II, no. 414, pp. 630–31.
33. Delbos to French Ambassadors in London and Brussels, July 17, 1936, *DDF*, 2e, II, no. 472, pp. 719–20. For a wider discussion of the reasons for the conference and what it was hoped it would accomplish, see "Note de la direction politique," July 21, 1936, *DDF*, 2e, III, no. 8, pp. 10–16.
34. Delbos to French Ambassadors in London and Brussels, July 17, 1936, *DDF*, 2e, II, no. 472, pp. 719–20.
35. "Conférence de Londres: Procès-verbal," July 23, 1936, *DDF*, 2e, III, nos. 18 and 19, pp. 38–46.
36. "Conférence de Londres: Communiqué final," July 23, 1936, *DDF*, 2e, III, no. 20, p. 46.
37. Cot, *Triumph of Treason*, pp. 338–39.
38. Blum's testimony in *Les Evénements*, I, 216.
39. Cot, *Triumph of Treason*, p. 339. The example most often cited in this case is Winston Churchill.
40. Colton, *Léon Blum*, p. 241.
41. Blum's testimony in *Les Evénements*, I, 216.
42. Colton, *Léon Blum*, p. 241.
43. Laugier interview.
44. Moch interview.
45. Blum's testimony in *Les Evénements*, I, 216; Moch, *Naissance et croissance*, pp. 45–46.
46. Moch interview.
47. Blum's testimony in *Les Evénements*, I, 216.

48. Ibid., pp. 216–17.
49. Cot, *Triumph of Treason*, p. 339.
50. Ibid., pp. 339–40.
51. *L'Action Française*, July 24, 1936.
52. Cot, *Triumph of Treason*, p. 340.
53. Cited by Renouvin, "La Politique extérieure," p. 332.
54. Delbos to Auriol, July 26, 1936, *DDF*, 2e, III, no. 33, p. 60; Delbos to Diplomatic Representatives in London, Rome, Washington, etc., July 27, 1936, *DDF*, 2e, III, no. 36, p. 64.
55. Colton, *Léon Blum*, p. 246.
56. Blum's testimony in *Les Evénements*, I, 217. See also Blumel, "La Non intervention," p. 462.
57. Cited in Renouvin, "La Politique extérieure," p. 333.
58. Blum's testimony in *Les Evénements*, I, 217.
59. Peyrouton (Rabat) to Delbos, July 30, 1936, *DDF*, 2e, III, no. 46, p. 79.
60. Renouvin, "La Politique extérieure," pp. 333–34.
61. Colton, *Léon Blum*, p. 246; Blum's testimony in *Les Evénements*, I, 217.
62. Blum's testimony in *Les Evénements*, I, 217.
63. *Débats, Chambre*, July 31, 1936, 2e séance, p. 2330.
64. Ibid.
65. Colton, *Léon Blum*, p. 247.
66. Bonnefous, *Vers la guerre, 1936–1938*, p. 46.
67. *L'Action Française*, Aug. 1, 1936. Maurras again played upon the French unpreparedness for war.
68. Colton, *Léon Blum*, p. 247.
69. Cot, *Triumph of Treason*, p. 342.
70. Straus (Paris) to Sec. of State, Aug. 2, 1936, *USFR, 1936*, II, 454–55.
71. Elizabeth R. Cameron, "Alexis Saint-Léger Léger," *in* Gordon A. Craig and Felix Gilbert, eds., *The Diplomats, 1919–1939* (Princeton, N.J.: Princeton University Press, 1953), p. 391.
72. Delbos to Diplomatic Representatives in London, Rome, Brussels, Aug. 2, 1936, *DDF*, 2e, III, no. 59, pp. 100–101; see also Memorandum by Foreign Minister (Neurath), Aug. 6, 1937, *DGFP*, D, III, no. 29, p. 29. A more definite text was submitted to Germany on Aug. 7. See the editors' note attached to the Memorandum by the Foreign Minister (Neurath), Aug. 7, 1936, *DGFP*, D, III, no. 32, p. 33.
73. Cot, *Triumph of Treason*, p. 343; Straus (Paris) to Sec. of State, Aug. 2, 1936, *USFR, 1936*, II, 455.
74. Cot, *Triumph of Treason*, p. 343; Renouvin, "La Politique extérieure," p. 334.
75. Cambon (London) to Delbos, Aug. 4, 1936, *DDF*, 2e, III, no. 71, pp. 114–15.
76. Delbos to Cambon (London), Aug. 5, 1936, *DDF*, 2e, III, no. 76, p. 119.
77. Delbos to Cambon (London), Aug. 5, 1936, *DDF*, 2e, III, no. 83, pp. 126–27.
78. Moch interview. See also Cot, *Triumph of Treason*, p. 343.

79. Moch interview. See also Blumel, "La Non intervention," p. 462.
80. Blum's testimony in *Les Evénements*, I, 217–18.
81. Moch interview. Most observers agree that Darlan, despite his shifts later, was at this time a sincere Republican concerned with the defense of France. See also Blumel, "La Non intervention," p. 462.
82. For a detailed account of the meeting between Darlan and Chatfield see "Compte-rendu," Aug. 5, 1936, *DDF*, 2e, III, no. 87, pp. 130–33.
83. There is no evidence that Chatfield considered that Franco was "a good Spanish patriot" as Blum testified in 1947.
84. Moch interview.
85. Ibid.; Moch, *Naissance et croissance*, p. 46.
86. Blum's testimony in *Les Evénements*, I, 218.
87. Blum's testimony in *Les Evénements*, I, 218–19; Léon Blum, *L'Oeuvre de Léon Blum, 1937–1940* (Paris: Editions Albin Michel, 1964), IV-A, 417. See also Thomas, *The Spanish Civil War*, pp. 258–59; Blumel, "La Non intervention," p. 463.
88. Clerk (Paris) to Eden, Aug. 7, 1936, UBFO 371, vol. 20528, no. W7964/62/41.
89. De Chambrun (Rome) to Delbos, Aug. 6, 1936, *DDF*, 2e, III, no. 90, pp. 140–41.
90. François-Poncet (Berlin) to Delbos, Aug. 5, 1936, *DDF*, 2e, III, no. 81, p. 124.
91. Clerk (Paris) to Eden, Aug. 7, 1936, UBFO 371, vol. 20528, no. W7964/62/41. On Aug. 10, after the French decision of Aug. 8, Clerk was assured by the British Foreign Office that "your language is approved and appears to have had good results." Foreign Office to Clerk (Paris), Aug. 10, 1936, UBFO 371, no. W7964/62/41. Hitherto, historians could only speculate upon the extent and nature of British pressure at this point in the crisis. Werth, *Which Way France?*, p. 378, alluded to British intimations that the Locarno guarantee would not be operative in the event of a general war over Spain stemming from France competing with Germany and Italy in sending aid to Spain. Patricia van der Esch (*Prelude to War: The International Repercussions of the Spanish Civil War, 1936–1939* [The Hague: Martinus Nijhoff, 1951], p. 54) also noted a "severe warning" from the British. She cited Alvarez del Vayo as her source. But she added that no further evidence of Clerk's visit existed, nor was a precise date available.
92. Clerk denied all knowledge of an impending meeting when he talked with Delbos. See Clerk (Paris) to Foreign Office, Aug. 8, 1936, UBFO 371, vol. 20528, no. W8055/62/41.
93. Colton, *Léon Blum*, p. 251.
94. The *Documents diplomatiques français* showed that this was not really the case. The German and Italian responses were less than promising, and Delbos showed considerable anxiety over their attitudes. See François-Poncet to Delbos, Aug. 7, 1936; de Chambrun to Delbos, Aug. 7, 1936; Del-

bos to de Chambrun, Aug. 8, 1936, *DDF*, 2e, III, nos. 103, 104, and 106, pp. 154–56, and 157.

95. Wilson (Paris) to the Sec. of State, Aug. 10, 1936, *USFR, 1936*, II, 476–77; Cot, *Triumph of Treason*, pp. 344–45; Colton, *Léon Blum*, pp. 251–52; Blum's testimony in *Les Evénements*, I, 219; Werth, *Which Way France?*, p. 378.

96. Cot, *Triumph of Treason*, pp. 344–45.

97. Moch interview; Blumel, "La Non intervention," p. 463. Both Moch and Blumel, Blum's Directeur du Cabinet, were close advisors and were therefore inside witnesses to the proceedings. For the best treatment of the Socialist attitudes, particularly those of Faure and Lebas, as well as a sound analysis of Daladier, see Greene, *Crisis and Decline*, pp. 80–81 and 111–30.

98. Delbos to Auriol, Aug. 9, 1936, *DDF*, 2e, III, no. 112, p. 163.

99. William L. Shirer, *The Collapse of the Third Republic: An Inquiry into the Fall of France in 1940* (New York: Simon & Schuster, 1969), p. 299.

100. See Esch, *Prelude to War; Puzzo, Spain and the Great Powers;* Thomas, *The Spanish Civil War;* William Laird Kleine-Ahlbrandt, *The Policy of Simmering: A Study of British Policy During the Spanish Civil War, 1936–1939* (The Hague: Nijhoff, 1962).

101. Cot, *Triumph of Treason*, p. 337.

102. Rathbone to Eden, June 24, 1937, UBFO 371, vol. 21342, no. W13939/7/41; in Oct., 1936, Eden had also denied British pressure on France when he replied to questions from G. R. Strauss, another Labor M.P. See G. R. Strauss to Eden, Oct. 1, 1936, UBFO 371, vol. 20579, no. W13010/9549/41.

103. UBCab. 23, vol. 86, 60(36)2, p. 7; Anthony Eden, *Facing the Dictators: The Memoirs of Anthony Eden, Earl of Avon* (Boston: Houghton Mifflin Co., 1962), p. 452.

104. Interviews with H. Bonnet; Blum, July 4, 1969; and Corbin.

105. *Le Temps*, Sept. 14, 1936.

106. Yvon Delbos, *Sunday Times* (London), June 12, 1938.

107. Ibid.

108. Quoted in Werth, *Which Way France?*, p. 377.

109. Blum, *L'Oeuvre*, IV-A, 418.

110. Phipps (Paris) to Eden, Oct. 29, 1937, UBFO 371, vol. 20687, no. C7481/18/17.

111. Ibid.

112. Larmour, *The French Radical Party*, p. 207.

113. Greene, *Crisis and Decline*, p. 83.

114. It is not the purpose of this work to detail the multitude of motives that determined Blum's decision. The topic has been treated at length in two excellent studies: Greene, *Crisis and Decline*, pp. 78–90, and Colton, *Léon Blum*, pp. 234–56.

115. Cameron, "Alexis Saint-Léger Léger," p. 391.

116. Massigli interview.

117. Phipps (Paris) to Eden, Oct. 29, 1937, UBFO 371, vol. 20687, no. C7481/ 18/17.

CHAPTER 4

1. Colton, *Léon Blum*, p. 254.
2. *L'Action Française*, May 28, 1936, quoted in Edward R. Tannenbaum, *The Action Française: Die-Hard Reactionaries in Twentieth-Century France* (New York: John Wiley & Sons, 1962), p. 217.
3. Cot and Moch interviews; see also Blum's testimony in *Les Evénements*, I, 219; Moch described the policy of *"non-intervention elastique"* in *Naissance et croissance*, p. 47.
4. Interviews with Moch, Cot, and Blum (June 26, 1969).
5. Colton, *Léon Blum*, p. 257; Furnia, *Diplomacy of Appeasement*, p. 229.
6. For discussions of those elaborate but fruitless efforts see Esch, *Prelude to War*, pp. 76–79 and 87–89; Furnia, *Diplomacy of Appeasement*, pp. 229–35.
7. Bullitt (Paris) to Sec. of State, May 31, 1937, *USFR, 1937*, I, 311–12. See also Furnia, *Diplomacy of Appeasement*, p. 259; Thomas, *The Spanish Civil War*, p. 441.
8. Bullitt (Paris) to Sec. of State, July 23, 1937, *USFR, 1937*, I, 335.
9. Ibid.
10. Ambassador Ulrich von Hassell (Rome) to Foreign Ministry, Aug. 5, 1937; and return from Ernst von Weizäcker (Berlin) to Embassy in Italy, Aug. 13, 1937, *DGFP*, D, III, nos. 408 and 409, p. 433.
11. Louis Fischer, *Men and Politics* (New York: Duell, Sloan & Pearce, 1941), p. 444.
12. Werth, *Twilight of France*, p. 179. It has been estimated that at the outbreak of hostilities the entire Spanish submarine fleet numbered twelve. Of these, the rebels seized only three. Consequently, it would have been impossible for the rebels to do so much damage themselves. See Norman J. Padelford, *International Law and Diplomacy in the Spanish Civil Strife* (New York: The Macmillan Co., 1939), p. 39.
13. Moch, *Naissance et croissance*, p. 50.
14. Ibid., p. 49.
15. See the list of appointments in Bonnefous, *Vers la guerre*, pp. 8–9 and 165–66. Jules Moch, however, does not agree that the new government represented a mere shuffling of the same men in different posts (Moch interview). Although one must agree with Moch that the spirit of the Popular Front had changed, the personnel remained essentially the same for the initial period of the Chautemps government. For the best treatment and analysis of Blum's action see Colton, *Léon Blum*, pp. 270–85.
16. Professor Georges Dupeux first suggested the possibility of a change in Delbos' attitude in a conversation with the author in Kent, Ohio, May, 1969. Jules Moch feels the change is partially explained by the strong control exercised by Blum over his ministers, whereas Chautemps allowed them

more flexibility (Moch interview). Robert Blum indicates that the closeness of viewpoint between Blum and Delbos might have made it appear that Delbos would not take decisive initiatives (interview, July 4, 1969). There is little doubt that Delbos disagreed with Chautemps' ideas on foreign policy at this time, particularly with regard to Italy. Perhaps this pushed him further to the fore. See Bullitt (Paris) to Sec. of State, Aug. 26, 1937, *USFR, 1937*, I, 118.

17. Furnia, *Diplomacy of Appeasement*, pp. 261–62. Furnia also cites an unpublished telegram from Bullitt (Paris) to Sec. of State of July 2, 1937, in which he reported that Delbos proposed a Franco-British attempt to thwart Italian and German objectives in the Mediterranean and Central Europe.

18. Bullitt (Paris) to Sec. of State, July 7, 1937, *USFR, 1937*, I, 356.

19. Bingham (London) to Sec. of State, July 14, 1937, *USFR, 1937*, I, 356.

20. Bullitt (Paris) to Sec. of State, July 15, 1937, *USFR, 1937*, I, 360–61. It appears that Delbos considered recognition of Franco as a weapon that could be used to bring about the withdrawal of Italian troops, quid pro quo.

21. Bullitt (Paris) to Sec. of State, Aug. 26, 1937, *USFR, 1937*, I, 118. Delbos considered that "Italy should be treated with contempt and disdain as a relatively unimportant jackal." This attitude will be explored in a later chapter.

22. Furnia, *Diplomacy of Appeasement*, p. 263.

23. Bullitt (Paris) to Sec. of State, July 7, 1937, *USFR, 1937*, I, 357.

24. Bullitt (Paris) to Sec. of State, July 30, 1937, *USFR, 1937*, I, 367.

25. Bullitt (Paris) to Sec. of State, Aug. 2, 1937, *USFR, 1937*, I, 369.

26. German Ambassador in France (Welczeck) to Foreign Ministry, July 22, 1937, *DGFP*, D, III, no. 400, p. 425.

27. Bullitt (Paris) to Sec. of State, Aug. 3, 1937, *USFR, 1937*, I, 369–70.

28. Bullitt (Paris) to Sec. of State, Aug. 28, 1937, *USFR, 1937*, I, 380–81.

29. Eden, *Facing the Dictators*, p. 516; Eden to Lloyd Thomas (Paris), Aug. 26, 1937, UBFO 371, vol. 21358, no. W16229/23/41.

30. Eden to Lloyd Thomas (Paris), Aug. 30, 1937, UBFO 371, vol. 21358, no. W16299/23/41.

31. Eden to Lloyd Thomas (Paris), Aug. 26, 1937, UBFO 371, vol. 21358, no. W16229/23/41.

32. Unpublished French document, Roger Cambon, French Chargé d'Affaires (London) to Eden, included in UBFO 371, vol. 21358, no. W16299/23/41.

33. Eden, *Facing the Dictators*, p. 519.

34. Ibid., p. 520; circular from Eden to Commonwealth governments, Sept. 3, 1937, UBFO, vol. 21404.

35. Eden to Lloyd Thomas (Paris), Sept. 2, 1937, UBFO 371, vol. 21358, no. W16521/23/41.

36. UBCab. 23, vol. 89, 34(37)2, p. 153. See also Sir G. Mounsey to Eden, Sept. 3, 1937, UBFO 371, vol. 21404, no. W16720/16618/41.

37. UBCab. 23, vol. 89, 34(37)3, p. 153; Eden to Lloyd Thomas (Paris), Sept. 3, 1937, UBFO 371, vol. 21359, no. W16608/23/41; Eden, *Facing the*

Dictators, p. 521. Eden was very concerned lest the differences between the two governments become public knowledge and weaken their effort at the conference.

38. Eden, *Facing the Dictators,* p. 521. Invitations went to Russia, Germany, Italy, Turkey, Greece, Yugoslavia, Rumania, Bulgaria, Albania, and Egypt.
39. Ingram (Rome) to Eden, Sept. 6, 1937, UBFO 371, vol. 21404, no. W16755/16618/41.
40. UBCab. 23, vol. 89, 34(37)3, p. 154.
41. Ingram (Rome) to Eden, Sept. 6, 1937, UBFO 371, vol. 21359, no. W16755/16618/41.
42. Ingram (Rome) to Eden, Sept. 6, 1937, UBFO 371, vol. 21359, no. W16781/23/41.
43. *L'Action Française,* Sept. 7, 1937, called attention to the *Pravda* attacks which it said recalled "the method of the pickpocket."
44. Ingram (Rome) to Eden, Sept. 7, 1937, UBFO 371, vol. 21359, no. W16854/23/41.
45. Sir G. Mounsey to British Embassy (Paris), Sept. 8, 1937, UBFO 371, vol. 21405, no. W16957/16618/41.
46. Lloyd Thomas (Paris) to Eden, Sept. 8, 1937, UBFO 371, vol. 21405, no. W16898/16618/41; and Sept. 7, 1937, no. W16874/16618/41.
47. UBCab. 23, vol. 89, 34(37)3, p. 154. Max Beloff, in *The Foreign Policy of Soviet Russia* (London: Oxford University Press, 1949), II, 97, believes that the Soviets feared that the conference would be used by the Axis powers to urge belligerent rights for Franco.
48. Ingram (Rome) to Eden, Sept. 9, 1937, UBFO 371, vol. 21405, no. W16932/16618/41; Memorandum to the British and French Embassies, Sept. 9, 1937, *DGFP,* D, III, no. 417, p. 442. The Germans also cited lack of Franco-British concern over the *Deutschland* and *Leipzig* incidents.
49. The evidence is that Delbos did not know of the impending Russian note. See Bullitt (Paris) to Sec. of State, Sept. 8, 1937, *USFR, 1937,* I, 389.
50. Eden to Lloyd Thomas (Paris), Sept. 7, 1937, UBFO 371, vol. 21405, no. W16874/16618/41.
51. Unpublished French Documents, Sept. 6, 1937, UBFO 371, vol. 21404, no. W16797/16618/41; Sept. 8, 1937, UBFO 371, vol. 21405.
52. See UBCab. 23, vol. 89, 34(37), app. 3, p. 193.
53. UBCab. 23, vol. 89, 34(37), app. 2, pp. 181–85.
54. Perhaps Delbos and Eden were anxious to avoid a situation that would find France, Britain, and the Soviet Union lined up ideologically against the Axis powers. Thus the emphasis upon the technical aspects of the problem. Eden, *Facing the Dictators,* p. 525; Lloyd Thomas (Paris) to Foreign Office, Sept. 10, 1937, UBFO 371, vol. 21405, no. W17031/16618/41.
55. Lloyd Thomas (Paris) to Eden, Sept. 2, 1937, UBFO 371, vol. 21358, no. W16518/23/41.
56. *Le Temps,* Sept. 3, 1937. *La Lumière,* Sept. 3, 1937, declared, "La Non-Intervention est morte."

57. Lloyd Thomas (Paris) to Eden, Sept. 2, 1937, UBFO 371, vol. 21358, no. W16518/23/41.
58. See *L'Humanité*, Sept. 6, 1937; *L'Oeuvre*, Sept. 6, 1937. Madame Geneviève Tabouis felt that the Axis powers would seize the opportunity to attack the Soviets.
59. *Le Temps*, Sept. 7, 1937.
60. See *L'Humanité*, Sept. 7, 1937; *L'Action Française*, Sept. 7, 1937. On the eighth the latter warned of creating a dangerous precedent by allowing Russian presence in the Mediterranean: "Russia and the Reich have as much interest in the Mediterranean as France and England in the Sea of Azov." On the tenth it warned that the Soviets' willingness to "light the spark that will inflame the world is evident." *Je suis partout*, Sept. 10, 1937, also invoked the fear that "never perhaps since the beginning of the Spanish war, has the danger of a European catastrophe been so near as in this second week of September." See also *Le Temps*, Sept. 8, 1937.
61. Fischer, *Men and Politics*, p. 445. It had been agreed that Geneva should not be the meeting place in order not to offend Italy. (The Italians associated Geneva with the League's condemnation of their Abyssinian War.) Nyon's proximity to Geneva would allow the delegates to be near enough for the opening of the League session on the thirteenth. Arnold J. Toynbee, ed., *The International Repercussions of the War in Spain*, vol. II of *Survey of International Affairs, 1937* (London: Oxford University Press, 1938), pp. 344–45. The countries attending included all those invited except Germany, Italy, and Albania.
62. Speech by Delbos, Verbatim Report of First Plenary Meeting (Public), Sept. 10, 1937, UBFO 371, vol. 21406, no. W17261/16618/41.
63. It should be noted that although his speech was uncompromising, he did not attempt to place any blame for the submarine attacks. Perhaps, as Toynbee suggests, *Survey*, p. 346, he was leaving the door open for Italian and German adherence at a later date.
64. Speech by Litvinov, First Plenary Meeting (Public), Sept. 10, 1937, UBFO 371, vol. 21406, no. W17261/16618/41.
65. Speech by Eden, ibid.
66. Eden, *Facing the Dictators*, p. 526; UBCab. 23, vol. 89, 35(37)2, p. 201.
67. Eden, *Facing the Dictators*, p. 526.
68. Ibid., pp. 526–28. France would supply twenty-eight destroyers, taking some out of reserve for the purpose. Britain would provide thirty-five.
69. Ibid., p. 527; Speech by Litvinov, Verbatim Report of Second Plenary Meeting (Public), Sept. 14, 1937, UBFO 371, vol. 21406, no. W17261/16618/41.
70. Eden, *Facing the Dictators*, p. 527.
71. British Delegation (Geneva) to Foreign Office, Sept. 11, 1937, UBFO 371, vol. 21405, no. W17095/16618/41.
72. UBCab. 23, vol. 89, 35(37)2, p. 201; Eden, *Facing the Dictators*, p. 527.
73. Eden, *Facing the Dictators*, p. 527.

74. The delay was caused by Litvinov, the only delegate who felt it necessary to refer the agreement to his government before signing it. Beloff, *Foreign Policy of Soviet Russia*, II, 99.
75. Speech by Delbos, Verbatim Report of Second Plenary Meeting (Public), Sept. 14, 1937, UBFO 371, vol. 21406, no. W17261/16618/41.
76. Verbatim Report of Third Plenary Meeting (Public) Sept. 17, 1937, UBFO 371, vol. 21406, no. W17261/16618/41.
77. Verbatim Report of Fourth Plenary Meeting (Private), Sept. 17, 1937, UBFO 371, vol. 21406, no. W17261/16618/41.
78. British Delegation (Geneva) to Foreign Office, Sept. 17, 1937, UBFO 371, vol. 21406, no. W17556/16618/41.
79. *L'Humanité*, Sept. 12, 1937, was convinced that the accord would lead to belligerent rights for Franco. Italy would be brought in and "the pirates would be called on to control the piracy." *L'Action Française*, Sept. 12, 1937, praised the Franco-British collaboration. *La Dépêche de Toulouse*, Sept. 13, 1937, concluded that the powers "have acted with resolution"; while *La Lumière*, Sept. 17, 1937, added that "for once the great western democratic powers have fulfilled . . . their obligations with regard to collective mankind and their national interests." *Le Populaire*, Sept. 12, 1937, declared that "all socialists and all democrats will rejoice."
80. Lloyd Thomas (Paris) to Eden, Sept. 15, 1937, UBFO 371, vol. 21406, no. W17324/16618/41.
81. *Le Temps*, Sept. 13, 1937. It added that the conference "is a solution of good faith taking account of all legitimate interests."
82. British Delegation (Geneva) to Foreign Office, Sept. 12, 1937, UBFO 371, vol. 21405, no. W17096/16618/41.
83. Ingram (Rome) to Foreign Office, Sept. 13, 1937, UBFO 371, vol. 21405, no. W17245/16618/41.
84. Eden and British Delegation (Geneva) to Foreign Office, Sept. 16, 1937, UBFO 371, vol. 21406, no. W17470/16618/41; Ingram (Rome) to Foreign Office, Sept. 17, 1937, UBFO 371, vol. 21406, no. W17511/16618/41. Von Neurath did warn Ciano that the British had intercepted Italian submarine messages. See Foreign Minister to Embassy (Italy), Sept. 12, 1937, *DGFP*, D, III, no. 418, p. 443.
85. The British representative in Rome felt this to be the more logical reason. Ingram (Rome) to Foreign Office, Sept. 19, 1937, UBFO 371, vol. 21406, no. W17553/16618/41.
86. British Delegation (Geneva) to Foreign Office, Sept. 15, 1937, UBFO 371, vol. 21406, no. W17416/16618/41. Both Eden and Vansittart agreed with the French viewpoint, which probably helped Delbos remain firm.
87. British Delegation (Geneva) to Foreign Office, Sept. 17, 1937, UBFO 371, vol. 21406. Once again Delbos' position had the support of Eden.
88. Ingram (Rome) to Foreign Office, Sept. 19, 1937, UBFO 371, vol. 21406, no. W17645/16618/41.
89. Ingram (Rome) to Foreign Office, Sept. 21, 1937, UBFO 371, vol. 21406,

no. W17767/16618/41. The news that Italy might abandon its uncompromising attitude was welcomed by the French press. Newspapers of the Left regarded it as a welcome result of Franco-British firmness, while those of the Right pointed out the dangers that would be avoided if Italy adhered. *Le Temps,* Sept. 21, 1937, hoped that the contact would develop happily. France and England, it stated, had never intended to overlook the rights of Italy in the Mediterranean. *La Dépêche,* Sept. 3, 1937, echoed these same sentiments. It judged that the Franco-British diplomacy had "achieved an incontestable victory." Of course, *L'Action Française,* Sept. 23, 1937, praised the adherence of Italy to the accords, while *L'Humanité,* Sept. 23, 1937, concluded that "Gribouille and Pierre Laval will applaud. Not the friends of peace."

90. Toynbee, *Survey,* p. 352.
91. Esch, *Prelude to War,* p. 97.
92. Taylor, *Origins of the Second World War,* p. 125.
93. Fischer, *Men and Politics,* pp. 445–47.
94. Eden later admitted that "Delbos had proved a good Chairman." UBCab. 23, vol. 89, 35(37)2, p. 200.
95. Yvon Delbos, *Sunday Times* (London), June 12, 1938.
96. *Le Temps,* Oct. 30, 1937.
97. *La Dépêche de Toulouse,* Oct. 30, 1937.
98. Fischer, *Men and Politics,* p. 446.
99. Puzzo, *Spain and the Great Powers,* p. 199.
100. Furnia, *Diplomacy of Appeasement,* p. 269, claims that evidence in unpublished U.S. State Department documents shows that Delbos threatened to open the Franco-Spanish frontier when the Italians continued to send troops to Spain. In fact, Furnia writes that after the Italians rejected a conciliatory Franco-British note on the volunteer problem, Delbos, Massigli, and Eden developed a plan for a joint naval takeover of Minorca. He adds that Chautemps and Chamberlain vetoed the plan.
101. Winston Churchill, *The Gathering Storm* (Boston: Houghton Mifflin Co., 1948), p. 248.
102. Quoted in Churchill, *Gathering Storm,* p. 246.

CHAPTER 5

1. Eden, *Facing the Dictators,* p. 418. In a letter to the author, May 28, 1969, Eden recalled, "I had the highest regard for both Léon Blum and Yvon Delbos and enjoyed working with them."
2. Harold Nicolson, "What France Means to England," *Foreign Affairs,* XVII (Jan., 1939), 351.
3. Sir Robert Vansittart, *Lessons of My Life* (London: Hutchinson, 1943), p. 21.
4. Ibid., pp. 21–22.
5. Pertinax (André Géraud), "What England Means to France," *Foreign Affairs,* XVII (Jan., 1939), 368–73.

6. Samuel M. Osgood, "Anglophobia and Other Vichy Press Obsessions," *Wiener Library Bulletin*, XXII, no. 3, New Series no. 12 (Summer, 1968), 14. The author analyzes French anti-English attitudes during the thirties as well as the historical legacy that promoted them. Particular attention is focused upon the rightist press. Osgood notes that "by keeping old sores open . . . the small core of Anglophobes were all too successful in perpetuating the myth of *Albion perfide*. In the process, they dampened what little enthusiasm there was among Frenchmen for an ally whom they did not really like very much, and whose reliability they trusted less." See also "The Antisemitism of the French Collaborationist Press," *Wiener Library Bulletin*, XXIII, nos. 2 and 3, New Series nos. 15 and 16 (1969), by the same author.
7. Nicolson, "What France Means to England," p. 353.
8. Arnold Wolfers, *Britain and France Between Two Wars* (New York: W. W. Norton & Co., 1966), p. 387.
9. This argument is put forth in detail by Wolfers.
10. W. M. Jordan, *Great Britain, France, and the German Problem, 1918–1939* (London: Oxford University Press, 1943), p. 207.
11. Ibid., p. 213.
12. Ibid., p. 154.
13. Wolfers, *Britain and France*, p. 380; Jordan, *Great Britain*, pp. 68–69.
14. John W. Wheeler-Bennett, *Munich: Prologue to Tragedy* (New York: Duell, Sloan & Pearce, 1948), p. 229.
15. John C. Cairns, *France* (Englewood Cliffs, N.J.: Prentice-Hall, 1965), p. 49.
16. Quoted in Pertinax, "What England Means to France," p. 369. Pierre-Etienne Flandin, testifying before the postwar Parliamentary Committee, made the accusation that "England literally ran after Germany to obtain an agreement with her." Yet the British had the nerve to accuse France of not having a policy of conciliation with Germany. Flandin's testimony in *Les Evénements*, I, 159.
17. Emile Mireaux, "Anglo-French Relations," *Nineteenth Century*, CXX (July, 1936), 2.
18. Quoted in Gaetano Salvemini, *Prelude to World War II* (Garden City, New York: Doubleday & Co., 1954), p. 495. Sir John Simon, Home Secretary at that time, later wrote that "France was more interested in finding a way to satisfy her Italian friends than in stopping Italian aggression." *Retrospect* (London: Hutchinson & Co., 1952), p. 212.
19. Salvemini, *Prelude to World War II*, p. 495.
20. For the most recent treatments of the Rhineland crisis see William L. Shirer, *Collapse of the Third Republic*, pp. 251–84; Duroselle, "France and the Crisis," pp. 244–68.
21. Mireaux, "Anglo-French Relations," p. 1.
22. Georges Lefranc, *Histoire du Front Populaire, 1934–1938* (Paris: Payot, 1965), p. 390. Lefranc noted that Blum felt it would be possible to negotiate a pact with Russia only after the entente with England had been

reestablished. This must be remembered when one seeks to understand the Popular Front's policy toward the Soviets.

23. For the text of the government's declaration see *Le Temps*, June 24, 1936. It is also reprinted in Blum, *L'Oeuvre de Léon Blum*, IV-A, 357–64. Blum continued to maintain that "the Anglo-French Entente is and remains the primordial condition of European peace." Reprinted from *Le Populaire*, June 24, 1938, in *L'Oeuvre*, IV-A, 411.

24. See Sir George Clerk (Paris) to Foreign Office, June 8, 1936, UBFO 371, vol. 19877, no. C4140/3511/17; Clerk (Paris) to Foreign Office, June 19, 1936, UBFO 371, vol. 19857, no. C4467/1/17. Clerk, the British Ambassador in Paris, added, "The outstanding feature of the French Government's attitude with regard to foreign affairs at the present moment is their almost pathetic desire to be given the lead by, and to be closely associated with, His Majesty's Government." Only four days after taking up his position at the Quai d'Orsay, Delbos had told Clerk of the French desire "to work in full agreement and loyalty" with Britain. The Blum government "felt that such an agreement was the first essential to a solution of the grave problems of Europe at this time." The Foreign Office held no illusions about the French capacity to act independently. The head of the Central Division, Ralph Wigram, noted, "I cannot believe that a government in as weak a position as that of M. Blum in France will be in a position to take any initiative in foreign policy."

25. René Massigli (Geneva) to Foreign Affairs Ministry (telephone), July 3, 1936, *DDF*, 2e, II, no. 386, p. 590. The British questionnaire attempted to establish the basis for negotiating a settlement with the Germans.

26. UBCab. 23, vol. 85, 53(36)1, p. 116. It is clear that the British were quite concerned about French weakness. Eden told the cabinet that "the weakness of France . . . was generally recognized at Geneva. As an example of this he gave a statement made to him by the well-informed Portuguese Foreign Minister that everyone knew that France did not count for much in Europe now." UBCab. 23, vol. 85, 50(36)2, p. 51.

27. Laroche (Brussels) to Delbos, July 8, 1936, *DDF*, 2e, II, no. 407, p. 613. See also UBCab. 23, vol. 85, 50(36)2, p. 61.

28. Delbos to French Ambassadors in Brussels, London, Rome, Berlin, July 9, 1936, *DDF*, 2e, II, no. 414, pp. 630–31. The British had some doubts that the French would agree to a meeting with the Germans due to Soviet pressure on them to refuse extending an invitation to the Germans. There is no evidence, however, to support this view. It is more logical, as was also suggested, that the commitments of the French in Eastern Europe would make it difficult for them to sit down with the Germans after the Rhineland coup. UBCab. 23, vol. 85, 50(36)2, pp. 53 and 57. In view of his antagonism toward Italy, a topic which will be explored in a later chapter, it is surprising that Delbos was somewhat more inclined to bring the Italians into the conference. See Delbos to French Ambassadors in Brussels, London, Rome, Berlin, July 9, 1936, *DDF*, 2e, II, no. 414, pp. 630–31. Perhaps he

felt the raising of sanctions against Italy on July 15 would be sufficient to bring that country back into the Western camp.

29. Corbin (London) to Delbos, July 17, 1936, *DDF*, 2e, II, no. 468, p. 716; Delbos to French Ambassadors in London and Brussels, July 17, 1936, *DDF*, 2e, II, no. 472, pp. 719–20.

30. The British favored holding the meeting in London both for reasons of prestige and because it would be less likely to arouse the suspicions of the Germans.

31. Corbin (London) to Delbos, July 20, 1936, *DDF*, 2e, III, no. 2, p. 4.

32. "Procès-verbal" of the London Conference, July 23, 1936, *DDF*, 2e, III, nos. 18 and 19, pp. 38–42.

33. Ibid., pp. 42–46.

34. "Communiqué final" of the London Conference, July 23, 1936, *DDF*, 2e, III, no. 20, pp. 46–47.

35. Werth, *Which Way France?*, p. 374.

36. For the full text of the British note see Corbin (London) to Delbos, Sept. 18, 1936, *DDF*, 2e, III, no. 265, pp. 384–85.

37. Furnia, *Diplomacy of Appeasement*, pp. 226–27.

38. UBCab. 23, vol. 86 (meeting number missing), 1936, Conclusion 4, p. 48.

39. Corbin (London) to Delbos, Nov. 20, 1936, *DDF*, 2e, IV, no. 4, p. 4.

40. *L'Oeuvre*, Nov. 21, 1936.

41. *Le Temps*, Nov. 21, 1936.

42. *Débats, Chambre*, Dec. 4, 1936, p. 3328.

43. Ibid.

44. See Werth, *Which Way France?*, p. 374. Werth points out that the government's critics felt it was going too far to please England. They believed that more attention should be paid to strengthening French ties with the Soviets and the Little Entente. At a time when passion over the Spanish Civil War ran high and the Axis violations of the Nonintervention Agreement became bolder, it seemed to many, particularly the Communists, that France was being too fearful of alienating the British. One might add that the Anglophobes of the Right were also in the vanguard of those denouncing the government's policy.

45. *Débats, Chambre*, Dec. 4, 1936, p. 3328.

46. See Delbos to Corbin (London), Nov. 16, 1936, *DDF*, 2e, III, no. 490, p. 771; Corbin to Delbos, Nov. 19, 1936, *DDF*, 2e, III, no. 511, p. 805; Corbin to Delbos, Nov. 24, 1936, *DDF*, 2e, IV, no. 30, pp. 43–44.

47. Corbin (London) to Delbos, Nov. 24, 1936, *DDF*, 2e, IV, no. 30, p. 43.

48. Blondel (Rome) to Delbos, Nov. 28, 1936, *DDF*, 2e, IV, no. 59, p. 81. Blondel to Delbos, Dec. 6, 1936, *DDF*, 2e, IV, no. 106, p. 163. Sir Eric Drummond, the chief British negotiator, did press the Italians for including France, but Ciano refused. See Blondel to Delbos, Dec. 19, 1936, *DDF*, 2e, IV, no. 177, p. 288.

49. Corbin (London) to Delbos, Dec. 9, 1936, *DDF*, 2e, IV, no. 121, p. 190; Delbos to Corbin, Dec. 18, 1936, *DDF*, 2e, IV, no. 170, p. 278.

50. Eden, *Facing the Dictators*, p. 484.
51. "Note du Ministre," Dec. 12, 1936, *DDF*, 2e, IV, no. 139, pp. 212–13.
52. Cambon (London) to Delbos, Dec. 31, 1936, *DDF*, 2e, IV, no. 231, p. 383; Cambon to Delbos, Jan. 2, 1937, *DDF*, 2e, IV, no. 234, pp. 395–96.
53. Cambon (London) to Delbos, Jan. 2, 1937, *DDF*, 2e, IV, no. 234, p. 396.
54. Quoted in Eden, *Facing the Dictators*, p. 486.
55. Clerk (Paris) to Eden, Jan. 3, 1937, UBFO 432, vol. 3, no. 1.
56. *L'Oeuvre*, Jan. 3, 1937.
57. *Le Temps*, Jan. 3, 1937.
58. *L'Humanité*, Jan. 3, 1937. At the other extreme, *L'Action Française*, Jan. 3, 1937, wondered in the light of Delbos' apparent approval of the agreement, whether the necessity of strengthening Franco-Italian relations had occurred to him.
59. Furnia, *Diplomacy of Appeasement*, p. 251.
60. *Le Temps*, Feb. 1, 1937.
61. Simon Harcourt-Smith (Brussels) to Eden, May 21, 1937, UBFO 371, vol. 20682, no. C3735/3372/4. Belgium, for example, was quite concerned about the French security system, particularly after the Rhineland crisis. The pro-French elements wanted French attention directed toward the West with its emphasis upon the entente with Britain. The lack of Franco-British cooperation in the face of German aggression did not stimulate Belgian resistance, and King Leopold's government had chosen to renounce its Locarno obligations and return to neutrality in Oct., 1936.
62. Furnia, *Diplomacy of Appeasement*, p. 253.
63. *La Dépêche de Toulouse*, Oct. 30, 1937.
64. Eden, *Facing the Dictators*, pp. 577–78; Wheeler-Bennett, *Munich*, pp. 17–18.
65. Eden, *Facing the Dictators*, p. 579.
66. Phipps (Paris) to Foreign Office, Nov. 22, 1937, UBFO 371, vol. 20698, no. C8039/3285/17. Other subjects that might be discussed would be the Italian question, the Far East, Spain, and European affairs generally.
67. UBCab. 23, vol. 90, 43(37)3, p. 163.
68. Foreign Office to Lindsay (Washington), Dec. 6, 1937, UBFO 371, vol. 20737, no. C8279/270/18.
69. Eden, *Facing the Dictators*, p. 584. As Eden notes, the statement could have meant one thing to Halifax and probably something quite different to Hitler.
70. Foreign Office to Lindsay (Washington), Dec. 6, 1937, UBFO 371, vol. 20737, no. C8279/270/18. Of course, it was not known that two weeks earlier Hitler had already disclosed his plans for conquering Austria and Czechoslovakia. See "Memorandum," Nov. 10, 1937, *DGFP*, D, I, no. 19, pp. 29–39.
71. Bullitt (Paris) to Sec. of State, Dec. 4, 1937, *USFR, 1937*, I, 186.
72. Bullitt (Paris) to Sec. of State, Dec. 1, 1937, *USFR, 1937*, I, 181.
73. Eden, *Facing the Dictators*, pp. 585–86; Keith Feiling, *The Life of Neville*

Chamberlain (London: The Macmillan Co., 1946), pp. 333–34. Later Delbos told Bullitt that neither France nor England would go to war in case Germany should act against Austria. On the other hand, neither would announce that they would not go to war. Only the event could prove what would happen. But he maintained that Czechoslovakia was different. France had treaty obligations to support Czechoslovakia at once in the event of German aggression. The British had declared that they were not disinterested but had made no promises. Bullitt (Paris) to Sec. of State, Dec. 1, 1937, *USFR, 1937,* I, 192.

74. UBCab. 21, vol. 552. This source is an unpublished folder apparently compiled by the Foreign Office for the cabinet. It pertains solely to the Franco-British conversations of Nov. 29 and 30, 1937. The folder contains telegrams and notes entering and leaving the Foreign Office, cabinet minutes concerned with the discussions, parliamentary debates, and newspaper clippings showing domestic and foreign reaction. These Franco-British meetings of November, 1937, must be considered by anyone interested in the Munich episode of nearly one year later. Many of the attitudes that led to selling out the Czechs were already becoming apparent.

75. UBCab. 21, vol. 552. The British concern over the colonial problem played nearly as an important role as the Central European developments, even though, with hindsight, it proved to be a short-term deviation for Hitler.

76. Ibid.

77. Bullitt (Paris) to Sec. of State, Dec. 1, 1937, *USFR, 1937,* I, 181.

78. Eden, *Facing the Dictators,* p. 587. Delbos reiterated his determination to pursue the policy of nonintervention.

79. UBCab. 21, vol. 552. It should be noted that the British were quite concerned about the inefficiency of French aircraft production. Phipps (Paris) to Foreign Office, Nov. 9, 1937, UBFO 371, vol. 20687, no. C7717/18/17. Georges Bonnet says that the British used the opportunity of the London conversations to warn the French that "in France you have no modern planes and you are not yet ready to manufacture a series. It is a great danger to your country." Georges Bonnet, *De Washington au Quai d'Orsay,* vol. I of *Défense de la Paix* (Geneva: Editions du Cheval Ailé, 1946), pp. 49–50. Chamberlain wrote that "[Chautemps] and Delbos were simply staggered when they heard what we were turning out in aeroplanes,—more than five times their output, I am sorry to say." Feiling, *Neville Chamberlain,* p. 334.

80. UBCab. 21, vol. 552; Bullitt (Paris) to Sec. of State, Dec. 1, 1937, *USFR, 1937,* I, 183. Since Delbos would speak on behalf of the British, the Foreign Office was quite concerned about what he would say in Prague. See Orme Sargent's note on UBFO 371, vol. 20712, no. C8370/3/18.

81. Bullitt (Paris) to Sec. of State, Dec. 1, 1937, *USFR, 1937,* I, 183.

82. UBCab. 21, vol. 552.

83. Phipps (Paris) to Foreign Office, Nov. 25, 1937, UBFO 371, vol. 20867, no. C8134/18/17.

84. *L'Humanité*, Dec. 1, 1937.
85. *Le Populaire*, Dec. 1, 1937.
86. *L'Oeuvre*, Dec. 1, 1937.
87. *Le Temps*, Dec. 1, 1937.
88. *L'Action Française*, Dec. 1, 1937.
89. Bullitt (Paris) to Sec. of State, Dec. 1, 1937, *USFR, 1937*, I, 183.
90. Chamberlain kept what he considered to be French weakness in mind while formulating his policy. In January he wrote to a friend:

> Unhappily France keeps pulling her own house down about her ears. We are on excellent terms with her. . . . But France's weakness is a public danger just when she ought to be a source of strength and confidence, and as a friend she has two faults which destroy half her value. She can never keep a secret for more than half an hour, nor a government for more than nine months!
>
> They [the British people] know that France though her army is strong, is desperately weak in some vital spots, and they are always alarmed lest out of loyalty to her we should be led into a quarrel over causes which are of little interest to us, and for which she could not give us decisive aid.
>
> Therefore our people see that in the absence of any powerful ally, and until our armaments are completed, we must adjust our foreign policy to our circumstances.

See Feiling, *Neville Chamberlain*, pp. 322–24.
91. Furnia, *Diplomacy of Appeasement*, pp. 274–75; Martin Gilbert and Richard Gott, *The Appeasers* (London: Weidenfeld & Nicholson, 1963), p. 76.
92. See above, p. 98.
93. Rock, *Neville Chamberlain*, pp. 121–22.
94. For discussions of the Eden resignation crisis see the following: Duff Cooper, *Old Men Forget* (London: Hart-Davis, 1953), pp. 210–13; Eden, *Facing the Dictators*, pp. 666–89; Wheeler-Bennett, *Munich*, pp. 268–72; Feiling, *Neville Chamberlain*, pp. 336–38; Bonnet, *Au Quai d'Orsay*, pp. 78–79; Lewis B. Namier, *Europe in Decay: A Study in Disintegration, 1936–1940* (Gloucester, Mass.: Peter Smith, 1963), pp. 159–60; Gilbert and Gott, *The Appeasers*, pp. 76–77. Lord Cranborne, the pro-French Undersecretary of State for Foreign Affairs, resigned with Eden. In January Sir Robert Vansittart, the Permanent Undersecretary of the Foreign Office, had been "kicked upstairs" to the impotent position of Chief Diplomatic Advisor to the Government. As Chautemps said, the three Englishmen closest to the Quai d'Orsay had been swept aside. Furnia, *Diplomacy of Appeasement*, p. 276.
95. Werth, *Twilight of France*, pp. 141–42.
96. Phipps (Paris) to Halifax, Feb. 28, 1938, UBFO 371, vol. 21590, no. C1384/13/17.
97. See enclosure to Phipps, ibid.
98. Phipps (Paris) to Halifax, Feb. 28, 1938, UBFO 371, vol. 21590, no. C1384/

13/17. The British did not take the French warnings about a governmental change in France too seriously. William Strang noted, "It is a familiar gambit of the French Foreign Ministers to tell us that unless we agree to do something or other the French Government will fall. We do not need to pay too much attention to it on this occasion." He also indicated that if the Chautemps government did fall, "and we were to see M. Chautemps instead of M. Delbos at the *Quai d'Orsay,* the change would be all to the good. M. Chautemps is much more in sympathy with, and has a greater understanding of, British policy than M. Delbos." Here, indeed, is a tribute to Delbos' opposition to appeasement from a man who headed the Central Department of the Foreign Office. See Strang's note attached to the telegram from Phipps (Paris) to Halifax, Feb. 25, 1938, UBFO 371, vol. 21590, no. C1300/13/17.

99. Werth, *Twilight of France,* p. 142.
100. Phipps (Paris) to Halifax, Feb. 28, 1938, UBFO 371, vol. 21590, no. C1384/13/17.
101. *Débats, Chambre,* Feb. 27, 1938, p. 630.
102. Even Pierre Cot, an ardent supporter of intervention on behalf of the Spanish Republicans who felt Britain had definitely told France not to intervene, believes that the orientation towards Britain was correct. Cot interview.
103. R. W. Seton-Watson, *Britain and the Dictators: A Survey of Post-War British Policy* (Cambridge, England: The University Press, 1938), p. 254.
104. Charles A. Micaud, *The French Right and Nazi Germany, 1933–1939* (New York: Octagon Books, 1964), pp. 222–23.
105. Seton-Watson, *Britain and the Dictators,* p. 413.

CHAPTER 6

1. Yvon Delbos, "Mon récent voyage en Russie" (a speech given by Delbos, upon his return, before the Société d'économie industrielle et commerciale, Feb. 17, 1933).
2. Yvon Delbos, *L'Expérience rouge* (Paris: Au Sans Pareil, 1933), p. 235.
3. Ibid., p. 241.
4. Ibid., p. 243.
5. Quoted in Scott, *Alliance Against Hitler,* p. 113.
6. Ibid., p. 251.
7. René Rémond, *The Right Wing in France from 1815 to de Gaulle* (Philadelphia: University of Pennsylvania Press, 1969), p. 301.
8. See Delbos, *L'Expérience rouge,* pp. 231–34.
9. Albrecht-Carrié, *Diplomatic History,* p. 480.
10. Shirer, *Collapse of the Third Republic,* p. 240; Rémond, *The Right Wing in France,* p. 301.
11. Maurice Gamelin, *Le Prologue du drama 1930–août 1939,* vol. II of *Servir* (Paris: Librairie Plon, 1946), p. 180.

12. Paul Reynaud, *La France a sauvé l'Europe* (Paris: Flammarion, 1947), I, 111–12 and 117–18. See also Reynaud, *Envers et contre tous*, II, 163–64.
13. *Le Temps*, June 24, 1936. Delbos and Blum told the Chamber and Senate that France "is assured of the powerful cooperation of our friends in the U.S.S.R. to whom we are united by a pact of assistance open to all and which is inspired by a common anxiety for peace." The government's statement is also reprinted in Blum, *L'Oeuvre*, IV-A, 357–64.
14. Renouvin, "La Politique extérieure," p. 347; Colton, *Léon Blum*, p. 210.
15. Blum's testimony in *Les Evénements*, I, 128.
16. Ibid.
17. Robert Coulondre, *De Staline à Hitler: Souvenirs de deux ambassades, 1936–1939* (Paris: Librairie Hachette, 1950), p. 15.
18. Ibid., p. 14.
19. Ibid., p. 20.
20. Ibid., pp. 20–22. Even one of Delbos' fellow Radicals, Edouard Herriot, warned Coulondre: "Beware of not putting the cart before the horse. We concluded successively two pacts with the U.S.S.R. The first in date is the pact of noninterference; the second the pact of assistance. This order must be respected. It is necessary that the engagement be observed, if they want the pact of assistance effectively executed." Blum took a more general view and was more positive in his assessment. He told Coulondre to express the willingness of France to assure the loyal application of the pact of assistance. Coulondre, *De Staline à Hitler*, pp. 14 and 18. As Paul Reynaud correctly noted, however, he did not give any instructions for Coulondre to respond to any Soviet offers to conclude a military pact. Reynaud said to Coulondre, "Look at the map. . . . On it is written our foreign policy. It is geography which arranged the alliance of the Third Republic with Tsarist Russia against the Germany of the Kaiser. It is what commands the alliance of the same Third Republic with the Russia of the Bolsheviks against the Germany of the Führer." Reynaud, *Mémoires*, II, 158; Coulondre, *De Staline à Hitler*, p. 17.
21. Coulondre, *De Staline à Hitler*, p. 13.
22. See Orme Sargent's note attached to the dispatch from Lloyd Thomas (Paris) to Eden, Oct. 15, 1936, UBFO 371, vol. 19880, no. C7262/92/62.
23. Ibid.
24. Coulondre, *De Staline à Hitler*, p. 44; Reynaud, *Mémoires*, II, 159–60. For an account of Coulondre's efforts to achieve a military agreement while he was Ambassador in Moscow, see Franklin L. Ford and Carl E. Schorske, "The Voice in the Wilderness: Robert Coulondre," pp. 556–61, *in* Gordon Craig and Felix Gilbert, eds., *The Diplomats* (Princeton, N.J.: Princeton University Press, 1953).
25. General Schweisguth may have been a particularly unwise choice to send to the maneuvers, but his views probably represented the majority opinion of the Command by this time. Colonel Beaumont-Nesbitt, the British Military Attaché in Paris, reported that in April, 1936, Schweisguth had

declared: "The pact had no military clauses and no military value for France. The Russians would have liked to have had conversations between the two General Staffs, but had received no encouragement. The sole factor which carried weight with the French General Staff was that they could not afford to allow Russia and Germany to combine." See enclosure by Colonel Beaumont-Nesbitt in the dispatch from Lloyd Thomas (Paris) to Eden, Oct. 15, 1936, UBFO 371, vol. 19880, no. C7262/92/62.

26. Blum's testimony in *Les Evénements*, I, 128.

27. Lucien Loizeau, "Une Mission militaire en U.R.S.S.," *Revue des deux mondes*, Sept. 15, 1955, p. 275.

28. "Rapport du Général Schweisguth, Chef de la Mission française," included in note from Daladier to Delbos, Oct. 13, 1936, *DDF*, 2e, III, no. 343, p. 513.

29. Blum's testimony in *Les Evénements*, I, 128.

30. For the best treatment of French military doctrine during the thirties see Philip C. F. Bankwitz, *Maxime Weygand and Civil-Military Relations in Modern France* (Cambridge, Mass.: Harvard University Press, 1967), chap. four.

31. Ibid., p. 260.

32. Ibid., pp. 250–51; Scott, *Alliance Against Hitler*, p. 140.

33. Blum's testimony in *Les Evénements*, I, 128.

34. See enclosure in the dispatch from Lloyd Thomas (Paris) to Eden, Oct. 15, 1936, UBFO 371, vol. 19880, no. C7262/92/62. The same document provides other indications of the General Staff's doubts about the value of the Red Army. General Giraud, commanding the Sixth Region, told Winston Churchill that the pact "conferred no benefit at all upon France, and that its repercussions were most unfortunate. So far as he [Giraud] was concerned, and he claimed also that he was speaking for the great majority of the French Command and Staff, it would be a very good thing if the Franco-Soviet Pact could be dropped." In October, 1936, General Le Goys, an officer of the Air Staff, after a meeting with Soviet Marshal Tukhachevsky, wondered "how was it possible to create efficient officers, when those officers lived perpetually under the shadow of such a system of political espionage." In Sept., 1936, General Gamelin acknowledged that he had "completely" changed his opinion of the Franco-Soviet Pact. This is interesting in view of his postwar assertion that he had earlier considered Russia as the "only great necessary eastern counterweight vis-à-vis Germany." *Servir*, II, 132.

35. Daladier to Delbos, Oct. 13, 1936, *DDF*, 2e, III, no. 343, p. 511.

36. Lloyd Thomas (Paris) to Eden, Oct. 15, 1936, UBFO 371, vol. 19880, no. C7262/92/62. Lloyd Thomas added that Alexis Léger, the Secretary General of the Quai d'Orsay, remarked that Laval's comment to Stalin that military conversations might take place was not the only time a Laval initiative had subsequently proved to be highly embarrassing. He added that although the Soviet Ambassador had received no encouragement, he never missed an opportunity to raise the question.

37. A bifurcation among politicians, quite apparent from the beginning of the

negotiations for the pact, was still much in evidence. By mid 1936 an increasingly large number, including such ardent early supporters as Edouard Herriot and Delbos, obviously opposed any further extension of the pact. Even Blum, who still hoped to revitalize it, was increasingly cautious and uneasy about closer ties. For a sampling of the spectrum of viewpoints see Reynaud, *Mémoires*, II, 153–65; Scott, *Alliance Against Hitler*. For the French Premier's position see Colton, *Léon Blum*, pp. 119–20 and 210–13.

38. "Notes d'audience de la Présidence du Conseil," Feb. 17, 1937, *DDF*, 2e, IV, no. 457, pp. 787–88. Potemkin stated that if Poland and Rumania agreed to the passage of Soviet troops, then the Soviet Union would lend full assistance to the Czechs. If Poland and Rumania refused, the Soviets would send air support to Czechoslovakia and ship ground troops by sea to France.

39. Gamelin, *Servir*, II, 286.

40. Reynaud, *Mémoires*, II, 162.

41. Renouvin, "La Politique extérieure," p. 348. According to Gamelin, no further military discussion occurred between the two powers. *Servir*, II, 287.

42. Blum's testimony in *Les Evénements*, I, 129.

43. Clerk (Paris) to Vansittart, Dec. 3, 1936, UBFO 371, vol. 19860, no. C8781/1/17.

44. Pierre Cot's testimony, in *Léon Blum: Chef de gouvernement*, pp. 366–67; Cot's testimony in *Les Evénements*, I, 273; Cot, *Triumph of Treason*, pp. 362–63.

45. Chilston (Moscow) to Eden, May 5, 1937, UBFO 371, vol. 20702, no. C3490/532/62; Daniel Brower, *The New Jacobins* (Ithaca, N.Y.: Cornell University Press, 1968), p. 188. Perhaps, as Brower notes, "in effect the Soviet leaders were warning the French that they were willing and able to do without the pact."

46. See the note by R. E. Barclay in the dispatch from Chilston (Moscow) to Eden, May 5, 1937, UBFO 371, vol. 20702, no. C3490/532/62.

47. Foreign Office Memorandum on Delbos-Eden conversation, May 15, 1937, UBFO 371, vol. 20702, no. C3685/532/62.

48. Coulondre, *De Staline à Hitler*, p. 127.

49. Phipps (Paris) to Eden, May 19, 1937, UBFO 371, vol. 20702, no. C3618/532/62.

50. Coulondre, *De Staline à Hitler*, p. 129.

51. Brower, *New Jacobins*, p. 207. Upon occasion, the British worried that the Soviets would exert pressure on France to act in a manner detrimental to British interests. For example, they felt that the Soviets would persuade France to reject British attempts to get France to agree to a meeting with the Germans to formulate a new Western pact. UBCab. 23, vol. 85, 2(50) 36, p. 53.

52. See Sargent's note attached to the dispatch from Lloyd Thomas (Paris) to Eden, Oct. 15, 1936, UBFO 371, vol. 19880, no. C7262/92/62.

53. Phipps (Paris) to Eden, May 13, 1937, UBFO 371, vol. 20702, no. C3620/532/62.

54. Foreign Office Memorandum on Delbos-Eden conversation, May 15, 1937, UBFO 371, vol. 20702, no. C3685/532/62.
55. Brower, *New Jacobins*, p. 207.
56. See above pp. 108–9.
57. Larmour, *The French Radical Party*, p. 213.
58. Werth, *Which Way France?*, pp. 401–2.
59. Renouvin, *Léon Blum*, p. 348.
60. This attitude is reflected in Coulondre's efforts in Moscow. He felt that he must make the Soviet government realize that it must choose between the exportation of its ideology to France and the preservation of the Franco-Soviet Pact. In his first meeting with Litvinov, he told the Soviet Commissar for Foreign Affairs, "I come to tell you: if things continue as they are going, before long there will be no assistance pact. French public opinion is sick and tired of Comintern meddling which, we know . . . is inspired if not also directly operated by the Soviet government itself." Coulondre warned, "Either Soviet interference shall cease, or the Pact will become . . . a dead letter." Coulondre, *De Staline à Hitler*, pp. 31–32.
61. Beloff, *The Foreign Policy of Soviet Russia*, II, 26.
62. *L'Humanité*, Dec. 11, 1937.
63. Ibid., Jan. 13, 1938.
64. Ibid., Jan. 15, 1938.
65. Phipps (Paris) to Eden, Jan. 20, 1938, UBFO 371, vol. 21598, no. C395/55/17. Evidently Litvinov was not above vigorously attacking Delbos himself. It was reported that he delivered a "violent diatribe" against Delbos to Luciani, *Le Temps* correspondent in Moscow. A similar outburst, delivered to Coulondre, appeared in *Le Petit Parisien* in the form of a Soviet demand that Delbos be ousted. See Chilston (Moscow) to Collier, Jan. 24, 1938, UBFO 371, vol. 22288, no. N499/97/38.
66. Feiling, *Life of Neville Chamberlain*, p. 334. Pierre Cot believed that William C. Bullitt, the American Ambassador in Paris, helped to foster the doubts about the Red Army. *Triumph of Treason*, pp. 357–58. Also see William E. Dodd, Jr., and Martha Dodd, eds., *Ambassador Dodd's Diary, 1933–1938* (New York: Harcourt, Brace & Co., 1941), pp. 376–77 for more evidence of Bullitt's anti-Soviet attitude.
67. D. W. Brogan, *The Development of Modern France*, rev. ed. (New York: Harper & Row, 1966), p. 720.
68. Phipps (Paris) to Eden, Nov. 25, 1937, UBFO 371, vol. 20687, no. C8134/18/17.
69. Wright (Paris) to Northern Department, Dec. 28, 1937, UBFO 371, vol. 20702, no. C8880/532/62.
70. Joseph Paul-Boncour's testimony in *Les Evénements*, III, 795–96.
71. Léon Noël, *L'Agression allemande contre la Pologne* (Paris: Flammarion, 1946), pp. 88–89.
72. Foreign Office Memorandum, "Summary of Recent Correspondence on the Value of the Franco-Soviet Pact," June 17, 1937, UBFO 371, vol. 21095,

228

NOTES TO PAGES 120–126

no. N3129/45/38. This is a particularly valuable document for indicating the opinions of the British representatives in Paris, Moscow, Warsaw, and Berlin.

73. Ibid.
74. General Gamelin, while attending the full-scale Rumanian Army maneuvers in Sept., 1937, received from King Carol a promise that he would let the Russians go through the northern part of his country to reach Czechoslovakia. *Servir,* II, 279. Paul-Boncour reported that the Rumanian King had promised him at the beginning of 1936 that he would come to an understanding on the subject. But in 1937 he made French passiveness during the Rhineland episode the pretext for withdrawing his promise. Joseph Paul-Boncour, *Entre deux guerres: souvenirs sur la Troisième République* (Paris: Librairie Plon, 1946), III, 60–61.
75. Lloyd Thomas (Paris) to Eden, Oct. 15, 1936, UBFO 371, vol. 19880, no. C7262/92/62.
76. Foreign Office Memorandum, June 17, 1937, UBFO 371, vol. 21095, no. N3129/45/38.
77. Ibid. This opinion had been expressed by Charles Alphand, the French Ambassador in Moscow prior to Coulondre.
78. Ibid.
79. Ibid.; Foreign Office Memorandum, "The Strength of the Franco-Soviet Pact, and the chances of a Rapprochement between Germany and Russia," n.d., UBFO 371, vol. 21626, no. C2209/95/62. This is a valuable document analyzing French, German, and Soviet opinion about the pact.
80. Foreign Office Memorandum, UBFO 371, vol. 21626, no. C2209/95/62.
81. Paul-Boncour's testimony in *Les Evénements,* III, 793.
82. Wright (Paris) to Northern Department, Dec. 28, 1937, UBFO 371, vol. 20702, no. C8880/532/62.
83. Ibid.
84. Coulondre, *De Staline à Hitler,* p. 45.
85. Quoted in Lewis B. Namier, *In the Nazi Era* (London: Macmillan Co., 1952), p. 172.

CHAPTER 7

1. *Le Temps,* June 24, 1936. This statement was made in the course of the Popular Front government's first foreign-policy statement.
2. For a good background study of Franco-Polish relations during the twenties and early thirties, see Noël, *L'Agression allemande,* pp. 91–120. See also Henry L. Roberts, "The Diplomacy of Colonel Beck," *in* Craig and Gilbert, eds., *The Diplomats,* pp. 556–61.
3. Piotr S. Wandycz, *France and Her Eastern Allies, 1919–1925* (Minneapolis: University of Minnesota Press, 1962), pp. 211–18.
4. Shirer, *Collapse of the Third Republic,* p. 415.

5. Roberts, "Diplomacy of Colonel Beck," p. 594. See Noël, *L'Agression allemande*, p. 102, for a summary of French obligations to Poland.
6. Roberts, "Diplomacy of Colonel Beck," p. 594.
7. Shirer, *Collapse of the Third Republic*, pp. 415–16; Noël, *L'Agression allemande*, pp. 114–15.
8. Roberts, "Diplomacy of Colonel Beck," p. 595.
9. Noël, *L'Agression allemande*, p. 119. Pierre-Etienne Flandin later wrote that the Poles "rejected with indignation the idea that the Red Army could move through Poland to bring aid to the Polish army in case of a conflict between Poland and Germany. Therefore, the Franco-Soviet Pact remained without practical value as long as Polish-Russian relations were not established on a better base" (*Politique française, 1919–1940* [Paris: Les Editions Nouvelles, 1947], p. 222). Daladier told the postwar Parliamentary Commission that "the interest of France was to reconcile Poland and Russia because, without the possibility of a *rapprochement* between these two countries, the Franco-Soviet Pact was a purely theoretical if not a profoundly illusory Pact" (*Les Evénements*, I, 42).
10. Beck informed the French that Poland "must reexamine its attitude towards the existing forms of international collaboration" (Noël, *L'Agression allemande*, p. 138).
11. Roberts, "Diplomacy of Colonel Beck," p. 599.
12. In interviews with the author, both Pierre Cot and André François-Poncet indicated their distaste for Beck's maneuvering. The latter even said that he believed that Beck's deviousness amounted to treason in view of its outcome. Robert Blum, the son of Léon Blum, noted that many left-wing Frenchmen, like the Socialists, disliked and distrusted Beck and Poland. They considered its form of military dictatorship particularly illiberal (interview, July 4, 1969). Noël wrote that "the League of Nations, collective security, the Little Entente, Czechoslovakia, Austria were the objects of constant maneuver by Joseph Beck" (*L'Agression allemande*, p. 105). The Poles held a similar distaste for the French, believing, particularly after the Rhineland occupation, that France sought to divert German aggression eastward. For a sampling of Polish antagonism, see Juliusz Lukasiewicz, *Diplomat in Paris, 1936–1939* (New York: Columbia University Press, 1970), p. 11.
13. Beloff, *Foreign Policy of Soviet Russia*, II, 74; Seton-Watson, *Britain and the Dictators*, p. 407. Poland, of course, recognized that the Rhineland coup had weakened France's potential as an ally. See Lukasiewicz, *Diplomat in Paris*, pp. 12–13. This is a fundamental fact that should be remembered when trying to assess Poland's actions during the period under consideration.
14. Blum, *L'Oeuvre*, IV-A, 384.
15. Blum's testimony in *Les Evénements*, I, 129.
16. Noël, *L'Agression allemande*, pp. 139–40.
17. Ibid. Noël gave the same account to the postwar Parliamentary Commission. See *Les Evénements*, IV, 853. Paradoxically, Smigly-Rydz already had the "distinct impression" that the French would seek to exploit the opportunity

to benefit from Polish internal division. Lukasiewicz, *Diplomat in Paris*, p. 12.

18. Blum's testimony in *Les Evénements*, I, 130.

19. Gamelin, *Servir*, II, 225 and 232–33. The Polish Ambassador in France, however, recalled that Gamelin did not bring up any political matters. See Lukasiewicz, *Diplomat in Paris*, p. 16.

20. Lukasiewicz, *Diplomat in Paris*, p. 19. It is conceivable that the French procrastination was designed to put pressure on the Poles so that Delbos' demand about Beck's removal would have its maximum effect.

21. Noël, *L'Agression allemande*, p. 145.

22. Gamelin, *Servir*, II, 233.

23. Colton, *Léon Blum*, p. 209.

24. Lukasiewicz, *Diplomat in Paris*, p. 19. Jules Moch, who served as Secretary-General of Staff Services for Blum, believes that an indication of French reluctance to make the loan can be seen in the fact that only a twelfth of the loan would be released to Poland every three months. This allowed France to stop the loan at any point if Beck stepped out of line. This was another indication of the French unwillingness to go too far with the Polish Foreign Minister. Moch interview.

25. Noël's testimony in *Les Evénements*, IV, 854; Noël, *L'Agression allemande*, p. 146.

26. Blum's testimony in *Les Evénements*, I, 130. See Gamelin, *Servir*, II, 234–38, for his account of the meeting and documents pertaining to it, especially on Czech-Polish relations. Noël wrote, "I had the conviction that the purifying of relations between our Prague and Warsaw allies was the *sine qua non* of the functioning of our alliance system" (*L'Agression allemande*, p. 145).

27. Noël, *L'Agression allemande*, p. 147. With the benefit of hindsight, Flandin and Georges Bonnet believed that the Rambouillet Conference represented a missed opportunity. Delbos and Blum should have insisted that the Poles clarify their position before granting the loan. Flandin felt that it could have been used as a lever to coerce Poland into making a common front with Czechoslovakia and Russia. Had Beck refused, France should have immediately concluded a new and meaningful alliance with Russia. See Flandin, *Politique française*, p. 222; Bonnet's testimony in *Les Evénements*, IX, 2668.

28. Albrecht-Carrié, *Diplomatic History*, p. 506. In a sense, Delbos and the French obtained something for their money. Poland did use it to initiate a rearmament program and to start construction of a steel-and-concrete defense network on its German frontier. On the other hand, the Poles also wished to build similar fortifications on their Russian frontier. The French were not eager for this. In any case, the Germans had no difficulty in overcoming the Polish defenses in 1939. William Orton, *Twenty Years Armistice, 1918–1938* (New York: Farrar & Rinehart, 1938), p. 274.

29. Lloyd Thomas (Paris) to Strang, Aug. 20, 1937, UBFO 371, vol. 20764, no. C6041/981/55.
30. "Compte rendu, des Conversations Delbos–Smigly-Rydz," Sept. 30, 1936, *DDF*, 2e, III, no. 301, pp. 441–42.
31. See Lukasiewicz, *Diplomat in Paris*, pp. 19–20.
32. Noël (Warsaw) to Delbos, Nov. 2, 1936, *DDF*, 2e, III, no. 433, pp. 668–69.
33. Ibid., p. 669.
34. De Lacroix (Prague) to Delbos, Oct. 8, 1936, *DDF*, 2e, III, no. 326, p. 488.
35. Roberts, "Diplomacy of Colonel Beck," p. 590.
36. Coulondre (Moscow) to Delbos, Feb. 9, 1937, *DDF*, 2e, III, no. 416, p. 725.
37. Memorandum by Eden, Jan. 7, 1937, UBFO 371, vol. 21136, no. R189/26/67. A note attached to this memorandum was rather ominous. Green wrote: "The Poles must know that *the odds* are that Czechoslovakia is doomed, and that any *rapprochement* that went far enough to satisfy Czechoslovakia and her friends would involve the risk of Poland having to fight Germany. . . . A few months ago I was all for the idea of a Czech-Polish *rapprochement*, but things have now deteriorated and clearly we cannot expect Poland to risk her neck on what must appear to be a well-nigh hopeless venture." This is a poignant indication of how at least part of the Foreign Office regarded Czechoslovakia's chances for survival, a year and a half before Munich.
38. Phipps (Paris) to Eden, June 15, 1937, UBFO 432, vol. 3, no. C4320/1/18.
39. See Lloyd Thomas (Paris) to Strang, Aug. 20, 1937, UBFO 371, vol. 20764, no. C6041/981/55; Kennard (Warsaw) to Eden, Oct. 6, 1937, UBFO 371, vol. 20764, no. C6975/981/55.
40. Kennard (Warsaw) to Foreign Office, Sept. 30, 1937, UBFO 371, vol. 20764, no. C6827/981/55; see also the Foreign Office Notes attached by Mallet and Strang.
41. Renouvin, "La Politique extérieure," p. 349; Foreign Office Memorandum, Jan. 6, 1937, UBFO 371, vol. 21136, no. R396/26/67.
42. Noël's testimony in *Les Evénements*, IV, 849.
43. Blum's testimony in *Les Evénements*, I, 128.
44. Ibid., p. 127; Payart (Moscow) to Delbos, Sept. 2, 1936, *DDF*, 2e, III, no. 228, pp. 329–30. Also see editor's note. The removal of Titulescu cast new doubt on whether the Red Army would be permitted on Rumanian soil in case of a conflict. Titulescu had promoted closer relations with Russia and had indicated a willingness for eventual military collaboration. Antonescu did not appear inclined to do so.
45. Thierry (Bucharest) to Delbos, Sept. 19, 1936, *DDF*, 2e, III, no. 266, p. 386.
46. Thierry (Bucharest) to Delbos, Oct. 16, 1936, *DDF*, 2e, III, no. 362, p. 553.
47. Blum's testimony in *Les Evénements*, I, 127.
48. De Dampierre (Belgrade) to Delbos, Sept. 30, 1936, *DDF*, 2e, III, no. 299, pp. 436–37.

49. Blum's testimony in *Les Evénements*, I, 127; de Lacroix (Prague) to Delbos, Nov. 6, 1936, *DDF*, 2e, III, no. 448, p. 703.
50. See de Lacroix (Prague) to Delbos, *DDF*, 2e, III, nos. 207, 352, and 448, pp. 288–89, 535–39, and 703. Blum also noted that the Czechs hinted about the need to find a common ground for a rapprochement with Germany (*Les Evénements*, I, 127). This was probably another attempt to urge the French to action.
51. Delbos to de Lacroix (Prague), Oct. 22, 1936, *DDF*, 2e, III, no. 391, p. 599.
52. Delbos to French Representatives in Belgrade, Prague, and Bucharest, Nov. 10, 1936, *DDF*, 2e, III, no. 457, pp. 715–16.
53. De Lacroix (Prague) to Delbos, Nov. 11, 1936, *DDF*, 2e, III, no. 468, pp. 736–37.
54. De Lacroix (Prague) to Delbos, Nov. 11 and 12, 1936, *DDF*, 2e, III, no. 467, p. 734.
55. Delbos to de Lacroix (Prague), Jan. 11, 1937, *DDF*, 2e, IV, no. 281, pp. 465–68.
56. De Lacroix (Prague) to Delbos, Nov. 11 and 12, 1936, *DDF*, 2e, III, no. 467, p. 733.
57. Delbos to de Lacroix (Prague), Jan. 11, 1937, *DDF*, 2e, IV, no. 281, p. 466.
58. United Kingdom Delegation (Geneva) to Foreign Office, Jan. 23, 1937, UBFO 371, vol. 21136, no. R547/26/67; R. Hoare (Bucharest) to Foreign Office, Mar. 25, 1937, UBFO 371, vol. 21136, no. R2211/26/67.
59. United Kingdom Delegation (Geneva) to Foreign Office, Jan. 23, 1937, 371, vol. 21136, no. R530/26/67.
60. Ibid.; "Note du Ministre de France à Bucarest," Jan. 23, 1937, *DDF*, 2e, IV, no. 344, p. 596.
61. "Note de la Direction politique," Jan. 21, 1937, *DDF*, 2e, IV, no. 334, p. 573.
62. Foreign Office Memorandum, Feb. 4, 1937, UBFO 371, vol. 21136, no. R396/26/67.
63. Campbell (Belgrade) to Foreign Office, Feb. 1, 1937, UBFO 371, vol. 21136, no. R758/26/67.
64. De Dampierre (Belgrade) to Delbos, Dec. 16, 1936, *DDF*, 2e, IV, no. 156, pp. 255–56.
65. Delbos to Corbin (London), Nov. 18, 1936, *DDF*, 2e, III, no. 503, p. 794.
66. Corbin (London) to Delbos, Dec. 23, 1936, *DDF*, 2e, IV, no. 203, p. 344.
67. Foreign Office Memorandum reviewing French relations with members of Little Entente, Jan. 29, 1937, UBFO 371, vol. 21136, no. R396/26/67. This file is replete with notes attached by the Foreign Office staff which indicate their distaste for Delbos' venture.
68. Ibid.
69. Corbin (London) to Delbos, Feb. 6, 1937, *DDF*, 2e, IV, no. 404, pp. 705–6. Given Delbos' unwillingness to alienate Britain, any resolute British opposition probably would have led him to abandon his proposal.
70. De Dampierre (Belgrade) to Delbos, Feb. 4, 1937, *DDF*, 2e, IV, no. 395, pp. 686–87.

71. De Dampierre (Belgrade) to Delbos, Feb. 5, 1937, *DDF*, 2e, IV, no. 400, p. 699.
72. Renouvin, "La Politique extérieure," p. 349.
73. Clerk (Paris) to Eden, Feb. 16, 1937, UBFO 371, vol. 21136, no. R1068/ 26/67.
74. Summary of an Interview between Stoyadinovitch and Delbos on the Occasion of the Former's Passage through France after his Visit to London, Nov. 16, 1937, UBFO 371, vol. 21201, no. R7626/2597/92.
75. Bullitt (Paris) to Sec. of State, May 6, 1937, *USFR, 1937*, I, 89.
76. Ibid.
77. Bullitt (Paris) to Sec. of State, May 5, 1937, *USFR, 1937*, I, 88.
78. Bullitt (Paris) to Sec. of State, May 6, 1937, *USFR, 1937*, I, 89.
79. Summary of the Stoyadinovitch-Delbos conversation, Nov. 16, 1937, UBFO 371, vol. 21201, no. R7626/2597/92.
80. Eisenlohr (Prague) to German Foreign Ministry, Dec. 21, 1937, *DGFP*, D, II, no. 38, p. 80.
81. Werth, *Twilight of France*, p. 34. Charles Corbin (interview) believed that it was quite possible that Delbos sought to repeat Barthou's success and reassure France's eastern allies.
82. Beloff, *Foreign Policy of Soviet Russia*, p. 111.
83. Phipps (Paris) to Eden, Dec. 20, 1937, UBFO 371, vol. 20698, no. C8744/ 7888/17; Werth, *Twilight of France*, pp. 134–35.
84. Kennard (Warsaw) to Eden, Dec. 14, 1937, UBFO 371, vol. 20764, no. C8668/981/55. Chautemps later described the official Polish attitude as "allied but not really friendly." Phipps (Paris) to Foreign Office, Dec. 11, 1937, UBFO 371, vol. 20734, no. C8529/237/18.
85. Noël, *L'Agression allemande*, p. 175.
86. Kennard (Warsaw) to Foreign Office, Dec. 5, 1937, UBFO 371, vol. 20764, no. C8369/981/55. Delbos later confided to the British Minister in Prague that he thought Polish allegations against the Comintern were merely a pretext. He believed the real reason for the Polish attitude was that they wished to divert German ambitions towards Czechoslovakia. Therefore, they preferred not to have cordial relations with Czechoslovakia. Newton (Prague) to Foreign Office, Dec. 16, 1937, UBFO 371, vol. 21140, no. R8564/770/67.
87. Kennard (Warsaw) to Foreign Office, Dec. 9, 1937, UBFO 371, vol. 20764, no. C8493/981/55.
88. Kennard (Warsaw) to Foreign Office, Dec. 5, 1937, UBFO 371, vol. 20764, no. C8369/981/55.
89. Kennard (Warsaw) to Eden, Dec. 14, 1937, UBFO 371, vol. 20764, no. C8668/981/55. The final communiqué issued from Cracow merely noted that Franco-Polish problems and the problem of European peace were reviewed in a spirit of loyal collaboration. Moreover, "it was agreed that the Polish-French Alliance concluded in 1921 constitutes a real and stable

234

factor in the policy of both countries." Kennard (Warsaw) to Foreign
Office, Dec. 7, 1937, UBFO 371, vol. 20764, no. C8509/981/55.
90. Kennard (Warsaw) to Eden, Dec. 14, 1937, UBFO 371, vol. 20764, no.
C8668/981/55.
91. Phipps (Paris) to Foreign Office, Dec. 11, 1937, UBFO 371, vol. 20734,
no. C8529/237/18.
92. Kennard (Warsaw) to Eden, Dec. 14, 1937, UBFO 371, vol. 20764, no.
C8668/981/55.
93. Interviews with Pierre Renouvin, Paris, June 28, 1969; François-Poncet; and
Cot.
94. Werth, *Twilight of France*, p. 136.
95. Loraine (Ankara) to Vansittart, Dec. 30, 1937, UBFO 371, vol. 22346, no.
R233/233/67. For a good example of Maurras' *"communiqué habituel,"*
see the final communiqué issued at the close of Delbos' visit on Dec. 11.
96. Phipps (Paris) to Foreign Office, Dec. 8, 1937, UBFO 371, vol. 21201,
no. R8229/2597/92; Phipps to Foreign Office, Dec. 15, 1937, UBFO 371,
vol. 21201, no. R8390/2597/92. The British even felt it might be necessary
to make it clear to Delbos that they would not support any intrigue against
Stoyadinovitch. They felt that, due to Stoyadinovitch's pro-Italian and pro-
German attitude, the French might support efforts to have him removed.
The British felt that his continuance in office was in the best interests of
France and Britain. Foreign Office Memorandum, Nov. 27, 1937, UBFO
371, vol. 21140, no. R7974/770/67.
97. Campbell (Belgrade) to Eden, Dec. 18, 1937, UBFO 371, vol. 21201, no.
R8611/2597/92; Werth, *Twilight of France*, pp. 136–37.
98. Werth, *Twilight of France*, p. 137.
99. Campbell (Belgrade) to Foreign Office, Dec. 14, 1937, UBFO 371, vol.
21199, no. R8386/244/92.
100. Phipps (Paris) to Eden, Dec. 20, 1937, UBFO 371, vol. 20698, no. C8744/
788/17. It must be noted, however, that in spite of their military inade-
quacies, Delbos considered the Yugoslav army leaders to be pro-French.
Therefore, for political reasons, he preferred that they remain at their posts
rather than be replaced by more efficient men who might be less friendly.
101. Campbell (Belgrade) to Eden, Dec. 18, 1937, UBFO 371, vol. 21201, no.
R8611/2597/92.
102. Ibid.
103. Werth, *Twilight of France*, p. 137.
104. Ibid.
105. Ibid.
106. Phipps (Paris) to Eden, Dec. 20, 1937, UBFO 371, vol. 20698, no. C8744/
7888/17.
107. Ibid.; Werth, *Twilight of France*, p. 138.
108. Eisenlohr (Prague) to German Foreign Ministry, Dec. 18, 1937, *DGFP*,
D, II, no. 34, p. 75.
109. Eisenlohr (Prague) to German Foreign Ministry, Dec. 21, 1937, *DGFP*,

D, II, no. 38, p. 80. The final communiqué said that "in their concern for the preservation of peace in Europe, both governments are prepared to support any action that might facilitate a rapprochement with all neighboring countries. Both governments are convinced that existing commitments are no obstacle to a rapprochement of this kind," pp. 81–82. Presumably the statement referred to Germany.

110. Ibid., p. 82.
111. Ibid., p. 80.
112. Werth, *Twilight of France*, p. 138.
113. Ibid., p. 133.
114. Eisenlohr (Prague) to German Foreign Ministry, Dec. 21, 1937, *DGFP*, D, II, no. 38, p. 80.
115. Werth, *Twilight of France*, pp. 135–36.
116. Sir Robert Hoare, the British Minister in Bucharest, noted that Delbos' visit might have inspired the parties of the Right to make a vigorous effort to attract voters. See the note by R. W. M. Ross attached to the dispatch from Loraine (Ankara) to Vansittart, Dec. 30, 1937, UBFO 371, vol. 22346, no. R233/233/67.
117. Noël, *L'Agression allemande*, pp. 180–81.
118. Loraine (Ankara) to Foreign Office, Dec. 30, 1937, UBFO 371, vol. 22346, no. R233/233/67.
119. Memorandum by the German Ambassador in the Soviet Union (Schulenburg), July 1, 1938, *DGFP*, D, I, no. 787, p. 1144.
120. Coulondre, *De Staline à Hitler*, p. 129.
121. Memorandum by Schulenburg, July 1, 1938, *DGFP*, D, I, no. 787, p. 1144.
122. Brower, *The New Jacobins*, p. 205.
123. Interviews with Corbin, François-Poncet, and G. Bonnet. Henri Laugier, who served in Delbos' cabinet, felt that by this time Italian actions had created too much of an impression in Eastern Europe for Delbos' trip to have any great impact (interview).
124. Corbin interview.

CHAPTER 8

1. Bullitt (Paris) to Sec. of State, Aug. 26, 1937, *USFR, 1937*, I, 118.
2. Delbos, *L'Expérience rouge*, p. 228.
3. Ibid.
4. Rome Chancery to Southern Dept., Apr. 23, 1937, UBFO 371, vol. 21182, no. R2828/2143/22. This document contains a particularly useful analysis of Franco-Italian relations.
5. See Foreign Office note attached to dispatch from Perth (Rome) to Eden, Dec. 6, 1937, UBFO 371, vol. 21182, no. R8064/2143/22.
6. Rome Chancery to Southern Dept., Apr. 23, 1937, UBFO 371, vol. 21182, no. R2828/2143/22; Colton, *Léon Blum*, p. 218.

7. Rome Chancery to Southern Dept., Apr. 23, 1937, UBFO 371, vol. 21182, no. R2828/2143/22.
8. Werth, *Which Way France?*, p. 371.
9. Memorandum on Eden-Blum Conversation, May 15, 1936, UBFO 371, vol. 19880, no. C3693/92/62; Eden also gave a good recapitulation of the meeting in *Facing the Dictators*, pp. 430–31. Eden believed that there were two alternative solutions to the Abyssinian problem. The powers could continue the sanctions until Italy was willing to negotiate a peace settlement, although such a path would almost certainly lead to war. Second, they could admit that the sanctions had failed, but refuse to recognize Italy's conquest. "M. Blum did not appear much attracted by either of these courses."
10. See UBCab. 23, vol. 84, 41(36) and 42(36), pp. 265 and 289. The British cabinet directed Eden to take the initiative at the next League meeting to propose raising the sanctions against Italy. See p. 295.
11. *Le Temps*, June 24, 1936.
12. Alexander Werth recorded that "certain members of the French Government—and particularly M. Delbos—believed that once sanctions were cleared out of the way, it would again be possible to make friends with Italy." *Which Way France?*, p. 371. It is difficult, however, to reconcile this statement with Delbos' subsequent attitude.
13. Blondel (Rome) to Delbos, June 23, 1936, *DDF*, 2e, II, no. 339, pp. 513–14.
14. De Chambrun (Rome) to Delbos, June 26, 1936, *DDF*, 2e, II, no. 359, pp. 538–39. A few days earlier Count Ciano had also suggested to Lagardelle the possibility of an entente with France once sanctions were removed. Blondel (Rome) to Delbos, June 20, 1936, *DDF*, 2e, II, no. 332, p. 501.
15. De Chambrun (Rome) to Delbos, June 24, 1936, *DDF*, 2e, II, no. 346, pp. 521–22.
16. Eden's Memorandum, May 15, 1936, UBFO 371, vol. 19880, no. C3693/92/62.
17. Blum's testimony in *Les Evénements*, I, 220.
18. Rome Chancery to Southern Dept., Apr. 23, 1936, UBFO 371, vol. 21182, no. R2828/2143/22.
19. Ibid.
20. See Lucien Lamoureux, "Mussolini et la France en 1936: Une Mission officieuse de M. J.-L. Malvy (député, ancien ministre)," *in* Edouard Bonnefous, *Vers la guerre*, pp. 410–11.
21. Renouvin, *Les Crises du XXe siècle*, p. 152. In this speech, Mussolini said, "It is obvious that as long as the French Government continues to adopt an attitude of waiting and reserve towards us, we can but do the same." Rome Chancery to Southern Dept., Apr. 23, 1937, UBFO 371, vol. 21182, no. R2828/2143/22.
22. Colton, *Léon Blum*, p. 221.
23. De Chambrun (Rome) to Delbos, Oct. 7, 1936, *DDF*, 2e, III, no. 318, p.

476; Rome Chancery to Southern Dept., Apr. 23, 1936, UBFO 371, vol. 21182, no. R2828/2143/22.

24. De Chambrun (Rome) to Delbos, Oct. 9, 1936, *DDF*, 2e, III, no. 329, p. 491.

25. Delbos to Corbin (London), Nov. 4, 1936, *DDF*, 2e, III, no. 440, p. 686.

26. Colton, *Léon Blum*, p. 222. André François-Poncet was finally sent to Rome only in the aftermath of Munich.

27. See Flandin, *Politique française*, p. 218; Bonnet, *Défense de la Paix*, I, 47.

28. *Débats, Chambre*, Dec. 4, 1936, 2e séance, p. 3329.

29. Clerk (Paris) to Eden, Jan. 3, 1937, UBFO 432, vol. 3, no. 1.

30. See the texts of Blum's and Delbos' speeches in *Le Temps*, Jan. 25 and Feb. 1, 1937.

31. Blum's testimony in *Les Evénements*, I, 220. Blum said that he considered Cerruti's attempt as "a little theatrical" and that it was a "pretty childish *ruse* at pushing us into complete neutrality in the Spanish affair and making easier and more effective the support that, for his part, Mussolini was determined to continue to furnish to Franco."

32. Renouvin, *Les Crises du XXe siècle*, p. 110.

33. Drummond (Rome) to Foreign Office, Feb. 12, 1937, UBFO 371, vol. 21136, no. R1014/26/67.

34. Bullitt (Paris) to Sec. of State, Aug. 5, 1937, *USFR, 1937*, I, 115.

35. Bullitt (Paris) to Sec. of State, Aug. 26, 1937, *USFR, 1937*, I, 118.

36. Perth (Rome) to Eden, Oct. 22, 1936, UBFO 371, vol. 21182, no. R7066/2143/22.

37. Phipps (Paris) to Foreign Office, Oct. 30, 1937, UBFO 371, vol. 21182, no. R7260/2143/22.

38. Perth (Rome) to Foreign Office, Nov. 25, 1937, UBFO 371, vol. 21182, no. R7877/2143/22.

39. Phipps (Paris) to Foreign Office, Nov. 29, 1937, UBFO 371, vol. 21182, no. R7928/2143/22.

40. Bullitt (Paris) to Sec. of State, Dec. 1, 1937, *USFR, 1937*, I, 182.

41. UBCab. 21, vol. 552. The Frenchmen did, however, agree to the desirability of improving relations with Italy. The British had argued in favor of some *démarche* to Italy. It was agreed that the Italian government should be informed that Britain was ready, with French consent, to begin negotiations. France would be brought into the conversations at the appropriate time. This was the occasion for Eden's meeting with Grandi.

42. Feiling, *Life of Neville Chamberlain*, p. 334.

43. Perth (Rome) to Eden, Dec. 1, 1937, UBFO 371, vol. 21182, no. R8064/2143/22. When an Italian newspaper, *Tribuna*, published an article advocating better relations with France, it was promptly confiscated.

44. Perth (Rome) to Foreign Office, Jan. 21 and Feb. 22, 1938, UBFO 371, vol. 22426, nos. R663 and R1893/240/22. The Italians placed a ban on importing certain French newspapers into Italy. After a short time, the French

responded by forbidding the entry of certain Italian newspapers into France. In a short time the restrictions on the French newspapers were relaxed.
45. *Débats, Chambre,* Feb. 26, 1938, p. 630. Delbos' statement may have been in response to a British suggestion. On January 24 the British cabinet expressed to Eden the "desirability of inducing M. Delbos to make an announcement of the French Government's approval of Anglo-Italian conversations whenever they are opened." UBCab. 23, vol. 92, 1(38)1, p. 2.
46. Adolf Hitler, *Mein Kampf,* trans. by Ralph Manheim (Boston: Houghton Mifflin Co., 1943), p. 624. Hitler also said: "Only in France does there exist today more than ever an inner *unanimity* between the intentions of the Jew-controlled stock exchange and the desire of the *chauvinist-minded national statesmen.* . . . This people . . . constitutes in its tie with the aims of Jewish world domination an enduring danger for the existence of the white race in Europe."
47. Delbos, *L'Expérience rouge,* p. 228.
48. Ibid., p. 227.
49. Ibid., p. 234.
50. E. H. Carr, *International Relations Between the Two World Wars, 1919–1939* (New York: Harper & Row, 1966), pp. 230–31; Albrecht-Carrié, *Diplomatic History,* p. 499.
51. Phipps (Berlin) to Foreign Office, June 15, 1936, UBFO 371, vol. 19877, no. C4372/3511/17. Phipps reported that Blum had said to André François-Poncet: "Hitler might rather be a genuine idealist working for what he thought to be the good of his own country."
52. *Débats, Chambre,* June 23, 1936, p. 1531.
53. Ibid., p. 1554.
54. Clerk (Paris) to Foreign Office, June 27, 1936, UBFO 371, vol. 19857, no. C4703/1/17.
55. Blum, *L'Oeuvre,* IV-A, 385.
56. Massigli (Geneva) to Foreign Affairs Ministry, July 3, 1936, *DDF,* 2e, II, no. 386, p. 590.
57. See Delbos to French Ambassadors in Brussels, London, Rome, Berlin, July 9, 1936; Corbin (London) to Delbos, July 7, 1936; Delbos to French Ambassadors in London and Brussels, July 17, 1936, *DDF,* 2e, II, nos. 414, 468, and 472, pp. 630–31, 716, and 719–20.
58. See "Procès-verbal" and "Communiqué final" of the London Conference, July 23, 1936, *DDF,* 2e, III, nos. 18–20, pp. 38–47.
59. Corbin (London) to Delbos, Sept. 18, 1936, *DDF,* 2e, III, no. 265, pp. 384–85.
60. "Memorandum allemand," Oct. 12, 1936, *DDF,* 2e, III, no. 337, pp. 502–3.
61. Delbos to Corbin (London), Oct. 22, 1936, *DDF,* 2e, III, no. 389, pp. 595–96; Delbos to François-Poncet (Berlin), Oct. 13, 1936, *DDF,* 2e, III, no. 339, p. 505.
62. André François-Poncet, *Souvenirs d'une ambassade à Berlin* (Paris: Flammarion, 1946), p. 281.

63. Ibid. It is difficult to evaluate Schacht's real influence with Hitler. Alan Bullock noted that Schacht's grasp of finance and economic problems made him useful to Hitler. But his influence on foreign policy could not have been so great. During 1936 and 1937, Goering, after entering the field of economic policy, began to supplant Schacht as the two men increasingly disagreed over economic policies. Consequently, Schacht's influence was probably on the wane during his two visits to Paris in 1936 and 1937. Finally his resignation was accepted by Hitler in December, 1937. *Hitler: A Study in Tyranny* (New York: Bantam Books, 1961), pp. 359–60.

64. Hjalmar Schacht, *Account Settled* (London: George Weidenfeld & Nicolson, 1949), pp. 92–93.

65. François-Poncet, *Souvenirs*, p. 281.

66. Schacht, *Account Settled*, p. 94; Earl R. Beck, *Verdict on Schacht: A Study in the Problem of Political "Guilt"* (Tallahassee, Fla.: Florida State University Press, 1955), pp. 106–7.

67. François-Poncet (Berlin) to Delbos, Aug. 24, 1936, *DDF*, 2e, III, no. 196, p. 275.

68. Eden (Paris) to Foreign Office, Sept. 20, 1936, UBFO 371, vol. 19859, no. C7626/5740/18 [C6636/G].

69. Moch interview.

70. Eden (Paris) to Foreign Office, Sept. 20, 1936, UBFO 371, vol. 19859, no. C7626/5740/18 [C6636/G].

71. Blum later told Eden that Schacht subsequently twisted his original statements. Schacht's report of the conversation indicated that Blum implied that if Germany ceased to be a menace to France, the Franco-Soviet Pact would lapse. Blum denied the statement that Schacht attributed to him. Eden (Paris) to Foreign Office, Sept. 20, 1936, UBFO 371, vol. 19859, no. C7626/5740/18 [C6636/G].

72. Blum later testified that Schacht wished to circumvent Eden and the Foreign Office by going directly to Baldwin. He told Blum, "If you want to settle this affair with the Foreign Office and with Eden you will fail, but if you, as is your right, insist on discussing only with M. Baldwin . . . you will be surprised to see that in the real ruling circles in England the solution to this question is much better prepared than you imagine." Blum's testimony in *Les Evénements*, I, 222.

73. For the best sources on the Blum-Schacht meeting see "Compte rendu," Aug. 28, 1936, *DDF*, 2e, III, no. 213, pp. 307–11; Eden (Paris) to Foreign Office, Sept. 20, 1936, UBFO 371, vol. 19859, no. C7626/5740/18 [C6636/ G]; Blum's testimony in *Les Evénements*, I, 221–22. Blum attached a note to the "Compte rendu" indicating that although the document was generally correct, it would be a mistake to assume that he dominated the conversation as the document suggests. Therefore, it is necessary to supplement it with Blum's subsequent accounts. The British document contains the first account that Blum gave Eden when the latter visited Paris in September.

The best secondary treatment is found in Colton, *Léon Blum,* pp. 213–16. Colton, however, did not have access to the French and British documents.

74. François-Poncet (Berlin) to Blumel, Chef de Cabinet du Président du Conseil, Oct. 10, 1936, *DDF,* 2e, III, no. 334, pp. 496–98.
75. Eden (Paris) to Foreign Office, Sept. 20, 1936, UBFO 371, vol. 19859, no. C7626/5740/18 [C6636/G].
76. Eden, *Facing the Dictators,* p. 568; Blum's testimony in *Les Evénements,* I, 222.
77. Blum's testimony in *Les Evénements,* I, 222.
78. Beck, *Verdict on Schacht,* p. 108.
79. Ibid., p. 109.
80. Eden (Paris) to Foreign Office, Sept. 20, 1936, UBFO 371, vol. 19859, no. C7626/5740/18 [C6636/G].
81. François-Poncet (Berlin) to Blumel, Oct. 10, 1936, *DDF,* 2e, III, no. 334, p. 497.
82. See the editor's note on "Compte rendu" of Blum-Schacht Meeting, Aug. 28, 1936, *DDF,* 2e, III, no. 213, p. 308.
83. *Débats, Chambre,* July 31, 1936, 2e séance, p. 2329.
84. Bullitt (Paris) to Sec. of State, Dec. 17, 1936, *USFR, 1936,* I, 382.
85. The Ambassador in France (Welczeck) to the Foreign Ministry, Dec. 24, 1936, *DGFP,* D, III, no. 164, pp. 180–81.
86. The Chargé d'Affaires in France (Forster) to the Foreign Ministry, Dec. 11, 1936, *DGFP,* D, III, no. 150, pp. 163–65.
87. The Ambassador in France (Welczeck) to the Foreign Ministry, Dec. 24, 1936, *DGFP,* D, III, no. 164, pp. 181–82.
88. Ibid., p. 181.
89. Bullitt (Paris) to Sec. of State, Dec. 17, 1936, *USFR, 1936,* I, 383.
90. Greene, *Crisis and Decline,* p. 94.
91. *Débats, Chambre,* Dec. 4, 1936, 2e séance, p. 3329. This debate was sparked by Communist Gabriel Péri's sharp attack on the government's nonintervention policy towards Spain. Péri believed that it favored the rebels, whose seizure of power would be contrary to French national interests. The debate and vote of confidence that followed must be seen as the first serious test of the government's foreign policy. Support for the government's policy was evident by its margin of victory of 350 votes to 171. An ominous development, however, was the Communists' decision to abstain. This reflected their dissatisfaction over the Spanish policy, which was the major question at stake in the vote.

The *Deutsche diplomatisch-politische Korrespondenz* criticized Delbos' speech for showing no new approach to the European situation. It expressed resentment at Delbos' promise, in this same speech, that French forces would be placed at Britain's disposal in the event of unprovoked aggression. The German newspaper saw this and the Franco-Soviet Pact as a proliferation of the very "bloc politics" that Delbos wished to avoid. Phipps (Berlin) to Foreign Office, Dec. 7, 1936, UBFO 371, vol. 19915, no. C8746/4/18.

92. *Le Temps*, Dec. 7, 1936.
93. Ibid., Jan. 25, 1937.
94. Ibid., Feb. 1, 1937.
95. Bullitt (Paris) to Sec. of State, Feb. 20, 1937, *USFR, 1937*, I, 49–50.
96. See "Memorandum du Gouvernement Britannique," Nov. 4 and 19, *DDF*, 2e, III, nos. 439 and 513, pp. 675–78 and 807–11.
97. Wilson (Paris) to Sec. of State, Mar. 16, 1937, *USFR, 1937*, I, 62.
98. Ibid.
99. Ibid., pp. 61 and 64. The Italian reply also rejected the British proposals.
100. Memorandum, Dec. 17, 1937, *DGFP*, D, I, no. 83, pp. 135–40. Blum's and Schacht's accounts of the meeting are reprinted in the German documents. For Schacht's account see no. 72, pp. 119–20.
101. Colton, *Léon Blum*, p. 217.
102. The German Foreign Ministry to the German Embassy in Paris, Dec. 24, 1937, *DGFP*, D, I, no. 91, pp. 159–60. It is difficult to understand what the Germans expected outside of a total capitulation to their desires. Delbos and Blum went as far as they could to persuade Germany to negotiate a settlement. Hitler's failure to respond to French overtures casts more doubt upon his desire at any time to undertake serious negotiations.
103. See above, chap. four, pp. 60–62.
104. Schacht, *Account Settled*, p. 95.
105. The German Foreign Ministry to the German Embassy in Paris, Dec. 24, 1937, *DGFP*, D, I, no. 91, pp. 159–60.
106. Colton, *Léon Blum*, p. 217.
107. *La Dépêche de Toulouse*, Oct. 30, 1937.
108. Phipps (Paris) to Foreign Office, Nov. 25, 1937, UBFO 371, vol. 20682, no. C8134/18/17.
109. See Bullitt (Paris) to Sec. of State, Nov. 6 and 22, *USFR, 1937*, I, 153 and 158. Indeed, the famous "Hossbach Memorandum" revealed that Hitler did not desire overseas colonies and he still regarded France as "the most dangerous opponent." "Memorandum," Nov. 10, 1937, *DGFP*, D, I, no. 19, pp. 29–39.
110. Eden, *Facing the Dictators*, p. 529.
111. UBCab. 21, vol. 552. For more on the London meeting see above, chap. five, pp. 95–98.
112. Bullitt (Paris) to Sec. of State, Dec. 1, 1937, *USFR, 1937*, I, 180–81. Eden apparently considered the colonial question moribund. As he told Joachim von Ribbentrop, the German Ambassador in London, the question was embedded in a number of other political questions that had been impossible to solve in the past. Britain and France would formulate their ideas and communicate them to the Germans. "But this process must take considerable time." Delbos' comments to Bullitt showed that he had no intention of formulating any new proposals. See UBCab. 21, vol. 552.
113. UBCab. 21, vol. 552.
114. See above, note 109.

115. Henderson (Berlin) to Foreign Office, Dec. 7, 1937, UBFO 371, vol. 20737, no. C8406/270/18; Phipps (Paris) to Foreign Office, Dec. 20, 1937, UBFO 371, vol. 20698, no. C8744/7888/17.

116. This is essentially the same question that Professor Renouvin asked in concluding his paper on Blum's foreign policy at the Colloquium on Léon Blum in 1965. See Renouvin, "La Politique extérieure," p. 353.

117. Interviews with Blum (July 4, 1969) and Cot.

118. Lloyd Thomas (Paris) to Eden, Apr. 14, 1937, UBFO 371, vol. 21182, no. R2559/2143/22. This is a particularly valuable document containing the British Chargé d'Affaires' analysis of Franco-Italian relations.

119. Interviews with Blum (July 4, 1969) and François-Poncet.

120. Massigli interview. Colton (Léon Blum, pp. 222–23) believes that Mussolini's overt aggression probably motivated Blum's attitude toward Il Duce.

121. Lloyd Thomas (Paris) to Eden, Apr. 14, 1937, UBFO 371, vol. 21182, no. R2559/2143/22.

122. Moch interview.

123. Ibid.; François-Poncet and Cot interviews. François-Poncet believed that Delbos and Blum missed a real opportunity for a rapprochement with Italy and that Mussolini had no real desire to be linked with Germany. Although Mussolini feared and distrusted the Germans, France would not take his pleas for Western unity seriously. Cot noted, however, that after the First World War many Frenchmen desired to cooperate with the new German democracy. This attitude of conciliation and cooperation was felt by some throughout the thirties. In fact, some of these people became collaborators during the war. Presumably this attitude did not exist with regard to Italy.

124. Foreign Office Memorandum by Sir Robert Vansittart, May 18, 1937, UBFO 371, vol. 20696, no. C3737/822/17.

125. United Kingdom Delegation (Geneva) to Foreign Office, Jan. 26, 1938, UBFO 371, vol. 21654, no. C535/42/18.

126. Lloyd Thomas (Paris) to Eden, Apr. 14, 1937, UBFO 371, vol. 21182, no. R2559/2143/22.

127. Clive (Brussels) to Sargent, Feb. 8, 1938, UBFO 371, vol. 22426, no. R1192/240/22.

128. Lloyd Thomas (Paris) to Eden, Apr. 14, 1937, UBFO 371, vol. 21182, no. R2559/2143/22.

129. Ibid.

130. Perth (Rome) to Foreign Office, Oct. 25, 1937, UBFO 371, vol. 21182, no. R7128/2143/22.

131. Lloyd Thomas (Paris) to Eden, Apr. 14, 1937, UBFO 371, vol. 21182, no. R2559/2143/22.

CHAPTER 9

1. Bullitt (Paris) to Sec. of State, Feb. 20, 1937, USFR, 1937, I, 52. See also Bullitt (Paris) to Sec. of State, Feb. 23, 1937, USFR, 1937, I, 54.

2. Bullitt (Paris) to Sec. of State, Apr. 22, 1937, *USFR, 1937,* I, 79. They both believed that Hitler had not decided upon his next move and was keeping all avenues open. While exploring the possible advantages of a policy of peace, he would simultaneously prepare for a policy of war.

3. Bullitt (Paris) to Sec. of State, Apr. 30, 1937, *USFR, 1937,* I, 85. Bullitt also noted that, at the same time, Delbos was urging Phipps to obtain Britain's definite promise to support Czechoslovakia. The British Ambassador replied that Britain could not make such a commitment in advance and could only act as it saw fit if a German invasion of Czechoslovakia actually occurred.

4. Bullitt (Paris) to Sec. of State, May 6, 1937, *USFR, 1937,* I, 89–92.

5. Ibid., p. 90.

6. Bullitt (Paris) to Sec. of State, Nov. 6, 1937, *USFR, 1937,* I, 152–53.

7. The German Ambassador in Austria (Papen) to the German Foreign Minister, Nov. 11, 1937, *DGFP,* D, I, no. 22, p. 44. See the enclosure attached.

8. Bullitt (Paris) to Sec. of State, Nov. 22, 1937, *USFR, 1937,* I, 158.

9. UBCab. 21, vol. 552.

10. Bullitt (Paris) to Sec. of State, Dec. 1, 1937, *USFR, 1937,* I, 182.

11. Bullitt (Paris) to Sec. of State, Dec. 23, 1937, *USFR, 1937,* I, 207.

12. François-Poncet, *Souvenirs,* pp. 285–86; Shirer, *Collapse of the Third Republic,* p. 327.

13. Churchill, *The Gathering Storm,* p. 263. For a good treatment of the meeting see Bullock, *Hitler,* pp. 369–71.

14. Kurt von Schuschnigg, *Ein Requiem in Rot-Weiss-Rot,* pp. 37 ff., quoted in Churchill, *The Gathering Storm,* p. 263.

15. Keith Eubank, *The Origins of World War II* (New York: Thomas Y. Crowell Co., 1969), pp. 93–94; Shirer, *Collapse of the Third Republic,* p. 327.

16. Lefranc, *Histoire du Front Populaire,* pp. 263–69.

17. Quoted in Werth, *Twilight of France,* p. 139.

18. Phipps (Paris) to Foreign Office, Jan. 25, 1938, UBFO 371, vol. 21598, no. C496/55/17. See also UBCab. 23, vol. 92, 11(38)6; Jacques Chastenet, *Declin de la Troisième, 1931–1938* (Paris: Librairie Hachette, 1962), p. 181.

19. Phipps (Paris) to Eden, Jan. 18 and 28, 1938, UBFO 371, vol. 21598, nos. C341 and C606/55/17.

20. See chap. six on policy towards the Soviet Union, pp. 118–19; *L'Humanité,* Jan. 15, 1938.

21. *L'Humanité,* Jan. 20, 1938.

22. Phipps (Paris) to Eden, Jan. 18, 1938, UBFO 371, vol. 21598, no. C341/55/17.

23. Phipps (Paris) to Eden, Jan. 20, 1938, UBFO 371, vol. 21598, no. C395/55/17.

24. Phipps (Paris) to Foreign Office, Jan. 21, 1938, UBFO 371, vol. 21598, no. C427/55/17.

25. Bullitt (Paris) to Sec. of State, Feb. 7, 1938, *USFR, 1938*, I, 16. Perhaps this misguided optimism was for public consumption. Werth, in *Twilight of France*, p. 141, speculated that certain members of the government "were anxious that French opinion should not become too worried about the developments in Germany." It was even rumored that a reassuring article in *Le Temps* had been authored by a high official at the Quai d'Orsay. Where Delbos stood in all of this is uncertain.
26. Werth, *Twilight of France*, p. 142.
27. Ibid., p. 141.
28. Phipps (Paris) to Halifax, Feb. 28, 1938, UBFO 371, vol. 21590, no. C1384/13/17.
29. Werth, *Twilight of France*, p. 142.
30. Phipps (Paris) to Halifax, Feb. 28, 1938, UBFO 371, vol. 21590, no. C1384/13/17.
31. Ibid., See the enclosure to the document.
32. Bullitt (Paris) to Sec. of State, Feb. 21, 1938, *USFR, 1938*, I, 28–29.
33. Phipps (Paris) to Halifax, Feb. 28, 1938, UBFO 371, vol. 21590, no. C1384/13/17. It should be noted that both William Strang and Orme Sargent at the Foreign Office hoped for a change at the Quai d'Orsay in favor of Chautemps. They believed that Chautemps was more sympathetic with British policy, and probably towards appeasing Mussolini, than Delbos. See the Foreign Office note attached to dispatch from Phipps (Paris) to Halifax, Feb. 25, 1938, UBFO 371, vol. 21590, no. C1300/13/17.
34. Phipps (Paris) to Halifax, Feb. 28, 1938, UBFO 371, vol. 21590, no. C1384/13/17; Werth, *Twilight of France*, p. 142.
35. Werth, *Twilight of France*, p. 151. For an account of his statement to the Foreign Affairs Commission, see *Le Temps* of Feb. 23, 1938.
36. *Débats, Chambre*, Feb. 26, 1938, pp. 631–32.
37. The German Ambassador in France (Welczeck) to the German Foreign Ministry, Mar. 1, 1938, *DGFP*, D, I, no. 133, p. 233. He noted that the French statements were decidedly more unequivocal about guaranteeing the independence of Czechoslovakia.
38. See *Débats, Chambre*, Feb. 26, 1938, pp. 638–49, for the speeches by Flandin and Reynaud. For a good *mise au point* of the most important aspects of their speeches see Werth, *Twilight of France*, pp. 149–51.
39. *Débats, Chambre*, Feb. 26, 1938, p. 655.
40. Ibid., pp. 660–62. Both Reynaud and Flandin abstained from voting.
41. Wilson (Paris) to Sec. of State, Mar. 1, 1938, *USFR, 1938*, I, 29.
42. Palairet (Vienna) to Halifax, Mar. 11, 1938, *DBrFP*, Third Series, I, no. 19, p. 10.
43. Halifax to Palairet (Vienna), Mar. 11, 1938, *DBrFP*, Third Series, I, no. 25, p. 13; UBCab. 23, vol. 92, 12(38)1, p. 2. Chamberlain recalled at the cabinet meeting on March 12, that Schuschnigg "had not asked advice before announcing the plebiscite which had caused so much trouble." By announcing the plebiscite, he "had given Herr Hitler an opportunity that

he would not miss." Hitler had been meaning to act for some time, and Schuschnigg's "blunder" gave him the opportunity.

44. The German Ambassador in France (Welczeck) to the German Foreign Ministry, Mar. 11, 1938, *DGFP*, D, I, no. 346, pp. 569–70.

45. Wilson (Paris) to Sec. of State, Mar. 14, 1938, *USFR, 1938*, I, 35.

46. Gamelin, *Servir*, II, 316.

47. Daladier's testimony in *Les Evénements*, I, 26. Halifax told the British cabinet on Mar. 12 that the "French asked if Britain would be willing (1) to make an inquiry in Rome as to the attitude of the Italian government (2) to make a protest to Berlin." This was certainly not a strong demand for action. UBCab. 23, vol. 92, 12(38)1, p. 2.

48. Daladier's testimony in *Les Evénements*, I, 26–27; Gamelin, *Servir*, II, 316.

49. Phipps (Paris) and Perth (Rome) to Halifax, Mar. 11, 1938, *DBrFP*, Third Series, I, nos. 27 and 43, pp. 14 and 20; UBCab. 23, vol. 92, 12(38)1, p. 2.

50. The French Ambassador in Germany (François-Poncet) to Reich Minister von Neurath, Mar. 11, 1938, *DGFP*, D, I, no. 356, pp. 578–79. Delbos told Daladier before the crisis broke that France was isolated. Daladier's testimony in *Les Evénements*, IX, 2888.

51. Eubank, *Origins of World War II*, pp. 96–97.

52. Renouvin, *Les Crises du XXe siècle*, pp. 124–25.

53. Feiling, *Life of Neville Chamberlain*, p. 341.

54. It is interesting to note that the British Foreign Office was scarcely elated over the new government. Orme Sargent made the following remarks: "This is the most deplorable ministry that could possibly be imagined in present circumstances. A typical *Front Populaire* administration, composed of little men in the wrong places. The appointment of Paul-Boncour to the Quai d'Orsay is particularly bad. We can only hope that they will fall very soon: indeed, the best thing of all would be for the Chamber to refuse to give them a vote of confidence when they present themselves this afternoon, but that, I am afraid, is too much to hope for." Alexander Cadogan observed that the government was "rather a broken reed." See the Foreign Office notes attached to the dispatch from Phipps (Paris) to Foreign Office, Mar. 13, 1938, UBFO 371, vol. 21598, no. C1728/55/17.

55. The verdict is still out on Chautemps' motives for resigning at such a particularly crucial time. Paul-Boncour scarcely concealed his doubts when he wrote that Chautemps resigned for reasons of domestic politics, "at least in appearance" (*Entre deux guerres* III, 81). Blum, in his testimony in *Les Evénements*, I, 252–53, however, gave him the benefit of the doubt by pointing to the complete secrecy of the operation until the last minute. But several facts are clear. Although none of the political prophets had predicted a long life for the Chautemps government, the crisis was opened rather than climaxed by his resignation. Just five days earlier the Chamber and Senate had unanimously adopted the government's bill for national defense. Phipps reported that "Chautemps' relinquishment of office . . . alike surprised and even shocked public opinion. . . . The reasons given

in his farewell speech in the Chamber, though not entirely lacking in cogency, were not regarded as justifying him in opening a political crisis at the present juncture. He seems, in fact, to have made up his mind to resign and then . . . to have deliberately created a situation in which his resignation became inevitable." See Phipps (Paris) to Halifax, Mar. 10 and 22, 1938, UBFO 371, vol. 21598, nos. C1660 and C1994/55/17. Perhaps Peter Larmour gave the best interim assessment of his resignation and its importance: "This was the third time that Chautemps had resigned as Premier when the going got rough; at no time was he defeated. . . . He was all nuance, suppleness, and compromise. In this critical moment of the declining Third Republic, his action assumed an almost symbolic cast; his abdication was, in a very real sense, the abdication of the Radical party, and through the Radical party, the abdication of France." *The French Radical Party*, p. 237.

56. Bonnefous, *Vers la guerre*, p. 282; see above, note 54.
57. Moch and Cot interviews; *La Dépêche de Toulouse*, June 17 and 28, 1938; Colton, *Léon Blum*, p. 259.
58. Moch, François-Poncet, and Corbin interviews. These men all gave some credence to this argument, although they could not be certain. François-Poncet doubted that anything serious had come between Delbos and Blum before the latter's second ministry.
59. Laugier interview.

CHAPTER 10

1. Wilson (Paris) to Sec. of State, Oct. 9, 1937, *USFR, 1937*, I, 137.
2. Bullitt (Paris) to Sec. of State, Dec. 1, 1937, *USFR, 1937*, I, 182.
3. Wilson (Paris) to Sec. of State, Oct. 9, 1937, *USFR, 1937*, I, 137. See also *La Dépêche de Toulouse*, Nov. 28, 1938; Eden to Lloyd Thomas (Paris), Aug. 30, 1937, UBFO 371, vol. 21358, no. W16299/23/41; Delbos to French Ambassadors in Tokyo, Washington, London, Berlin, Moscow, Dec. 9, 1936, *DDF*, 2e, IV, no. 120, p. 189.
4. *La Dépêche de Toulouse*, Nov. 17, 1938.
5. Ibid., July 25, 1938.
6. It must be admitted, however, that the British Foreign Office frequently showed scant respect for the French position, anxieties, and susceptibilities.
7. *La Dépêche*, July 25, 1938.
8. See virtually all editorials he wrote during the next six months.
9. *La Dépêche de Toulouse*, July 25, 1938.
10. Ibid.
11. Ibid., June 17, 1938.
12. Thomson, *Democracy in France*, pp. 205–6.
13. Renouvin, *Les Crises du XXe siècle*, p. 112.
14. See *La Dépêche* for May 27, Aug. 31, and Sept. 21, 1938.
15. Ibid., Oct. 3, 1938.

16. Paul Reynaud, "The Parliamentary System Failed to Function," *in* Samuel M. Osgood, ed., *The Fall of France, 1940: Causes and Responsibilities* (Boston: D. C. Heath & Co., 1965), p. 23.
17. Pierre Cot, "The Breakup of the Franco-Russian Alliance," *in* Osgood, *The Fall of France,* p. 48.
18. Renouvin, *Les Crises du XXe siècle,* p. 127.
19. Colton, *Léon Blum,* p. 200.

Bibliography

A. INTRODUCTORY NOTE

Few unpublished French sources exist for a study of Yvon Delbos. Pierre Renouvin, president of a commission established to collect and publish documents relating to the origins of World War II, and Robert Clergerie, Delbos' private secretary, have assured this writer that Delbos' private papers were destroyed during the last hectic days of the debacle of 1940. Large numbers of documents were burned in the courtyard of the Quai d'Orsay, and many of those that were saved became lost either at Bordeaux or later at sea. Unfortunately, the Delbos papers, which had been collected and deposited at the Foreign Ministry, were among those destroyed.

In order to gain insight into Delbos as an individual and to ascertain his role in formulating French foreign policy during the Popular Front period, particularly great importance has been attached to the personal testimony of his lifelong acquaintances and his colleagues of the interwar years. A series of interviews conducted by this writer in France during the summer of 1969 have, therefore, become the basis for an understanding of the character of Yvon Delbos. These testimonies have been supplemented with various unpublished *souvenirs* written about Delbos by some of his long-time friends, which, to my knowledge, have been untapped by scholars of the period. The Association Les Amis d'Yvon Delbos undertook to collect and publish these essays, which treat briefly with diverse phases of his career and character, but the project was interrupted by the death of its editor, Albert Châtelet. One can only hope that the Association, under the presidency of Henri Laforest, will resume this endeavor in the future. Finally, Delbos' writings, speeches, and dispatches are significant sources for tracing and evaluating his role as Foreign Minister.

The testimonies by key governmental leaders before a postwar Parliamentary Commission of Inquiry have been an indispensable source, both for the opinions expressed and the documents revealed. The publication of French diplomatic documents for the period has not yet been completed, and volume five appeared too late to be incorporated into this work. Therefore, the published American, British, and German documents have been relied upon to provide various essential details. Of special value have been the unpublished British Foreign Office and Cabinet papers which recently became available for the period encompassed by this study. Several weeks spent at the Public Records Office in London disclosed some revealing details and opinions as expressed by the British observers in Paris and the Foreign Office officials in London.

Several Frenchmen who were associated with French foreign policy during the period, in one capacity or another, have published their memoirs, journals, or diaries. Although they frequently differ greatly in their interpretations, accuracy, and usefulness, they, along with various newspaper accounts, parliamentary debates, and records of party congresses, help to round out the picture.

B. PRIMARY SOURCES

1. Major Writings and Speeches of Yvon Delbos

Delbos, Yvon. "Address in the Chamber of Deputies, November 19, 1937." *In* James W. Gantenbein. *Documentary Background of World War II, 1931–1941.* New York: Columbia University Press, 1948, pp. 462–70.

———. "Après Munich," *La Dépêche de Toulouse,* Oct. 3, 1938.

———. "La Défense de la Paix," *La Dépêche de Toulouse,* June 17, 1938.

———. "L'Eclipse de Genève," *La Dépêche de Toulouse,* June 17, 1938.

———. "L'Epreuve tchécoslovaque," *La Dépêche de Toulouse,* May 27, 1938.

———. *L'Expérience rouge.* Paris: Au Sans Pareil, 1933.

———, et al. *The Family of Nations.* Addresses delivered from New York, Brussels, Paris, London, and Warsaw on Armistice Day, 1936, over the Columbia Broadcasting System and allied systems, New York, 1936.

———. "France et Angleterre," *La Dépêche de Toulouse,* June 28, 1938.

———. "Heureuses journées," *La Dépêche de Toulouse,* July 25, 1938.

———, et al. *Manifestation de solidarité franco-polonaise, November 26, 1937.* Bordeaux: Imprimerie centrale, n.d.

———, et al. *Manifestation en l'honneur de l'alliance et de l'amitié, February 4, 1937.* Bordeaux: Imprimerie centrale, n.d.

———. *Message de la France aux Nations Américaines.* Paris: Institute des Etudes Américaines, June, 1937.

———. "Mon récent voyage en Russie." Société d'économie industrielle et commerciale. Compte rendu de la Reunion du 17 Février 1933.

———. "The Powers and Spain: French View of Nonintervention," *Sunday Times* (London), June 12, 1938.

———. "Rassemblement nationale," *La Dépêche de Toulouse,* Oct. 28, 1938.

———. "La Rôle de l'Amérique," *La Dépêche de Toulouse,* Nov. 17, 1938.

———. "La Tchécoslovaquie et l'équilibre européen," *La Dépêche de Toulouse,* Aug. 31, 1938.

———. "Tragique Epreuve," *La Dépêche de Toulouse,* Sept. 21, 1938.

————. "De l'Ukraine à la Mediterranée," *La Dépêche de Toulouse*, Dec. 17, 1938.

————. "La Visite des ministres anglais," *La Dépêche de Toulouse*, Dec. 28, 1938.

2. Unpublished Documents

Great Britain. Foreign Office, Unpublished State Papers, May, 1936, to March, 1938.

Great Britain. Public Records Office, Unpublished Cabinet Records, May, 1936, to March, 1938.

3. Published Documents

France. *Documents diplomatiques français, 1932–1939*, 2e série (1936–1939). Tomes II–IV, 17 mars 1936–19 février 1937. Ministère des affaires étrangères, Commission de publication des documents relatifs aux origines de la guerre 1939–1945. Paris: Imprimerie nationale, 1964–1967.

France. *Les Evénements survenus en France de 1933 à 1945: Témoignages et documents recueillis par la Commission d'Enquête Parlementaire.* 9 vols. Paris: Presses Universitaires de France, 1947–1954.

France. *Journal Officiel, Chambre des Députes, Débats Parliamentaires, 1936–1938.* Paris: Imprimerie des Journaux Officiels, 1936–1938.

Germany. *Documents on German Foreign Policy, 1918–1945*, Series D, vols. I–III (1936–1938). London: His Majesty's Stationery Office, 1949–1951.

Great Britain. *Documents on British Foreign Policy, 1919–1939.* Third Series, vol. I (Mar. 9, 1938–July 23, 1938). Edited by E. L. Woodward and Rohan Butler. London: His Majesty's Stationery Office, 1949.

Parti Républicain Radical et Radical-Socialiste. *33e Congrès du Parti Républicain Radical et Radical-Socialiste tenu à Biarritz.* Les 22, 23, 24, et 25 Octobre 1936. Paris: Au Siège du Comité Exécutif, 1936.

————. *34e Congrès du Parti Républicain Radical et Radical-Socialiste tenu à Lille.* Les 27, 28, 29, 30, et 31 Octobre 1937. Paris: Au Siège du Comité Exécutif, 1937.

United States. *Foreign Relations of the United States: Diplomatic Papers*, 1936, vols. I–II; 1937, vols. I–II; 1938, vols. I–II. Washington, D.C.: United States Government Printing Office, 1953–1955.

4. Interviews and Correspondence

Bastid, Paul. Interview, Paris, July 3, 1969.

Blum, Robert. Interviews, Paris, June 26 and July 4, 1969.

Bonnet, Georges. Interview, Paris, July 11, 1969.

Bonnet, Henri. Interview, Paris, Aug. 30, 1969.

————. Letter, March 23, 1972.

Clergerie, Robert. Interview, Boulogne s/Seine, France, Aug. 28, 1969.

Corbin, Charles. Interview, Paris, Aug. 25, 1969.

Cot, Pierre. Interview, Paris, July 7, 1969.

Eden, Anthony, Earl of Avon. Letter, May 23, 1969.

François-Poncet, André. Interview, Paris, July 9, 1969.

Laugier, Henri. Interview, Antibes, France, July 8, 1969.

Massigli, René. Interview, Paris, July 7, 1969.

Mayer, Daniel. Interview, Paris, June 30, 1969.

Moch, Jules. Interview, Chataigneraie, France, Aug. 28, 1969.

5. Other Unpublished Sources, Association Les Amis d'Yvon Delbos, Paris

Barsalou, Joseph. MS.
Bonnet, Henri. MS.
Bouvier, Emile. MS.
Communiqué de l'Association Les

Amis d'Yvon Delbos (Typescript).
Drouart, Léon. MS.
Massigli, René. MS.
Romains, Jules. MS.

6. Memoirs, Diaries, and Published Papers of Contemporaries

Alvarez del Vayo, Julio. *Freedom's Battle*, trans. by Eileen E. Brooke. New York: Alfred A. Knopf, 1940.

Blum, Léon. *L'Oeuvre de Léon Blum*. Vols. IV-A and IV-B. Paris: Editions Albin Michel, 1964–1965.

Blumel, André. "La Non intervention en Espagne." Pp. 460–66 in Georges Lefranc. *Histoire du Front Populaire*. Paris: Payot, 1965.

Bonnet, Georges. *De Washington au Quai d'Orsay*. Vol. I of *Défense de la Paix*. Geneva: Les Editions du Cheval Ailé, 1946.

———. *Le Quai d'Orsay sous trois républiques, 1870–1961*. Paris: Librairie Arthème Fayard, 1961.

Chautemps, Camille. *Cahiers secrets de l'armistice, 1939–1940*. Paris: Librairie Plon, 1963.

Churchill, Winston. *The Gathering Storm*. Vol. I of *The Second World War*. Boston: Houghton Mifflin Co., 1948.

Ciano, Galeazzo. *Ciano's Hidden Diary, 1937–1938*, trans. by Andreas Mayor. New York: E. P. Dutton & Co., 1953.

Cooper, Alfred Duff. *Old Men Forget*. London: Hart-Davis, 1953.

Cot, Pierre. "La Politique extérieure de la Troisième République." Pp. 39–66 in Jean Benoît-Levy, Gustave Cohen, et al. *L'Oeuvre de la Troisième République*. Montreal: Les Editions de l'Arbre, 1943.

———. *Triumph of Treason*, trans. by Sybille and Milton Crane. Chicago and New York: Ziff-Davis Publishing Co., 1944.

Coulondre, Robert. *De Staline à Hitler: souvenirs de deux ambassades, 1936–1939*. Paris: Librairie Hachette, 1950.

Dodd, William E., Jr., and Dodd, Martha, eds. *Ambassador Dodd's Diary, 1933–1938*. New York: Harcourt, Brace & Co., 1941.

Eden, Anthony. *Facing the Dictators: The Memoirs of Anthony*

Eden, Earl of Avon. Boston: Houghton Mifflin Co., 1962.

———. Foreign Affairs. London: Faber & Faber, 1939.

Fischer, Louis. Men and Politics: An Autobiography. New York: Duell, Sloan & Pearce, 1941.

Flandin, Pierre-Etienne. Politique française, 1919–1940. Paris: Les Editions Nouvelles, 1947.

François-Poncet, André. Souvenirs d'une ambassade à Berlin. Paris: Flammarion, 1946.

Gamelin, Maurice. Le Prologue du drame, 1930–août 1939. Vol. II of Servir. Paris: Librairie Plon, 1946.

Halifax, Lord (Edward). Fullness of Days. New York: Dodd, Mead & Co., 1957.

Henderson, Nevile. Failure of a Mission: Berlin, 1937–1939. New York: G. P. Putnam's Sons, 1940.

Herriot, Edouard. D'Une guerre à l'autre, 1914–1936. Vol. II of Jadis. Paris: Flammarion, 1952.

Hitler, Adolf. Mein Kampf, trans. by Ralph Manheim. Boston: Houghton Mifflin Co., 1943.

Hull, Cordell. The Memoirs of Cordell Hull. Vol. I. New York: The Macmillan Co., 1948.

Lamoureux, Lucien. "Mussolini et la France en 1936: Une Mission officieuse de M. J.-L. Malvy (député, ancien ministre). Pp. 410–11 in Edouard Bonnefous, Vers la guerre, 1936–1938. Vol. VI of Histoire politique de la Troisième République. Paris: Presses Universitaires de France, 1965.

Loizeau, Lucien. "Une Mission militaire en U.R.S.S.," Revue des Deux Mondes, Sept. 15, 1955, pp. 252–76.

Lukasiewicz, Juliusz. Diplomat in Paris, 1936–1939. Edited by Waclaw Jedrzejewicz. New York: Columbia University Press, 1970.

Moch, Jules. Naissance et croissance du Front Populaire. Paris: Editions du Parti socialiste S.F.I.O., 1966.

Noël, Léon. L'Agression allemande contre la Pologne. Paris: Flammarion, 1946.

Paul-Boncour, Joseph. Entre deux guerres: souvenirs sur la Troisième République. Vol. III. Paris: Librairie Plon, 1946.

Pertinax (André Géraud). The Gravediggers of France. Garden City, N.Y.: Doubleday, Doran & Co., 1944.

Reynaud, Paul. Envers et contre tous, 7 mars 1936–16 juin 1940. Vol. II of Mémoires. Paris: Flammarion, 1963.

———. La France a sauvé l'Europe. Vol. I. Paris: Flammarion, 1947.

———. In the Thick of the Fight. New York: Simon & Schuster, 1955.

Schacht, Hjalmar. Account Settled. London: George Weidenfeld & Nicolson, 1949.

Simon, Viscount (John). Retrospect: The Memoirs of the Rt. Hon. Viscount Simon. London: Hutchinson & Co., 1952.

Strang, Lord (William). Home and Abroad. London: A. Deutsch, 1956.

Templewood, Viscount (Sir Samuel Hoare). *Nine Troubled Years*. London: Collins, 1954.

Vansittart, Lord (Robert). *Lessons of My Life*. London: Hutchinson & Co., 1943.

————. *The Mist Procession: The Autobiography of Lord Vansittart*. London: Hutchinson & Co., 1958.

Zay, Jean. *Souvenirs et solitude*. Paris: R. Julliard, 1946.

C. SECONDARY SOURCES

1. Selected Books and Articles Consulted

Albrecht-Carrié, René. *A Diplomatic History of Europe Since the Congress of Vienna*. New York: Harper & Row, 1958

Bankwitz, Philip C. F. *Maxime Weygand and Civil-Military Relations in Modern France*. Cambridge, Mass.: Harvard University Press, 1967.

Baumont, Maurice. *La Faillite de la Paix (1918–1939)*. Paris: Presses Universitaires de France, 1945, 1950.

Beck, Earl R. *Verdict on Schacht: A Study in the Problem of Political "Guilt."* Tallahassee, Fla.: Florida State University Press, 1955.

Bell, J. Bowyer. "French Reaction to the Spanish Civil War, July–September, 1936." Pp. 276–96 *in* Lillian Parker Wallace and William C. Askew, eds. *Power, Public Opinion, and Diplomacy*. Durham, N.C.: Duke University Press, 1959.

Beloff, Max. *The Foreign Policy of Soviet Russia, 1929–1941*. Vol. II. London: Oxford University Press, 1949.

Birkenhead, The Earl of. *Halifax: The Life of Lord Halifax*. Boston: Houghton Mifflin Co., 1966.

Bodin, Louis, and Touchard, Jean. *Front Populaire, 1936*. Paris: Librairie Armand Colin, 1961.

Bonnefous, Edouard. *Vers la guerre, 1936–1938*. Vol. VI of *Histoire politique de la Troisième République*. Paris: Presses Universitaires de France, 1965.

Brogan, D. W. *The Development of Modern France*. Rev. ed., New York: Harper & Row, 1966.

Brower, Daniel. *The New Jacobins*. Ithaca, N.Y.: Cornell University Press, 1968.

Bullock, Alan. *Hitler: A Study in Tyranny*. Rev. ed., New York: Bantam Books, 1961.

Cairns, John C. *France*. Englewood Cliffs, N.J.: Prentice-Hall, 1965.

Cameron, Elizabeth R. "Alexis Saint-Léger Léger." Pp. 378–405 *in* Gordon A. Craig and Felix Gilbert, eds. *The Diplomats, 1919–1939*. Princeton, N.J.: Princeton University Press, 1953.

Carr, E. H. *International Relations Between the Two World Wars, 1919–1939*. New York: Harper & Row, 1966.

Chastenet, Jacques. *Declin de la Troisième, 1931–1938*. Vol. VI of *Histoire de la Troisième République*. Paris: Librairie Hachette, 1962.

———. *Vingt ans d'histoire diplomatique, 1919–1939*. Geneva: Editions du Milieu du Monde, 1945.

Cobban, Alfred. *France of the Republics, 1871–1962*. Vol. III of *A History of Modern France*. Baltimore, Md.: Penguin Books, 1965.

Colton, Joel. *Léon Blum: Humanist in Politics*. New York: Alfred A. Knopf, 1966.

Cot, Pierre. "The Breakup of the Franco-Russian Alliance." Pp. 47–49 *in* Samuel M. Osgood, ed. *The Fall of France, 1940: Causes and Responsibilities*. Boston: D. C. Heath & Co., 1965.

Craig, Gordon A., and Gilbert, Felix, eds. *The Diplomats, 1919–1939*. Princeton, N.J.: Princeton University Press, 1953.

De Tarr, Francis. *The French Radical Party from Herriot to Mendès-France*. London: Oxford University Press, 1961.

Dictionnaire biographique français contemporain. Paris: Pharos, 1950, p. 183.

Dictionnaire des parlementaires français: notices biographiques sur les ministres, députés et senateurs français de 1889 à 1940. Vol. IV, pp. 1310–12. Paris: Presses Universitaires de France, 1966.

Dupeux, Georges. *Le Front Populaire et les élections de 1936*. Paris: Librairie Armand Colin, 1959.

Duroselle, Jean-Baptiste. "France and the Crisis of March 1936." Pp. 244–68 *in* Evelyn M.

Acomb and Marvin L. Brown, Jr., eds. *French Society and Culture Since the Old Regime*. New York: Holt, Rinehart & Winston, 1966.

———. *Histoire diplomatique de 1919 à nos jours*. Paris: Librairie Dalloz, 1953.

Esch, Patricia A. M. van der. *Prelude to War: The International Repercussions of the Spanish Civil War, 1936–1939*. The Hague: Nijhoff, 1951.

Eubank, Keith. *The Origins of World War II*. New York: Thomas Y. Crowell Co., 1969.

Feiling, Keith. *The Life of Neville Chamberlain*. London: Macmillan & Co., 1946.

Flottes, Pierre. "Yvon Delbos." Pp. 49–52 in *L'Annuaire de l'Ecole Normale Supérieure*. Paris: Association Amicale des Anciens Elèves de l'Ecole Normale Supérieure, 1958.

Ford, Franklin L., and Schorske, Carl E. "The Voice in the Wilderness: Robert Coulondre." Pp. 555–78 *in* Gordon A. Craig and Felix Gilbert, eds. *The Diplomats*. Princeton, N.J.: Princeton University Press, 1953.

Friedlander, Robert A. "Great Power Politics and Spain's Civil War: The First Phase," *Historian*, XXVII (Nov., 1965), pp. 72–95.

Furnia, Arthur H. *The Diplomacy of Appeasement: Anglo-French Relations and the Prelude to World War II, 1931–1938*. Washington, D.C.: The University Press, 1960.

Gadrat, F., and Renouvin, P. "Les

Documents diplomatiques français," *Revue d'histoire de la deuxième guerre mondiale*, no. 71 (juillet, 1968), pp. 1–11.

Gantenbein, James E. *Documentary Background of World War II, 1931–1941*. New York: Columbia University Press, 1948.

Gathorne-Hardy, Geoffrey. *A Short History of International Affairs, 1920–1939*. 4th ed., New York: Oxford University Press, 1950.

George, Margaret. *The Warped Vision: British Foreign Policy, 1933–1939*. Pittsburg: University of Pittsburg Press, 1965.

Gilbert, Felix. "Ciano and His Ambassadors." Pp. 512–36 *in* Gordon A. Craig and Felix Gilbert, eds. *The Diplomats*. Princeton, N.J.: Princeton University Press, 1953.

Gilbert, Martin, and Gott, Richard. *The Appeasers*. London: Weidenfeld & Nicolson, 1963.

Goldberg, Harvey. *The Life of Jean Jaurès*. Madison, Wis.: University of Wisconsin Press, 1962.

Grayson, Jasper Glenn. "The Foreign Policy of Léon Blum and the Popular Front Government in France." Ph.D. dissertation. University of North Carolina, 1962.

Greene, Nathanael. *Crisis and Decline: The French Socialist Party in the Popular Front Era*. Ithaca, N.Y.: Cornell University Press, 1969.

Hughes, H. Stuart. *Contemporary Europe: A History*. Englewood Cliffs, N.J.: Prentice-Hall, 1966.

Joll, James. "The Making of the Popular Front." Pp. 36–66 *in*

James Joll, ed. *The Decline of the Third Republic*. London: Chatto & Windus, 1959.

Jordan, W. M. *Great Britain, France, and the German Problem, 1918–1939*. London: Oxford University Press, 1943.

Kleine-Ahlbrandt, William Laird. *The Policy of Simmering: A Study of British Policy During the Spanish Civil War, 1936–1939*. The Hague: Nijhoff, 1962.

Knapp, W. F. "The Rhineland Crisis of March 1936." Pp. 67–85 *in* James Joll, ed. *The Decline of the Third Republic*. London: Chatto & Windus, 1959.

Langer, William L., and Gleason, S. Everett. *The Challenge to Isolation, 1937–1940*. Harper & Row, 1952.

Larmour, Peter J. *The French Radical Party in the 1930's*. Stanford, Calif.: Stanford University Press, 1964.

Laurens, Franklin D. *France and the Italo-Ethiopian Crisis, 1935–1936*. The Hague: Mouton & Co., 1967.

Lee, Dwight E. *Ten Years: The World on the Way to War, 1930–1940*. Boston: Houghton Mifflin Co., 1942.

Lefranc, Georges. *Histoire du Front Populaire, 1934–1938*. Paris: Payot, 1965.

Léon Blum: Chef de gouvernement, 1936–1937. Paris: Librairie Armand Colin, 1967.

Lévy, Louis. *The Truth about France*, trans. by W. Pickles. Harmondsworth, Middlesex, England: Penguin, 1941.

Marcus, John T. *French Socialism*

in the Crisis Years, 1933–1936: Fascism and the French Left. New York: Frederick A. Praeger, 1958.

Micaud, Charles A. The French Right and Nazi Germany, 1933–1939. New York: Octagon Books, 1964.

Mireaux, Emile. "Anglo-French Relations," Nineteenth Century and After, CXX (July, 1936), 1–9.

Namier, Lewis B. Europe in Decay: A Study in Disintegration, 1936–1940. Gloucester, Mass.: Peter Smith, 1963.

———. In the Nazi Era. London: Macmillan & Co., 1952.

Nicolson, Harold. "What France Means to England," Foreign Affairs, XVII (Jan., 1939), 351–61.

Orton, William. Twenty Years Armistice, 1918–1938. New York: Farrar & Rinehart, 1938.

Osgood, Samuel M. "Anglophobia and Other Vichy Press Obsessions," Wiener Library Bulletin, XXII, no. 3, New Series no. 12 (Summer, 1968), pp. 13–18.

———. "The Antisemitism of the French Collaborationist Press," Wiener Library Bulletin, XXIII, nos. 2 and 3, New Series nos. 15 and 16 (1969), pp. 51–55.

———, ed. The Fall of France, 1940: Causes and Responsibilities. Boston: D. C. Heath & Co., 1965.

———. "The Front Populaire: Views from the Right," International Review of Social History, IX, pt. 2 (1964).

———. "The Third French Republic in Historical Perspective."

Pp. 53–83 in Gerald N. Grob, ed. Statesmen and Statecraft of the Modern West. Barre, Mass.: Barre Publishers, 1967.

Padelford, Norman J. International Law and Diplomacy in the Spanish Civil Strife. New York: The Macmillan Co., 1939.

Pertinax (André Géraud). "France and the Anglo-German Naval Treaty," Foreign Affairs, XIV (Oct., 1935), 51–61.

———. "What England Means to France," Foreign Affairs, XVII (Jan., 1939), 362–73.

Puzzo, Dante A. Spain and the Great Powers, 1936–1941. New York: Columbia University Press, 1962.

Rémond, René. The Right Wing in France from 1815 to de Gaulle, trans. by James Laux. Philadelphia: University of Pennsylvania Press, 1969.

———, and Coutrot, Aline. Les Catholiques, le communisme, et les crises, 1929–1939. Paris: Librairie Armand Colin, 1960.

Renouvin, Pierre. Les Crises du XXe siècle, 1929 à 1945. Vol. VIII of Histoire des relations internationales. Paris: Librairie Hachette, 1958.

———. "La Politique extérieure du premier gouvernement Léon Blum." Pp. 329–53 in Léon Blum: Chef de gouvernement, 1936–1937. Paris: Librairie Armand Colin, 1967.

Reynaud, Paul. "The Parliamentary System Failed to Function." Pp. 20–25 in Samuel M. Osgood, ed. The Fall of France, 1940: Causes and Responsibilities.

Boston: D. C. Heath & Co., 1965.

Roberts, Henry L. "The Diplomacy of Colonel Beck." Pp. 579–614 in Gordon A. Craig and Felix Gilbert, eds. *The Diplomats.* Princeton, N.J.: Princeton University Press, 1953.

Rock, William R. *Neville Chamberlain.* New York: Twayne Publishers, 1969.

Salvemini, Gaetano. *Prelude to World War II.* Garden City, N.Y.: Doubleday & Co., 1954.

Scott, William E. *Alliance Against Hitler: The Origins of the Franco-Soviet Pact.* Durham, N.C.: Duke University Press, 1962.

Seton-Watson, R. W. *Britain and the Dictators: A Survey of Post-War British Policy.* Cambridge, England: The University Press, 1938.

Sherwood, John M. *Georges Mandel and the Third Republic.* Stanford, Calif.: Stanford University Press, 1970.

Shirer, William L. *The Collapse of the Third Republic: An Inquiry into the Fall of France in 1940.* New York: Simon & Schuster, 1969.

Sieburg, Friedrich. "Persons and Personages: Yvon Delbos," *Living Age,* CCCLII (Mar., 1937), 48–52.

Soulié, Michel. *La Vie politique d'Edouard Herriot.* Paris: Librairie Armand Colin, 1962.

Suarez, Georges. *Nos Seigneurs et maîtres.* Paris: Editions de France, 1937.

Tannenbaum, Edward R. *The Action Française: Die-hard Reac-*

tionaries in Twentieth-Century France. New York: John Wiley & Sons, 1962.

Taylor, A. J. P. *The Origins of the Second World War.* Greenwich, Conn.: Fawcett Publications, 1961.

Thomas, Hugh. *The Spanish Civil War.* New York: Harper & Row, 1961.

Thomson, David. *Democracy in France Since 1870.* New York and London: Oxford University Press, 1964.

———. "Third Republic versus the Third Reich," *Contemporary Review,* CLIX (June, 1941), 668–75.

Tint, Herbert. *The Decline of French Patriotism, 1870–1940.* London: Weidenfeld & Nicolson, 1964.

Touchard, Jean, and Bodin, Louis. "L'Etat de l'opinion au début de l'année 1936." Pp. 49–68 in *Léon Blum: Chef de gouvernement, 1936–1937.* Paris: Librairie Armand Colin, 1967.

Toynbee, Arnold J., ed. *Survey of International Affairs, 1936.* London: Oxford University Press, 1937.

———, ed. *The International Repercussions of the War in Spain.* Vol. II of *Survey of International Affairs, 1937.* London: Oxford University Press, 1938.

Wandycz, Piotr S. *France and Her Eastern Allies, 1919–1925.* Minneapolis, Minn.: University of Minnesota Press, 1962.

Warner, Geoffrey. *Pierre Laval and the Eclipse of France.* London: Eyre & Spottiswoode, 1968.

Weber, Eugen. *Action Française: Royalism and Reaction in Twentieth-Century France.* Stanford, Calif.: Stanford University Press, 1962.

Werth, Alexander. *France and Munich: Before and after the Surrender.* New York: Harper & Brothers, 1939.

———. *The Twilight of France, 1933–1940.* New York: Howard Fertig, 1966.

———. *Which Way France?* New York: Harper & Brothers, 1937.

Wheeler-Bennett, John W. *Munich: Prologue to Tragedy.* New

York: Duell, Sloan & Pearce, 1948.

Windell, George C. "Léon Blum and the Crisis over Spain, 1936," *Historian,* XXIV (Aug., 1962), 423–49.

Wiskeman, Elizabeth. *Europe of the Dictators, 1919–1945.* New York: Harper & Row, 1966.

Wolfers, Arnold. *Britain and France Between Two Wars: Conflicting Strategies of Peace from Versailles to World War II.* New York: W. W. Norton & Co., 1966.

Wright, Gordon. *France in Modern Times: 1760 to the Present.* Chicago: Rand McNally & Co., 1960.

2. Newspapers

L'Action Française.
Dépêche du Midi.
La Dépêche de Toulouse.
Le Figaro.
Gringoire.
L'Humanité.
Je suis partout.
La Lumière.

The Manchester Guardian.
Le Monde.
The New York Times.
Le Populaire.
The Sunday Times (London).
Le Temps.
The Times (London).

Index

Abyssinia, 31, 83, 84, 108, 141, 236n.9; and Franco-Italian relations, 151–53, 157, 158, 178

Action Française, 4, 177

L'Action Française: and Spain, 35, 40, 43; and Nyon Conference, 68, 73, 215n.79, 216n.89, 220n.58; and London Conference of November, 1937, 99; and Mediterranean Conference, 213n.43, 214n.60

Adowa, 179

Albert, André, 185

"Albion perfide," 80

Algeria, 59

Almeria, 57, 174–75

Alphand, Charles, 228n.77

Anglès, Raoul, 5

Anglo-German Naval Agreement, 83

Anglophobes, 217n.6

Anschluss. See Austria

Anti-Comintern Pact, 180

Antonescu, Victor, 133, 148; opposes Eastern European Mutual Assistance Pact, 135–36; and passage of Soviet troops, 136; discussions with Delbos, 143–44

Appeasement, 93, 100, 102; Delbos' resistance to, 60, 93, 99

Archimbaud, Léon, 179

Armée de métier, 111

Asua, Ximines de, 46

Auriol, Vincent, 23, 41, 128, 162, 163; and Spain, 39, 49, 56

Austria, 176, 181; and Halifax's trip to Germany, 95; discussed at London Conference of November, 1937, 96, 176; and Italy, 140; Anschluss, 142, 189–90, 194; Nazi party in,

183–84; Hitler's plans for conquering, 220n.70; and Franco-British policy toward, 221n.73. See also Schuschnigg

Axis. See Germany; Italy; Rome-Berlin Axis

Baldwin, Stanley: and London Conference of July, 1936, 36

Balearic Islands, 35, 154, 178

Balkan Entente, 140

Barsalou, Joseph, 16

Barthou, Louis, 93, 107, 141, 148, 150

Bastid, Paul, 8, 49

Beaumont-Nesbitt, Colonel, 224n.25

Beck, Earl, 166

Beck, Colonel Joseph, 131; and France, 126, 128–29, 132, 140, 229n.12, 230n.24; and Germany, 126, 132, 148; and Rambouillet Conference, 128–29; and Czechoslovakia, 131; visits Rumania, 140; interested in colonies for Poland, 142; tendency toward neutrality, 229n.10

Bedouce, Albert, 23, 49

Belgium, 85, 86, 161; and neutrality, 170, 220n.61

Beloff, Max, 118

Benes, Eduard, 129; warns of Soviet General Staff relations with Germany, 113, 116, 119; on Poland, 131; discussions with Delbos, 145–47; and Sudeten question, 145–46; and Germany, 146–47

Bidault, Georges, 12, 13

Bilbao, 157

Blomberg, Field Marshal Werner von, 183

tance Pact, 137–38; view of Delbos, 223n.98; and Chautemps, 223n.98, 244n.33; on Czechoslovakia, 231n.37; and Delbos' trip through Eastern Europe, 232n.67; and second Blum government, 245n.54

Brogan, D. W., 119

Brower, Daniel, 149

Brussels Conference, 149

Bulgaria, 63, 139

Bullitt, William C., 61, 95, 98, 99, 151, 156, 167, 169, 171, 177, 181, 182, 187, 227n.66, 243n.3; Anti-Soviet attitude, 227n.66

Bullock, Alan, 239n.63

Cadogan, Alexander, 137, 245n.54

Caillaux, Joseph, 6

Cambon, Roger, 62–63

Cameroons, 172

Campbell, Sir Ronald, 145

Campinchi, César, 157–58

Canary Islands, 35

Caporetto, 179

Cárdenas, Juan F. de, 35

Carol, King of Rumania, 143, 228n.74

Cecil, Lord Robert, 83

Central Europe: topic of discussion at London Conference of November, 1937, 95–96. *See also* Austria; Czechoslovakia; Germany

Cerruti, Vittorio, 154–55, 157, 237n.31

Chamberlain, Neville, 63, 141; reaction to Rhineland crisis, 11; and Spanish Civil War, 46, 216n.100; and appeasement, 60; and Italy, 77, 100, 156, 158; and France, 92, 101, 187, 221n.79, 222n.90; attitude concerning Eastern and Central Europe, 92, 95, 96; cross purposes with Delbos, 93; and Germany, 94; and London Conference of November, 1937, 95–98; and Eden's resignation, 100–101,

186–87; speech on collective security, 187; and Anschluss, 244n.43

Chambrun, Count Charles de, 153, 154, 157

Chanak episode, 83

Charles-Roux, François, 158

Chatfield, Lord Admiral of the Fleet, 45, 209n.82, 209n.83

Chautemps, Camille, 8, 9, 38–39, 40, 141, 156, 162, 185, 194, 205n.9, 212n.16, 216n.100; as leader in Radical party, 7, 9; candidate for Foreign Ministry, 26; becomes Premier, 60; supports appeasement, 60; and London Conference of November, 1937, 95, 97; opinion of Halifax's trip, 95; on Delbos' trip to Eastern Europe, 147; and Italy, 155; and Central Europe, 182, 188–89; and cabinet crisis of January, 1938, 184–85; and Hitler's reshuffle of military and diplomatic corps, 186; and Eden's resignation, 186–87, 222n.94; and Austrian Anschluss, 189–90; resignation of March, 1938, 189, 191, 245–46n.58

Chilston, Lord, 120

Churchill, Winston, 19, 117, 225n.34; on Nyon Conference, 78

Ciano, Count, 141, 215n.84; and Nyon Conference, 64–65, 74–75; on Franco-Italian relations, 151; and new Mediterranean pact with France, 153, 236n.14; and Rome-Berlin Axis, 154; and ambassadorial dispute with France, 154; and Anschluss, 190

Clemenceau, Georges, 19

Clerk, Sir George, 46–47, 51, 90, 113, 209n.91, 209n.92, 218n.24

Cogniot, 185

Collective security, 84–85, 146, 178. *See also* Britain; France; League of Nations

government, January, 1936, 10; and Soviet Union, 10, 28, 105–22, 140, 149, 159, 185–86, 196–97, 226n.37; reaction to German occupation of Rhineland, 11, 28, 160–61, 207n.32; and Munich crisis, 11, 196; and World War II, 11–12, 202n.38; post–World War II political activity, 12–14, 202n.52; death (November 15, 1956), 14; character of, 14–15, 19–20; reason for political ascent, 14; rejects premiership, January, 1936, 14–15; management of Quai d'Orsay, 15; close relationship with Sarrauts, 16; in domestic politics, 17; personal life, 17–18; relationship with Socialists, 17; marriage, 18; and religion, 18; oratorical abilities, 18–19; and Dordogne constituents, 20; selected as Foreign Minister of Popular Front government, 26–29; personal relationship with Blum, 27; agreement with Blum on conception of foreign policy, 27–28, 191, 212n.16; attacks Hoare-Laval Plan, 28; supporter of League of Nations and collective security, 28–29; and Britain, 29, 36–38, 40, 43–44, 48, 51–52, 61, 63, 79, 84–103, 116–17, 137, 190, 194–95, 218n.24, 221n.73, 243n.2; and outbreak of Spanish Civil War, 35–38; and London Conference of July, 1936, 36–38, 85–88, 160–61, 207n.32, 218–19n.28; and nonintervention in Spanish Civil War, 39–54, 56, 58, 60–62, 97, 157, 168, 175, 178, 191, 195, 209n.94, 212n.20, 216n.100; and opposition to appeasement, 60, 93, 99; remains Foreign Minister in Chautemps government, 60; and Mediterranean crisis of 1937, 60–63, 212n.17; and Nyon Confer-

ence, 63–77, 194–95, 213n.49, 213n.54, 214n.63; relations with Eden, 79, 90–91, 216n.1; and Czechoslovakia, 86, 95–96, 115, 132, 134–35, 142–47, 181, 188, 221n.73, 243n.3; and Anglo-Italian Gentleman's Agreement, 90–91, 155, 158; speech at Châteauroux, 92, 155, 171; and Eastern Europe, 92–93, 96, 99, 121–22, 125–50, 177, 181, 188, 194, 196; and Chamberlain, 93, 156; trip to Eastern European capitals, 93, 97–99, 116, 141–50, 181–83, 185; and Halifax's trip, 94–96; at London Conference of November, 1937, 95–99, 141, 176–77, 182; and Germany, 95–96, 105–6, 109, 114–15, 151, 158–62, 167–80, 181–83, 186–91, 196–97, 207n.32, 243n.2; impact of Eden's resignation on, 101–2, 186–87, 192, 197; offers resignation, turned down, 101, 187, 197; and Nazi-Soviet relations, 114–15; and Litvinov, 115, 149, 185; and French Communist party, 117–18, 185–86; and French Communist party press attacks against, 118, 185–86, 192, 197; and Poland, 125–32, 142–43; and Beck, 127–29, 132, 142–43; and Rambouillet Conference, 128–30; and Polish-Czech relations, 130–32, 142, 233n.86; and Little Entente, 132–41; and Eastern European Mutual Assistance Pact, 134–39, 147, 156; and Yugoslavia, 136–40, 144–45, 178, 234n.100; and Italo-Yugoslav Nonaggression Pact of 1937, 138–39; meeting with Neurath, 142, 177; and Rumania, 143–44; and Italy, 151–58, 177–80, 197, 212n.21, 216n.100, 236n.12; on Mussolini, 151, 156, 178–79; and ambassadorial dispute with